A USER'S GUIDE
TO THOUGHT AND
MEANING

A USER'S GUIDE TO THOUGHT AND MEANING

RAY JACKENDOFF

WITH ILLUSTRATIONS BY NEIL COHN, BILL GRIFFITH, AND OTHERS

OXFORD
UNIVERSITY PRESS

OXFORD

UNIVERSITY PRESS

Great Clarendon Street, Oxford OX2 6DP

Oxford University Press is a department of the University of Oxford.
It furthers the University's objective of excellence in research, scholarship,
and education by publishing worldwide in

Oxford New York

Auckland Cape Town Dar es Salaam Hong Kong Karachi
Kuala Lumpur Madrid Melbourne Mexico City Nairobi
New Delhi Shanghai Taipei Toronto

With offices in

Argentina Austria Brazil Chile Czech Republic France Greece
Guatemala Hungary Italy Japan Poland Portugal Singapore
South Korea Switzerland Thailand Turkey Ukraine Vietnam

Oxford is a registered trade mark of Oxford University Press
in the UK and in certain other countries

Published in the United States
by Oxford University Press Inc., New York

British Library Cataloguing in Publication Data
Data available

Library of Congress Cataloging in Publication Data
Data available

Typeset by SPI Publisher Services, Pondicherry, India
Printed in Great Britain
on acid-free paper by
Clays Ltd, St Ives plc

ISBN 978–0–19–969320–7

1 3 5 7 9 10 8 6 4 2

In memory of some great teachers in my life: Sam Flanders, Lou Bloom, Joseph Gigliotti, Hans Moennig, Allan Glatthorn, Ed Klima, Bobby Koff. Some of them knew they were teaching me, some didn't.

Contents

Foreword

This book lays out a particular path through a range of issues I've been thinking and writing about for over thirty years. If I'd tried to write it as a traditional scholarly treatise, it would have been a thousand pages long, I probably would never have finished it, and even if I had, you probably would never have read it. Instead, I've taken a chance and written it in a fashion that I hope will be accessible to anyone curious about thought and meaning. I trust that specialists can forgive the informality and find some interest in the way the book connects themes from linguistics, philosophy, cognitive science, and art. Many parts of the story, but not all, appear in fuller form in my books *Semantics and Cognition*, *Consciousness and the Computational Mind*, *Foundations of Language*, and *Language, Consciousness, Culture*.

In the interests of a smoother read, I've relegated references and suggestions for further readings to endnotes. Academic that I am, I still couldn't resist some comments and digressions in footnotes.

I'm grateful to numerous people for help and encouragement on various chunks of the book. Steve Levinson told me it was time to write a short book, and he was right. Cormac McCarthy, Avner Baz, Maryanne Wolf, and students in my 2009 Semantics course at Tufts gave me detailed comments on major portions of it. Dan Dennett, Peter Culicover, David Aaron, Eva Wittenberg, Ari Goldberg, Anita Peti-Stantić, Neil Cohn, Chelsey Ott, Naomi Berlove, Martin Paczynski, my wife Hildy Dvorak, my editor John Davey, and several anonymous reviewers read through the whole thing in one version or another and offered invaluable advice. Peter Bloom, Carol Hetrick, Susan Russinoff, Jim Giles, Sara Bershtel, and my brother Harry Jackendoff all helped a lot too.

The first full draft of the book was completed while I was in residence at the Santa Fe Institute in spring 2009. For that fabulous opportunity I must especially thank Chris Wood. I also want to acknowledge my other wonderful colleagues there: Geoff West, David Krakauer, Jessica Flack, Sam Bowles, Murray Gell-Mann, Tanya Elliott, Mark Newman, Dan Hruschka, Willemien Kets, and Karoline Wiesner, as well as staff members Carolyn Resnicke, Ronda Butler-Villa, Nate Metheny, Della Uli-barri, and Patrisia Brunello.

Many of the illustrations were created by Neil Cohn. Being able to plan the book with his talents in mind made the enterprise a lot more fun. I am pleased to thank Bill Griffith for his permission to use three *Zippy the Pinhead* cartoons. I am grateful also for permission to include the following illustrations:

M. C. Escher's "Waterfall" © 2011 The M.C. Escher Company-Holland. All rights reserved. www.mcescher.com

Johann Georg Edlinger, "Wolfgang Amadeus Mozart," ca. 1790. Photo Credit: bpk, Berlin / Gemaeldegalerie, Staatliche Museen, Berlin, Germany / Photo: Jörg P. Anders / Art Resource, NY

René Magritte, "The Treachery of Images" © 2011 C. Herscovici, London / Artists Rights Society (ARS), New York

Many many thanks also to my editor John Davey for all he has done to help make this book happen, and to Teresa Salvato, who keeps the Center for Cognitive Studies at Tufts running so smoothly. And of course my deepest gratitude goes to my family: Hildy, Amy, Tom, Beth, Dan, and Olive, who make it all worthwhile.

We were beguiled into thinking that language is to the mind as the ark is to the Torah.

(S. J. Keyser, June 17, 2002)

Language lets us say things that have perfectly good meanings, but we have a hard time saying how they could be true.

(Peter Culicover, October 24, 2006)

The thing was that Earth was the only place in the whole known Universe where language was used. It was a unique Earthling invention. Everybody else used mental telepathy, so Earthlings could get pretty good jobs as language teachers just about anywhere they went.

The reason creatures wanted to use language instead of mental telepathy was that they found out they could get so much more *done* with language. Language made them so much more *active*. Mental telepathy, with everybody constantly telling everybody everything, produced a sort of generalized indifference to *all* information. But language, with its slow, narrow meanings, made it possible to think about one thing at a time—to start thinking in terms of *projects*.

(Kurt Vonnegut, God Bless You, Mr. Rosewater)

Part One
Language, Words, and Meaning

1

Why do we need a User's Guide to thought and meaning?

What's the connection between your language and your thought? Everybody seems to have an opinion about this, from philosophers to scientists to the general public. But to answer this question, we first have to ask: What is language? And what is thought? And of course, everybody has opinions about these questions too.

I'm going to chew over these questions—work out *my* opinions—from what I'll call the "cognitive perspective," a sort of "brain's-eye view" on speaking and thinking. The cognitive perspective puts the question this way: What's going on in our heads when we're thinking, when we turn our thoughts into speech, and when we understand what other people say?

Many expositions of this cognitive perspective on language have focused on grammar—the way words are arranged into sentences. Here, though, I'll concentrate much more on *meanings*—the thoughts expressed by language. If there's a connection between language and thought, it's through meanings. I'll explore what meanings must be like to do the jobs they do, and I'll show that meanings are flexible, adaptive, and a lot more complicated than people give them credit for.

These explorations lead to even more basic questions, such as: What's going on in our heads when we perceive the world, talk about it, and act in it? For instance, I sit here at my computer, I think of something I want to say, I feel my fingers punching the keys, and I see the text appear on the screen. Next to my computer I see my coffee mug with a frog painted on it. I reach for it, pick it up, and take a sip. All of this seems so perfectly simple. We take it entirely for granted. But how does my brain actually do it? And especially, since we're asking about the connection of language and thought, what's going on in my brain when I "think of something I want to say"?

Contemporary neuroscience tells us that when you're looking at something, you use *these* particular parts of your brain. When you're afraid, this *other* part of your brain is active. When you're making decisions, this *other* part lights up. These discoveries are fascinating, but they only get us started on answering the question. They don't tell us how those parts of the brain do what they do—how they *work*.

Just to see how hard this question is, compare: How does pressing the keys on your computer make letters appear on the screen? It seems so simple. We take it for granted. But how does the computer actually do it? The people who write the programs know part of the answer, and the people who design the hardware know another part of the answer, but most of us computer users don't know any of it. And understanding how your brain works is lots harder than understanding how your computer works.

One of the hardest parts of the problem is figuring out how a collection of neurons could give rise to our experiences—how we come to be *conscious* of the world and of ourselves. The more we find out about the mechanisms behind language, thought, and perception, the less they look like the way we experience things. All the seeming simplicity disappears in a tangle of detail. So we end up concluding that most of what the brain does is unconscious, and only a small part is conscious. Which parts are conscious, and why? I'm not going to be able to "explain" consciousness here, but I will be able to make some progress on this last question.

The answer turns out to be important to my story, because I'm going to try to convince you that *thought and meaning are almost completely unconscious*. What we consciously experience as rational thought—the kind of thought we prize the most, the kind of thought that distinguishes us from the animals—is only a pale reflection of what's going on in our brains. And much of our thinking is entirely invisible to experience. We call such thinking "intuition," "gut feelings," "insight," or "inspiration"—or "irrational" or "emotional," depending on whether we like it or not.

This conclusion may seem strange and uncomfortable. I urge you to please bear with me as we pick our way through the intellectual mine-fields. As you can already see, I've taken on a lot of interwoven themes here. Because things have to come in linear order, I can't tell the full story of any one theme before moving on to the next—I have to develop many of them simultaneously. So I often have to start with rather vague formulations of things and sharpen them as I go along. I think the results are worth the discomfort.

For instance, we'll be able to see why language and thought seem so transparent, and why, even so, they've been so resistant to philosophical investigation. We'll understand why so-called "rational" or "conscious" thought is beneficial, and also where it goes awry. At the end I want to mull over what this conclusion might mean for human endeavors such as science, the arts, and education, and reflect on the limits of human understanding.

2
What's a language?

In the last chapter I asked "What is language?" I'd like to start working on that by posing (I hope) a more concrete question: What is *a* language? For instance, what is English?

English speakers often talk as though there's something called "correct English" that we conform to when we speak "correctly." We talk about the English language changing since the time of Shakespeare, and people often complain that it's degenerating under the onslaughts of teenagers or immigrants. We sometimes say that languages like Classical Latin or Northern Pomo are "dead," as though a language is a sort of organism. And sometimes we say they're extinct, as though a language is like a species.

Unlike with organisms and species, though, it's odd to speak of a language's "location" or "habitat." *Where* is English? Here the analogy with organisms and species breaks down. It seems odd to say, "Japanese is in Japan, Serbian is in Serbia, Hausa is in Nigeria, and English is everywhere in the world." It makes more sense to say "Japanese is *spoken* in Japan" and so on. We say language is changing when we notice that people *speak* it differently. And when a language like Northern Pomo is "dead," it's because nobody speaks it anymore. So the notion of people *speaking* a language seems central to understanding what a language is.

All right then: What are people *doing* when they're speaking English or Hausa or Serbian? They're making complex sounds that express their thoughts. (Speakers of signed languages make complex gestures instead of sounds.) Speakers are constantly expressing all sorts of new thoughts by making new sounds, for instance:

I'm really Olympic'd out.
I'm outgrowing my narcolepsy.
This is the kind of house that people sell their big houses in Belmont and downsize to.
Pure religion is as hard to find as pure science.
Every book should have a reference to bowling.

These utterances were made up on the spot (by my daughter and my wife, as it happens) to express some new idea. Neither they nor I had ever heard them before. The sentences weren't sitting there preassembled in our heads, just in case we ever wanted to say them—or in case we had to understand someone else saying them. So where did they come from?

Since our brains can only store a finite (if very large) amount of information, this unlimited novelty has to come from a finite amount of information stored in our heads. Part of this information, of course, is a finite list of words. But the part that gives us the power of unlimited expression is a system of principles that enables speakers to combine and recombine words in an unlimited number of ways. Linguists call this system a "mental grammar."[1]

Speakers don't just produce novel sounds. Matched with (nearly) every utterance is a meaning—a thought that the utterance expresses. We typically create new utterances like the ones above because we have new thoughts we want to express. And where do all the new thoughts come from? The same considerations come into play: The only way a finite brain can produce an unlimited number of novel thoughts is by storing a finite system. Part of this system is a large collection of stored parts, which we might call "concepts." But, again, in order to be able to produce an unlimited number of different thoughts, the system must also have principles that can combine and recombine concepts in an unlimited number of ways. And in order to allow us to express our thoughts, the system must also include ways of associating combinations of concepts with combinations of words.

So suppose you have some new thought, and using your vocal cords, tongue, and lips, you make a complex sound that your mental grammar associates with that thought. Then people whose mental grammars are similar to yours can associate your noise with a thought, which they then attribute to you. In other words, they can "understand" what you "mean." Other people, with different mental grammars in their heads (that is, who speak different languages), won't be able to understand you.[2]

(At this point you may be asking, "What do you mean by 'understand what I mean'?" Patience, please.)

---

[1] This paragraph summarizes an argument that serves as the foundational premise of modern linguistics. It has been made most forcefully by the pioneering linguist Noam Chomsky in myriad publications.

[2] This represents the ideal situation. People still manage to misunderstand each other even when they share a language, often because speakers and hearers have different unspoken agendas or subtexts. That's what a lot of marriage counseling is about, for instance. See Chapter 12 for some of the many ways language conveys more than is in the words.

Could we possibly have *entirely* different systems in our heads and still be convinced we understand each other? I don't think so, at least not with a system as rich and nuanced as a human language.

Actually, even people who take themselves to speak the same language don't have the *exact same* system in their heads. For one thing, everybody's vocabulary is different. For another, we routinely converse with people who have different accents—slightly different patterns in the sounds they make. But still, our mental grammars are close enough that we can usually understand each other pretty well. Linguists use the term "speech community" to refer to a collection of people who all code thoughts into sounds similarly enough to be able to understand each other, and we can give a name, say "English" or "Japanese," to the system that they more or less share.

Often members of a speech community can understand each other, but people from one part notice that people from other parts use slightly different patterns of sounds or words. Then we say that these parts of the community speak different *dialects* or *varieties* of the same language. For instance, speakers of "standard" English might say *Bill and I aren't coming*, while speakers of another variety of English express the same thought as *Me and Bill ain't comin'*. The latter isn't a "careless" version of the former. Rather, it reflects a systematic and internally consistent mental grammar, just a slightly different one.

The distinction between dialects and languages is slippery, because it's so often overlaid with political connotations. The linguist Max Weinreich is famous for saying: "A language is a dialect with an army and a navy." Many of the varieties of the "language" called Arabic are mutually incomprehensible. So are many of the varieties of Chinese, even though they use the same mutually intelligible writing system. So it might make sense to talk about the Arabic and Chinese "families" of languages. For a different sort of case, once upon a time there was a language called Serbo-Croatian, spoken in a place once called Yugoslavia. This language had different but mutually intelligible "dialects" spoken in Belgrade and Zagreb, though these dialects happened to be written most of the time in different alphabets. When Yugoslavia disintegrated in the civil war of the 1990s, suddenly these "dialects" were regarded as two official *languages*, Serbian and Croatian, even though nothing had changed in the way people spoke them—until various political authorities tried to officially (and artificially) create greater differences.

Of course, many people have two or more systems at their disposal—either different languages or different varieties of the same language—and they can switch back and forth when it's socially appropriate (say from the *Bill and I aren't coming* style to the *me and Bill ain't comin'* style). And there are subtler differences of *register*—the way you talk with people professionally, or with your kids, or with your friends at the corner bar. Each of these is a slightly different system too.

Children in the process of *learning* language also have different systems from the people they're learning it from. We notice this and say they "still talk baby talk" or they "still make mistakes," such as thinking toiletries are a kind of tree, saying *lip-sank* for the past tense of *lip-synch*, or saying *I hope this shirt didn't ruin in the wash* (real examples produced by my children at around 8 years old). Nevertheless children *do* have a system, just one different from that of the adults. We might think of children learning to talk as trying to "tune up" their system so they can understand and be understood.

Viewed from this perspective, "the English language" is an idealization over the mental grammars of English speakers, for convenience treating them as uniform and overlooking the differences. Where is the English language, then? If anywhere, in the heads of its speakers.

Sometimes it's claimed that a language isn't in the head, that it's "socially constructed" by the community. However, except for artificial languages such as Esperanto and Klingon, no one *deliberately* constructs languages. And a language, even a deliberately constructed one, only exists in a society because it exists in the heads of speakers whose systems are close enough that they can understand each other.[3]

[3] An interesting test case is the emergence of Nicaraguan Sign Language since the 1980s. This is a language that sprang up in a newly established school for the deaf, in a community of deaf individuals who had no previous experience with language, spoken or signed. The language is still developing rapidly, and it's an interesting question what parts its speakers conceive of themselves as having deliberately constructed, and what parts have "just happened" and no one knows why.

A related idea is that the English language isn't in the head, it's a set of conventions. This suggests that language is something people agree upon or consent to. For instance, the philosopher David Lewis writes: "[The] belief that the others conform to [the convention] gives everyone a good and decisive reason to conform to [it] himself." Hmm. I don't think I ever looked for reasons to conform to the system that constitutes English. Well, okay, I may have decided not to say *ain't* in situations that call for "proper speech." But I sure didn't look for reasons to "conform to the convention" of putting the direct object of my sentences after the verb. Most of the "conventions" of language aren't things people tell you to do, like driving on the right-hand side of the road or wearing appropriate clothes to a wedding.

Some philosophers assure me that Lewis didn't mean we're instructed in these conventions or that we *consciously* decide to follow them. Maybe we're just unconsciously copying what other people do, and in that way conforming to the convention. In fact, in a very rough sense, that *is* what children are doing as they learn to speak. But then these unconscious "conventions" that we conform to raise the same problem as "language." What are they, and where could they be, other than in people's heads? You might say they're in the practices of the community. But members of the community can only conform to these practices because of something in their heads. Their cats are surrounded by these practices too, but *they* don't conform to them, because they have different kinds of minds. So whatever we may think about the role of the community in maintaining languages and conventions, we still have to explain how each individual member of the community manages to learn them and utilize them.

Sometimes it's said that a system doesn't count as a language unless it's *written*. But in fact most of the languages ever spoken in the world haven't been written down. There's something odd and dismissive about saying they don't count as "real" languages. And even for the languages that *are* written, remember that until the last century or so, most people couldn't read. I don't think we'd want to conclude that maybe they didn't count as "real" speakers of the language. Sure, there's no question that writing is a vital element of our culture and many others. But in terms of defining what a language is, writing doesn't play an essential role. It is more like a wonderful add-on that enhances the uses of language—but only an add-on. In contrast, spoken language, unlike reading and writing, is found in every culture.

With this view of what a language is, let's return to the questions from the beginning of the chapter.

- How can a language have a continuing existence over time? Answer: There is a community of speakers who use (approximately) the same system for relating sound and meaning, and new speakers learn it as older speakers die off.
- How does a language die off? Answer: It dies when all the speakers that use that system die and no new ones learn it—as is happening with a large proportion of the languages of the world today, the so-called endangered languages.
- How does a language change over time? Answer: Some people (maybe teenagers or movie stars or politicians) start using a slightly different system, not so different as to prevent understanding—they may introduce some new vocabulary or pronounce some vowels a little differently—and other people imitate them. And after a while, the people who used the older system either switch to the new system or die out. Eventually, the result is still a community of people who understand each other. But the system they use is different from what people fifty years ago used.
- What's "correct English"? Answer: It's just the version of the system that happens to be used by the socially dominant segment of the speech community. About the most important markers of social identity are the way we look and the way we talk. So speaking "correctly" marks you as belonging to that elite. Speaking "incorrectly" marks you as *not* belonging. You may not be able to help it because you grew up speaking another language or another

variant, but you might also *choose* to speak "incorrectly" to show solidarity with your rebellious (or cool) peers. Of course, this issue of "correctness" isn't confined to English. It shows up in other languages as well, where for instance borrowings from English and from the languages of immigrant communities may be strongly disparaged.

An aside: Over the centuries, the more powerful segments of a society have typically enforced their dominance by preventing other people from talking the way they're used to, say by forbidding the use of Spanish or Navajo or Cambodian in school or at work or in public. Members of the dominant subculture don't understand the other people very well, and might be a little afraid of them ("They're talking about us!"), so they say things like "Those guys are stupid (or careless or illogical or barbarous), and we'd better protect our culture from their influence." Actually, one reason the other folks are hard to understand is that they have a different system for understanding each other. And one reason they may seem stupid is that they can't understand *us* very well.

3

Perspectives on English

One way to interpret the story I've been telling about English (and other languages) would be to say there's really *no such thing* as English—there's only a hodgepodge of systems in the heads of hundreds of millions of speakers. A slightly different way to interpret it would be: English exists all right, but most people are mistaken about what it is: it's actually a hodgepodge of systems in the heads of hundreds of millions of speakers.

Neither of these interpretations makes me very happy. They don't leave any room for what we might call the "ordinary perspective" on English, the view that people typically take: English is a single structured entity out there in the world that you can use sort of like a tool, if you learn how to.

But the last chapter changed the focus a little. Instead of asking "What is English?" I asked "What is *speaking* English?"—what role does "English" play in what people say and how they understand other people? From this standpoint, speaking English involves using a system in our head that lets us communicate with people who have similar systems in *their* heads. "English" is then an approximation, an average, or an idealization of all the systems in all these speakers. If we want to get more specific, say to study different dialects or how children talk, we can drop this idealization. But even so, we're always thinking in terms of systems in speakers' heads.[1] I'll call this the "cognitive perspective" or "functional perspective"—how language functions in the mind. And from this perspective, English looks quite a bit different than from the ordinary perspective.

The ordinary and cognitive perspectives aren't the only ways to look at language, either. All the systems in a person's head—not just the language system, but also the visual system, the motor system, the motivational system, and so on—ultimately function because of the activity of the neurons in the speaker's brain. In this "neural perspective," there's no longer a distinct unit we can call "English." English is just some subset of chemically and electrically mediated firings, scattered among huge networks of neurons.

The scientific study of language makes use of each of these perspectives. Many philosophers—and a few linguists—root their approach in the ordinary perspective, and they maintain (or at least assume) that language is an abstract object that exists apart from any of its speakers.[2]

[1] What I'm calling the ordinary perspective on language corresponds more or less to what Noam Chomsky calls "E-language" (or External language); the cognitive perspective is roughly what he calls "I-language" (Internalized language).

In the cognitive perspective, the system that constitutes English actually has a number of layers, because it draws on everything else going on in the head. So we can ask: How much of what governs our speaking English is due to *English* specifically, or to *language* more generally? And how much of it comes from our general way of understanding the world, how much from more general systems of social interaction, how much from the way memory and attention work, and so on? From this viewpoint, much of "English" might dissolve into other aspects of mental functioning.

[2] For instance, the logician Gottlob Frege argued strenuously against treating language (especially meaning) as internal to speakers; his approach underpins most Anglo-American philosophy of language. More recently, David Lewis treats a language as a mapping between sound and meaning. Speakers are not part of this mapping, but they adopt the convention of "trusting" this mapping. The philosopher of language Jerrold Katz, a former Chomskyan, explicitly argues that language is an abstract Platonic object. Among linguists, Terence Langendoen and Paul Postal champion Katz's view.

On the other hand, by far the majority of linguists who are explicit about it adopt the cognitive perspective, treating language as a system in a speaker's head. They do differ in how much they idealize the system across the community. For instance, if you're interested in dialect differences, language change, or the role of language in society, you tend to take account of variation among different speakers' systems more than if you're mostly concerned with details of the linguistic capacity in an individual speaker.

Finally, many linguists, psycholinguists, and neurolinguists work within the neural perspective as well, studying the location and timing of language use in the brain, and the effects of brain damage on the details of language ability.

It's also common for linguists to shift freely among perspectives, using one perspective to help explain certain properties of another. This is what I did in the last chapter, when I moved to the cognitive perspective in order to explain certain properties of the ordinary perspective, such as how languages change over time.

Sometimes such changes of perspective are called "reductions" of one theory to another (the biologist E. O. Wilson calls it "consilience"). The idea behind reduction is that all phenomena in one perspective can be explained entirely in terms of the other. A classic case in the history of science is the explanation of heat transfer in terms of the statistics of molecular motion.

I don't think this is quite the right way to think about the various perspectives on language. It's true that all use of language depends on the operation of neural circuitry, and this might tempt us to try to reduce everything about language to neurons. But we can't explain everything we might want to know about language from looking at neurons. Issues from the ordinary and cognitive perspectives don't all go away. For instance, could a neural perspective help us understand how the Norman Conquest led to changes in English? Well, it might tell us *something*, but probably not the kind of things a lot of people find most interesting, such as why *beef* and *pork* got borrowed from Norman French to refer to the meat of good old Anglo-Saxon *cows* and *pigs*. This is probably a job for the ordinary perspective.

The cognitive and neural perspectives aren't totally irrelevant to this problem, though. For instance, they may well be able to tell us about how *in general* the systems in people's heads—especially in the heads of language learners—respond to multilingual input. And this may turn out to be relevant to how English changed in the 12th and 13th centuries.

Once again, so what *is* English? It depends on which perspective you're taking. Which one is the *right* perspective? That depends on your interests and goals.

4

Perspectives on sunsets, tigers, and puddles

It's not as though this choice among ordinary, cognitive, and neural perspectives is a peculiarity of the term *English*. What's a sunset? In the ordinary perspective, the sun goes down. From an astronomical perspective, the earth turns and sunlight ceases to fall where we are. From a cognitive perspective, we might want to explain why it *looks* as though the sun is going down. From a physical perspective, there are just photons striking or failing to strike certain molecules in retinal cells and so on. Should we take from this that there's *no such thing* as a sunset, or that people talking about sunsets are simply wrong or misguided? I hope not. After all, the time of sunset can be found in newspapers and on the internet, and people rely on these sources for various things they do. It's odd to say everyone is just making a big mistake. The philosopher of science Thomas Kuhn points out that the ordinary perspective is actually the best one for navigation by the stars.

Another well-known example of dependence on perspective is *money*. Like language, money is only used by people. The physical form of money—coins, bills, checks, and bits in the bank's computer—is only relevant if these objects *count* as money and can therefore be used in monetary transactions. With money, then, a functional perspective is where the interesting action is—how much of it you need to pay for things. A physical perspective only comes into play when we're discussing things involving the physical form of money, like how big a wallet has to be, how to detect counterfeiting, and of course where you stashed your spare cash.[1]

In his influential essay "The meaning of 'meaning'," the philosopher Hilary Putnam argues that most people don't know the meaning of a word like *gold*. Its 𝕽eal 𝕸eaning, he says, is known only to experts— metallurgists and chemists—who can determine its atomic composition. Similarly, the 𝕽eal 𝕸eaning of *tiger* has something to do with its DNA. The implication (although Putnam conveniently doesn't point it out) is that, until the advent of modern chemistry and biology, *no one at all* knew what these words meant! Come on!

I think a better approach is to say that atomic composition and DNA signatures belong to the interests and goals of a "physicalist" perspective, and that it is this perspective the scientists (and Putnam) are talking about. Indeed, most people don't associate their words *gold* and *tiger* with these scientific concepts. But for as long as people have encountered gold and tigers, they have always had ordinary concepts of them, which have been perfectly adequate for most everyday interests and goals. And these ordinary concepts are what are associated with the words *gold* and *tiger* in people's minds.

Here's another sort of response to Putnam: What's the meaning of the word *puddle*? Of course there's an ordinary way of thinking about puddles, but is there any other way? It's hard to imagine what a functionalist or physicalist perspective on puddles could contribute to the ques-

---

[1] The philosopher Wilfrid Sellars calls the ordinary understanding of the world the "manifest image," contrasting this to a "scientific perspective" which encompasses my cognitive, neural, and physicalist perspectives. The philosopher John Searle uses the term "institutional facts" for the use of money in transactions, along with other phenomena such as points in a game and boundary markers. He contrasts these with "brute physical facts" such as the size and color of a $10 bill.

tion about what constitutes a puddle—what some future science would have to say about them, what a "puddlologist" would find worth studying.

In the same vein, what's the meaning of *laundry*? Of *junk*? Of *buddy*? Everyone knows what they are, the same way they know what *tiger* means. They probably can't give you an airtight definition (as we'll see in Chapter 11). But they certainly react appropriately when someone says "Look out for the puddle!" or "Let's get this junk out of here"—just as they react appropriately when someone says "Look at that gorgeous sunset" or "Look out for the tiger!" The only difference is that, unlike *English* and *sunset*, words like *puddle, laundry, junk,* and *buddy* don't lend themselves to perspectives other than the ordinary one.

On the flip side, some words *don't* have an ordinary conceptualization, and can only be understood from one technical perspective or another. Three examples are *c-command* (a technical term of syntactic theory), *differentiable* (a technical term of mathematics), and *eruv* (a Hebrew word borrowed into English as a technical term of Judaism). These are words for which, unlike *puddle*, only certain people are in the know.

It seems to me that Putnam's argument grows out of a long-standing philosophical tradition: real knowledge can only be attained through the scientific method. This is why his approach to meaning might kind of make sense for words like *gold* and *tiger*—words for things that there are scientific theories about—but has nothing to say about words like *puddle* and *laundry*.

I'm not just worrying here that Putnam's approach to meaning only accounts for some words but not others. I'm also concerned that it has the curious effect of delegitimating our ordinary way of understanding the world. On one hand, this approach may be useful and even fun, because it "makes the familiar strange" and invites us to think in new ways. On the other hand, some people might think it's a way of asserting power—the power conferred by knowledge. This sort of rhetorical move dates back to Socrates ("I'm wiser than you, because at least I know what I don't know"). Here, I'd like to show more respect for ordinary conceptualizations, because after all, they're conceptualizations too—ways of understanding the world that often do the job quite well, thank you.

I want to draw three points out of this little discussion of gold and puddles. First, we see that treating the word *English* in terms of multiple perspectives isn't a fluke—I haven't made it up just for this one case. Rather, this approach helps us understand what's going on with all sorts of words. In this respect, *English* isn't so different from any other word.

Second, in the chapters coming up, I'll be asking what meanings are. Here we've learned something important about meanings: the meaning of a word is partly dependent on the perspectives it can be embedded in.

Third, it's important to notice when we're operating in multiple perspectives, and which perspective is most useful for which purposes. I guess this too is a perspective. We might call it the "perspectival perspective."

5

What's a word?

Before we can tackle meaning, we have to dig a bit deeper into what a language is. Obviously, an important part of language is *words*. So our next question is: "What's a word?"

From the ordinary perspective, words have some of the same peculiarities as languages. The word *puddle* may seem like something out in the world that speakers use. But where is it? It's not in puddles![1]

How should we think about words, then? Does the word *puddle* exist all the time, or only when somebody uses it? I think it seems to exist all the time. Fine, but now a trickier question: What kind of thing *is* the word *puddle*? Sometimes we talk about a word as if it's something like a hammer—we pull it out of the drawer whenever we need it. ("Okay, I'll need to use *puddle* in my next sentence." "You should have used *intelligent* instead of *smart* in that paragraph.") But sometimes we talk about a word as though it's more like an endless supply of identical nails, and we can use a new one each time. ("I used four *puddles*, including this one, in this paragraph.") These comparisons may seem silly, but they give us a sense of what an odd thing a word is.

---

[1] Even so, we may have a feeling that the word is an inherent property of the object it names. For instance, one of my daughters, at the age of 7 or 8, asked me, "If people weren't around when the dinosaurs were alive, how do we know what they were called?"—as though a stegosaurus's name was as natural a property as its size and and its diet. (She did catch on, though, when I told her that people made the name up.)

People sometimes say it's not a real word unless it's in a dictionary (or in "the" dictionary)—as though dictionaries have some deep or magical authority about the "real" language out there in the world. But dictionaries don't come down from heaven. *People* write them, after observing how other people *use* words in speech and writing. And, as we'll see in the next chapter, people writing dictionaries face a delicate juggling act in deciding how many meanings a word has and in writing definitions for them all—just compare different dictionaries' treatment of the same word (try *double*, *doubt*, and *down*, for example).

A new word "comes into the language" because someone makes it up and other people use it. It gets into the dictionary because some editor notices that people use it, and especially when it appears in print enough times.[2] It gets its "official meaning"—its dictionary definition—because some lexicographer writes it, following policies set out by the editor. So the authority we grant to dictionaries shouldn't come from a sense of their "objectivity," it should be based on our trust in the editors' judgments. (This is only one of the problems with dictionaries. A more serious one turns up at the end of Chapter 11.)

Anyhow, the dictionary isn't the place where words exist. As I mentioned in Chapter 2, there are plenty of languages that aren't written. If they aren't written, they don't have dictionaries. But their words still exist in the same peculiar way that words of English do.

Words aren't the only things with these odd properties. We find similar peculiar symptoms in other sorts of things that, like words, take place in time. For instance, the song "Row, Row, Row Your Boat" exists, and it has existed ever since someone made it up. But there is no *place* that it

---

[2] In June 2009, the press made a small fuss over the addition of the "millionth word of English," which, according to an organization called the Global Language Monitor, was *Web 2.0*. Their rather arbitrary criterion for inclusion was 25,000 appearances on the internet. And then, various bloggers got upset that the millionth word was so prosaic. What was all *that* about? Exactly how do you count the words of English anyway? One difficulty, as we'll see in the next chapter, is that it's not always clear when we have two (or six) different words rather than two (or six) uses of the *same* word.

exists. Where is it when no one happens to be singing it? Is it out there in "music space" to be pulled out whenever someone wants to sing it? Or is it an endless supply of copies somewhere out there, and one copy gets used up every time someone sings it? Neither choice makes a lot of sense.

Days and months like Tuesday and Valentine's Day and September are something like this too. Sometimes we say, "Tuesday's here again," as though it's the very same day that's gone away and come back. And sometimes we say, "Aargh, another Tuesday!" as though there's an endless supply of Tuesdays somewhere (in the future?), and right now another one is with us until it's over. Neither way of thinking about Tuesday seems to be the "right" way.[3]

So let's go back to words, and see what the cognitive perspective has to say. Here, words are part of the system in people's heads that they use to build messages. Even when you're not uttering *puddle* or listening to someone say it, it's still there in your memory. In order for people to understand each other, they have to have a substantial shared stock of words in their heads. Let's call each person's stock of words their own personal "mental dictionary." If you use a word that's not familiar to me—that's not part of my mental dictionary—I may be baffled, and I may have to guess what message you have in mind. Of course, this is also what kids learning language have to do all the time (and what we often have to do when little kids are talking to us).

---

[3] George Lakoff and others in cognitive linguistics propose that our conceptualization of time is metaphorical, and that it's modeled on our understanding of space. Some of the basic evidence for this claim is that in many languages, most prepositions for time are also prepositions for space: *at* 10:00, *on* Tuesday, *before* breakfast, *after* the concert, *in* five minutes, and so on. (On the other hand, English also has *during*, *until*, and *since*, which can only be used for time, not for space; and it also has *to the left of*, *behind*, and *beneath*, which can only be used for space, not time.) We've just seen that the way we think about temporal entities such as words, songs, and Tuesdays doesn't fit the mold of spatial entities like screwdrivers and nails very well. So although there are definite parallels, our understanding of entities that take up time can't be entirely modeled on or derived metaphorically from our understanding of entities that take up space.

From the cognitive perspective, then, the notion of, say, "the word *tomato*" is a lot like "the English language." It's an abstraction or idealization of something stored in the heads of the members of a speech community, as part of their mental dictionaries, and they can use it as part of their communication with each other. What each speaker stores may or may not be exactly the same as what the others store—you say *tomayto* and I say *tomahto*—but it's usually safe to assume it is. A word "stays in the language" over time if new speakers keep learning it and using it. It becomes "obsolete" when no one uses it anymore and all the people who used to use it die off (though it still may be recorded in dictionaries).

I want to compare this approach with a physicalist perspective, in which a word is basically just a sound. This perspective makes it hard to characterize words at all. For one thing, it can't tell us how people use words to convey meanings. But even at the level of sound there are problems. When *you* say *tomato* and *I* say *tomato* (even if we both say *tomayto*, not *tomahto*), our voices are acoustically different, so we make different sound waves. I myself make different sound waves when I whisper *tomato* and when I scream *tomato*. And when I say *you say tomato*, there's no separation in the sound between *you* and *say*, or between *say* and *tomato*, even though we understand the words as separate.

The late Alvin Liberman, one of the founders of modern acoustic phonetics, used to talk about the early attempts to get computers to understand speech, back in the late 1940s. He and his colleagues thought you could just segment the acoustic signal into speech sounds, say "p," "ah," and "t," and you'd put them together and get *pot* (as pronounced by a speaker of "standard" American English). It turned out that this didn't work at all, and Liberman devoted his career to finding out why. He and his colleagues found that the acoustic correlate of each speech sound depends not only on the speaker's voice, but also on the acoustics of the speech sounds around it. For instance, the sound "ah" is acoustically different in *pot*, *top*, *mob*, and so on—even though it sounds the same to us.

In addition, speakers tend to "swallow up" a lot of acoustic detail, and they unconsciously rely on hearers to make sense of the message anyway. For an extreme example, you can (sort of) understand someone talking with their mouth full, despite the mangled acoustics. On the other hand, if you *only* have acoustics to go on—say if you're trying to take dictation in a language you don't know—it's pretty much impossible to tell what sounds you're hearing, much less tell where one word ends and the next begins.

It turns out that you identify what words you're hearing partly by finding the best match between the sound and the words you already know, and partly by guessing what the speaker might be talking about—all completely unconsciously. In other words, your understanding of speech relies heavily on identifying not just the acoustics but also the meaning. Although we know how to get computers to deal with acoustics pretty well by now, meaning is still elusive. This is one reason that after sixty years of research on computer understanding of spoken language, there's still quite a way to go.

The acoustic problems only get worse when we add accents to the mix. If you speak "standard" American English, you pronounce the "r" in *park*. If you're from Boston, you may say "pahk"; if you're from New York you may say "pawk." Yet they all count as the word *park*, because the systems they belong to differ consistently in the same way ("heart" vs. "haht" vs. "hawt", "guard" vs. "gahd" vs. "gawd" and so on). That's not all: in the context of different systems, the very same sound may count as a different word. We understand "gahd" spoken by a midwesterner to be *god*; spoken by a Bostonian, *guard*; by a Texan, *guide*. As long as we can "tune into" the accent, we can interpret it in terms of our own accent. So what counts as the same word depends on what system (or version of the system) it's in, in this case the accent it's spoken with. The word gets its identity partly from its place in the system—what other words it contrasts with, what other words it rhymes with, and so on. At the same time, the system is only a system because of the parts that make it up, including the words. Is this circular? Yes.

But it's not a *vicious* circularity. Notice that something similar is going on with *Tuesday*. What makes a particular day Tuesday? Only that it follows Monday, precedes Wednesday, and is seven days after the last Tuesday. If there weren't people naming days, there wouldn't be Tuesdays (right?). But as long as we're all operating inside the same system, we understand each other fine.

You might say Tuesday is a "convention." But like putting our direct objects after our verbs, we don't normally have a choice whether to adopt it or not. One part of this convention is when Tuesday *starts*. We normally take it for granted that it begins at midnight (which in turn depends on conventions like clock time and time zones). But in the traditional Jewish reckoning of time, the new day begins at sunset (which is why Genesis says "And the evening and the morning were the first day"). This way works just as well, at least for religious purposes.

The point of all this is that a physicalist perspective doesn't give us a useful way to talk about words. What does it take to identify two sounds as the same word? We have to abstract away from each individual speaker's voice quality, their tone of voice on any particular occasion, and their accent. And to abstract away from their accent, we need a notion of the sound system in which it's embedded. None of this makes sense purely in terms of acoustics. It only makes sense in terms of the systems in people's heads, as described from the cognitive perspective.

6

What counts as the same word?

A whole other set of issues about words comes up when we try to take into account what they *mean*. These issues are stock in trade for linguists like me, and I'd like to give you a feel for how tricky they can be.

Let's start with an easy case. Do these two sentences have the same last word?

> She went down to the river and stood on the bank.
> She went to town to take some money out of the bank.

If we're playing Scrabble, only the spelling makes a difference, so the answer doesn't matter. But if we care about what the word means, there are two ways to describe the situation. One way is to say that the same word *bank* has two meanings. The other is to say there are two words with different meanings that happen to be pronounced and spelled the same. Compared to the cases we'll look at next, the second way turns out to make more sense, so I'll say there are two different words pronounced *bank*. The technical term is that the two *banks* are "homonyms."

What about these four sentences? Is the last word the same?

> The ice will melt.
> Every spring the ice melts.
> The ice is melting.
> The ice has melted.

In Scrabble, these count as different words. But traditional grammars— and psycholinguistic experiments—tell us that in some sense they're the *same* word, but in different *grammatical forms* (infinitive, third person singular present tense, present participle, and past participle).

How about the word *smoke* in these six sentences?

(1) The fire gave off a lot of smoke.
(2) The fire smoked a lot.
(3) Bill smoked the cigar.
(4) Bill smoked the fish.
(5) Do you have a smoke?
(6) Let's smoke him out.

At first this may look like the same situation as the two *banks*. But this time the six uses are related in meaning. When a fire smokes (#2), it gives off smoke (#1). When you smoke a cigar (#3), you make it smoke (#2), by holding the end of the smoking object in your mouth, sucking the smoke in, and puffing it out. Smoking a fish or a ham (#4) is quite different: you don't make it give off smoke (#1) by puffing on it, you make smoke go *into* it, by putting it in an enclosure with a fire.

Moving right along, a smoke (#5) is something you smoke (#3), like a cigarette. It's definitely not something that you smoke (#4), like a salmon. Finally, smoking someone out (#6) is making them come out from a closed place such as a house or cave, by forcing smoke (#1) *into* the place—or metaphorically, making them reveal themselves. Looking at this list as a whole, we could put it in either of two ways: we could say

29

that these are six different but related words, or that they're different senses of the same word. The technical term for this situation is that *smoke* is "polysemous," as though it's the same word with six related senses. (Some people would rather say it's two words—a noun and a verb—each of which is polysemous.)[1]

Going a little further afield, think about the word *smoker*, which has the suffix *–er* tacked onto *smoke*. It can be used for someone who habitually smokes (#3), or for a device in which you smoke things (#4). These two uses are distant cousins, related to each other only because they both have something to do with smoke (#1). *Smoker* also used to have a third use, now pretty much obsolete: a railroad car in which people were allowed to smoke (#3). What we see overall for *smoke* and *smoker*, then, is a network of nine related words, some pronounced exactly the same, and some pronounced in related ways. And of course, we could extend this network further by adding words such as *smoky* and *smoked*.

None of these issues arise in the way people ordinarily think of what counts as a word. Still, it's strange to say that people don't know what words really *are*. I'd rather say there are different perspectives on words, suitable for different purposes. For the purpose of spelling bees or counting the words in a written document, the ordinary perspective works pretty well. But for the purpose of looking into the relation of language to thought and meaning, we need to be aware of the distinctions we've just explored:

---

[1] I actually don't care for this terminology, for the following reason. English has some polysemous words in which one meaning denotes an object or substance, and the other denotes the process of removing that object or substance. For instance, to *dust* the house is to remove *dust* from it; to *scale* a fish is to remove its *scales*. But, there are other cases where the same meaning relation is conveyed by a different word with a related form: one *de-claws* a lobster and *beheads* a person. Treating polysemy as something special obscures (or at least de-emphasizes) the fact that all four of these pairs exhibit the same meaning relation. So I'd prefer to think of cases like *smoke*, *dust*, and *scale* as separate words with related meanings and identical pronunciation. In this way they differ minimally from pairs of words with related meanings that differ in form only by a prefix or suffix. I don't think it makes any difference for what we're doing here, though.

- Homonyms—two words that sound the same but aren't related at all in meaning (*bank, bank*)
- Different forms of the same word (*melt, melting*)
- Polysemous words, which have two or more related meanings (*smoke #1, smoke #2*, etc.)
- Words that are related in sound and related in meaning (*smoke, smoker*)

These distinctions make a difference in dictionaries. Homonyms typically get two separate entries. Different forms of the same word aren't even mentioned, unless they're irregular (such as *think* and *thought*). Polysemous words often have separate subentries under a single word. Words related in sound and meaning may appear as subentries, or one may be used in the definition of the other (for instance: "Smoker: a person who smokes").

Turning to the cognitive perspective, what about in people's *mental* dictionaries? I think it's safe to say that the people who write dictionaries classify words the way they do because it corresponds to their sense of how closely different words and meanings are related in people's heads. And linguists and psycholinguists spend a lot of effort trying to further clarify the character of relations among words. We've only scratched the surface here. For instance, there's a substantial literature on the many senses of the word *over*. Is it the same word *over* in *somewhere over the rainbow* and *he turned the pancake over*? Or are they homonyms? How about the *over* in *overeat* and *overthrow the government*?

People sometimes have a preconception that if it's spelled the same, it must be the same word. For *bank* and *smoke*, it's easy enough to see that this isn't so, and it's no big deal. I'm going through these complications because they'll serve as a baseline when the same symptoms turn up with words with more philosophical weight, such as *meaning, consciousness*, and *true*. If *smoke* is this complicated, why should we expect *meaning* to be simple?

7
Some uses of *mean* and *meaning*

It's time to start thinking about what meaning is. But wait! Are we thinking about 𝕽𝖊𝖆𝖑 𝕸𝖊𝖆𝖓𝖎𝖓𝖌 in some profound sense? Or just the word *meaning*? Well, we'll have to think about both. I'd like to proceed first the way we did with *language*, *word*, and *smoke* in the previous chapters, looking at how the word is used in the ordinary perspective. We'll then turn to the cognitive perspective in Chapter 9.

If we want to find out what meaning is, what should we be looking *at*, and what should we be looking *for*? In his *Philosophical Investigations*, the prominent early 20th-century philosopher Ludwig Wittgenstein famously said, "Don't look to the meaning, look to the use." People often take him to be saying we should just look at the use of language and then stop, because *there is no such thing* as meaning, aside from the use of linguistic expressions in context. I take home a different message. I think he's saying we shouldn't be trapped by our prejudices about what the meaning of a word *ought* to be, based on a few well-worn traditional examples. We should be gathering evidence, searching out all the word's uses—not just for their own sake, but in an effort to see the larger patterns. "One cannot guess how a word functions. One has to look at its use and learn from that." In other words, be a linguist.

(There is some justice in the standard interpretation of Wittgenstein, though. Like many philosophers of his time, he believed that a scientific account of language could not rely on such unobservable entities as minds. So for him, explanation from a cognitive perspective was unthinkable.)

The *Investigations* are full of creative and playful examination of data. But Wittgenstein didn't give us any analytical techniques for going beyond the data. In fact, he painfully rejects his own earlier formal techniques, and says "We must do away with all *explanation*, and description alone must take its place." Personally, I think this amounts to giving up. How can you arrive at understanding without trying to explain things? The past half century of linguistics and cognitive science has developed some tools that can help out a bit. So here we go with some more linguistics, looking at the uses of *mean* and *meaning*. You might want to fasten your seat belt.

Let's start with the basic grammatical frame *X means Y*. In this frame, the word *means* is sort of like *smoke*—it has a number of related senses. In one family of senses, the object of the sentence (*Y*) is used to explain or interpret the subject of the sentence (*X*), which the speaker presumes the hearer is less familiar with.

Interpretation uses of *X means Y*

(The German word) *Rauch* means *smoke*.	(Translation)
Slithy means *lithe and slimy*.	(Definition)
(Humpty Dumpty in *Through the Looking Glass*)	
Osculating means doing *this*.	(Demonstration)
A red light means you should stop.	(Explanation of symbols)

Because the subject of the sentence is supposed to be less familiar than the object, we can't reverse these sentences and put the more familiar item first. ('*' is linguists' notation for recording that a sentence sounds odd. '?' and '??,' which I use below, mean the sentence doesn't sound absolutely terrible, but it doesn't sound great, either.)

*Smoke means *Rauch*.[1]
*Lithe and slimy means *slithy*.
*Doing *this* means osculating.
*That you should stop means a red light.

---

[1] Well, we *might* say this sentence if we're speaking English to a German speaker who doesn't happen to know this particular English word. But then, as in the other cases, the subject of the sentence is unfamiliar and the object is familiar.

When we speak of the meaning of a word, phrase, or sentence, we're usually talking about definition or translation. A dictionary of English gives the meanings of English words in the definition sense. A German–English dictionary gives the meanings of German words in the translation sense.

A different use of *X means Y* expresses a linkage of some sort between the subject of *means* and the object:

Linkage uses of *X means Y*
Smoke means fire.
A sharp pain in your left side may mean appendicitis.
It doesn't mean you're top dog just because your ass is bleeding.
   (Norman Mailer, quoted in Newsweek, 4 September 1989)
This means war!

Smoke is a result of fire, and therefore is evidence that there may be a fire. Likewise, pain is a result of appendicitis, and therefore is evidence that you may have appendicitis. Similarly, Mailer is saying that bleeding is *not* evidence that you're top dog. But in the last example, the relation is reversed: *this* (whatever it is) isn't the result of war, but rather the reason or cause or motivation for it.[2]

---

[2] This reversible relation of cause and effect is not unique to the word *mean*. It also shows up with the words *reason* and *why*. For instance, in these two sentences, the situation in the first clause is a result of the situation in the second clause.

The reason that leaves are green is that (or because) they have chlorophyll.
Why are leaves green? Because they have chlorophyll.

But in the next two sentences, the situation in the second clause is a result of the situation in the first.

The reason that leaves have chlorophyll is to be able to metabolize carbon dioxide.
Why do leaves have chlorophyll? So they can metabolize carbon dioxide.

In some cases, the difference is marked by the grammatical form of the second clause: a tensed clause denotes a cause, and an infinitival (*to be able*) or modal (*can*) clause denotes a result. If we exchange the tense in the first and third examples above, the sentences say something odd:

??The reason that leaves are green is to have chlorophyll.
??The reason that leaves have chlorophyll is that they're able to metabolize carbon dioxide.

Is it the same word *mean* in all these uses? Or are some of them just related senses, like the six *smokes*, or even homonyms, like the two *banks*? To get some perspective, here are three uses of *mean* that are obvious homonyms:

What does he mean to do next?	[= 'intend']
That's one mean and ugly dog.	[= 'nasty']
The mean temperature in Lower Slobbovia is minus 6.	[= 'average']

In comparison to these last three uses, all of the interpretation uses and the linkage use seem pretty close.

But they're not quite all the same either. One way to see this is by looking at two other grammatical frames. In some of the uses, the new grammatical frames say the same thing as our original frame. But in other uses, the new frames simply sound odd.

Frame A: *The meaning of X is Y*

The meaning of *Rauch* is *smoke*.	
[=*Rauch* means *smoke*]	(Translation)
The meaning of *slithy* is *lithe and slimy*	
[=*Slithy* means *lithe and slimy*]	(Definition)
?The meaning of *osculate* is doing *this*.	(Demonstration)[3]
?The meaning of a red light is that you	
should stop.	(Explanation of symbols)
*The meaning of smoke is fire.	(Linkage)

Frame B: *X has the same meaning as Y*

(The German word) *Rauch* has the same	
meaning as (the English word) *smoke*.	(Translation)
Slithy has the same meaning as *lithe and slimy*.	(Definition)
Osculate has the same meaning as doing *this*.	(Demonstration)
*A red light has the same meaning as that	
you should stop.	(Explanation of symbols)
*Smoke has the same meaning as fire.	(Linkage)

So these frames appear to divide the five uses into three groups: the translation and definition uses, which sound fine in Frames A and B; the

---

[3] Some speakers think this example and the next sound fine, but others don't.

demonstration and symbol explanation uses, which sound so-so in Frame A and pretty bad in Frame B; and the linkage use, which sounds really bad in both frames.

But we're not done. Another use of *mean* appears in the grammatical frame *X means Y for Z*. Here, *Y* describes how some situation *X* affects *Z*. I'll call this the "impact" use. In these examples, I've underlined the affected character.

Impact use: *X means Y for Z*
What the stock market decline means for <u>us</u> is that we can't retire soon.
What do the latest insights of brain imaging mean for <u>music theory</u>?

Another use might be called "emotional impact." This one talks about *how much* something means, and we can use the adjective *meaningful*.

Emotional impact use: *X means a lot/a little to Z;*
X is meaningful to Z
Your thank-you note meant a great deal to <u>my wife</u>.
The situation in Rwanda means very little to <u>most Americans</u>.
Graduating from Tufts was very meaningful to <u>Karen</u>.

If we try to force the interpretation and linkage uses into the grammatical frame for the emotional impact use, we get nonsensical sentences. This shows how different the emotional impact use is from the others.

Rauch means *smoke* very much to Sam.
*A red light means that you should stop a great deal to Igor.
*Smoke is very meaningful to fire.

Just to be as complete as I can: What's the sense of *mean* in *what it means to be human* or *what it means to be an American Jew*? I think this is a combination of the linkage sense—one is looking for all the consequences of being human—and the impact sense—how being human matters for one's existence. This sense also appears in another grammatical frame: *To be human means to suffer*.

And where does the expression *the meaning of life* fit in? The best paraphrases I can come up with are 'what life is for,' 'the purpose of life,' or possibly 'the deep value of life.' The last of these is sort of like the emotional impact use in *Your thank-you note meant a lot to my wife.*

Then there's the use found on bottled water: *Poland Spring: What it means to be from Maine.* (I didn't make this up!) I can't make any sense of this at all, beyond general atmospherics of profundity. I think you're supposed to take from it that Poland Spring exhibits all the quintessential good qualities that one associates with Maine, but I'm not sure how it says this.

You may be finding this analysis of *mean* and *meaning* outrageously baroque. "Surely there has to be a simpler explanation—after all, it's only one word." This attitude is just the sort of preconception that Wittgenstein is ranting about.[4] If it's any consolation, I want to assure you that *mean* is quite ordinary. Practically any random word gets us into the same sort of difficulty. We've already seen some of the complexity of *language*, *word*, and *smoke*. We'll see more of this sort of thing as we go along.

---

[4] The logicians Jon Barwise and John Perry based a whole theory, Situation Semantics, on the hypothesis that the explanation use of *mean* (*Slithy means lithe and slimy*) can be understood in terms of the the linkage use (*Smoke means fire*). From the analysis here, we can see that this is like trying to understand how to smoke a cigar in terms of how you smoke a herring.

8
"Objective" and "subjective" meaning

We're not quite done with *mean*. In addition to all its uses in the last chapter, it's also used to describe a character's subjective take on a situation. I'll call this character the "interpreter."

This further use has two subcases. Here's the first one, in a variety of grammatical frames. (I've underlined the interpreter in each example.)

Subjective interpretation of a word, phrase, or sentence
In <u>Bill</u>'s opinion, *"All trespassers will be shot"* means anyone but him [. . . will be shot].
In the *Investigations*, *language game* means any use of language in a context.
Language means something different to <u>linguists</u> than it does to <u>computer scientists or philosophers</u>.
"No" may mean *"yes"* to <u>you</u>, but it means *"no"* to <u>me</u>!
When I say *"no,"* <u>I</u> MEAN *"no"*!
By *reference*, <u>David Lewis</u> means reference in all possible worlds.
By *"look to the use,"* <u>Wittgenstein</u> means that we shouldn't be trapped by our preconceptions.
<u>I</u> meant by *impenetrability* that we've had enough of that subject, and it would be just as well if you'd mention what you mean to do next, as I suppose you don't mean to stop here all the rest of your life.
(Humpty Dumpty again; notice that he also uses *mean* to mean 'intend')

Like the interpretation use of *mean* in the last chapter (such as *"Rauch means smoke"*), this use provides an interpretation or explanation of some word or phrase. But, unlike the use in the last chapter, it points out that this interpretation is just the way the *interpreter* understands this phrase. The person uttering the sentence may not agree that this is the right interpretation, and may be implying that not everyone understands the phrase the same way. So we might call this a "subjective" use of *mean*—it describes the interpreter's point of view.

By contrast, the interpretation use of *mean* in the last chapter presents the interpretation of a phrase as a fact: it's a fact that *Rauch* means 'smoke,' and anyone who doesn't think so is just wrong. So I'll call this the "objective" interpretation sense.

The second new use of *mean* also describes someone's understanding, this time their understanding of a linkage between situations.

Subjective linkage between two situations
In some people's minds, the president's behavior means that he's losing his grip.

To me, the look on Bill's face means that we'd better get out of here fast.

Again, this differs from the linkage use we discussed in the last chapter. It adds that this linkage is someone's interpretation of the relation between the two situations. And again, our original linkage sense presents the linkage as simply a fact: smoke simply means fire. So I'll call this previous use the "objective" linkage sense.

I'm putting "objective" in scare quotes because, of course, the speaker is only expressing his or her own take on the situation. We, the hearers, might well disagree. The sentence *presents* the interpretation as a fact, but saying it's a fact doesn't make it so.

This duality of "objective" and "subjective" uses is actually pretty common among words of English. (By now, you might have guessed I was going to say that!) Think about these examples, which involve a number of different grammatical frames.

Tom adores Olive.
Tom enjoys playing checkers.
   (also *detests*, *hates*, *loathes*, and many others)
Syntax is fascinating to Noam.
Syntax fascinates Noam.
Noam is fascinated with syntax.
   (also *terrifying/terrifies/terrified of*, *surprising/surprises/surprised at*, *disgusting/disgusts/disgusted with*, *exciting/excites/excited about*, and many others)

These convey the attitude of some person (here, Tom or Noam) toward some thing or activity. The person uttering the sentence doesn't necessarily hold the same attitude, and may be implying that other people see things differently. So these examples parallel the "subjective" uses of *mean*.

But the same or related words can also be used to convey an evaluation pure and simple:

Olive is adorable.
Playing checkers is enjoyable.
Syntax is fascinating.
   (also *detestable*, *hateful*, *loathsome*, *terrifying*, *surprising*, *disgusting*, *exciting*, and many others)

Here the speaker is conveying a "fact" about Olive, playing checkers, and syntax. Again, I put "fact" in scare quotes, because the person hearing the sentence might well disagree, and think the speaker is wrong about Olive, playing checkers, or syntax. So these examples are like the "objective" uses of *mean*.

This distinction between "subjective" and "objective" is interesting in itself. I bring it up, though, because it will also loom large in Part Three, when we discuss what truth (or 𝕿𝖗𝖚𝖙𝖍) might be.

9

What do meanings have to be able to do?

So far we've been talking about the words *mean* and *meaning*. Now it's time to ask what 𝕽eal 𝕸eaning could be like, if there is such a thing. Over the next few chapters, I want to show you that it can't just be a matter of working up a better dictionary with better definitions.

Let's start with a puzzling question raised by Wittgenstein. What does the word *this* mean?—not when we're pointing at anything, just the plain word *this* on its own. None of the uses of *mean* we talked about in Chapter 7 do the trick. We can't define *this* in terms of something more familiar, as when we say "*Slithy* means 'lithe and slimy.'" And we can't demonstrate it, as when we say "*Osculating* means doing *this* [demonstrating]." So we don't know how to answer. We certainly don't want to say the word *this* is *meaningless*, that it's a nonsense syllable like *bliff* and *thit*. It *isn't* a nonsense syllable, and of *course* it's meaningful.

In what sense is it meaningful, though? We say that jobs and love affairs can be meaningful or meaningless—in the sense of having emotional impact. But the meaningfulness of *this* doesn't have anything to do with its emotional impact. What *does* it have to do with?

Here are some sentences that raise a similar puzzle.

> *"The bear was chased by the lion"* means the same thing as *"The lion chased the bear."*

> *"It appears that the war is lost"* means the same thing as *"The war appears to be lost."*

And I just can't resist this example:

> *"X and Y mean the same thing"* means the same thing as *"X means the same thing as Y."*

Here we're talking not about the meanings of words, but about the meanings of sentences. What is this *thing* that these pairs of sentences both mean? What's the same about them?

It's not just that they have the same words in them. After all, these next two sentences have the same words, but they don't mean the same thing:

> The lion chased the bear.
> The bear chased the lion.

And these next two sentences have the same words, but the second one doesn't mean anything at all (in English, anyway).

> It appears that the war is lost.
> *The it appears war lost is that.

There's something about how the words are put together that plays a role in what sentences mean.

I think we sense something deeper, something hidden behind the words and sequences of words. It's not just a definition in terms of other words. When we say the word *this* is meaningful, we're saying that, unlike *thit*, it has a meaning—whatever a meaning might be. But here's where the trouble begins. What could this hidden, deeper something be?

Plato thought the meaning of a word like *dog* is a sort of timeless essence of "dogginess," something we can never experience directly. But he didn't talk about the meanings of *sentences*, and he also didn't talk about the meaning of the word *this* (or its Greek equivalent)—what could the essence of "thisness" be like? Other philosophical approaches have tried to explicate word and sentence meanings in terms of kinds (the meaning of *dog* is the natural kind 'dog'), sets (the meaning of *dog* is the set of all dogs), and sets in all possible worlds (the meaning of *dog* is the set of all dogs in all possible worlds). And some approaches in linguistics have tried to identify word and sentence meanings in terms of abstract Deep Structures or Logical Forms. As different as these approaches to meaning are, they agree on one thing: we have no direct perceptual access to meanings—they are indeed hidden from us.

I'd like to work gradually toward describing what meanings are by asking: Whatever meanings of words and sentences might be, what do they have to *do*? What are the design specs for meanings? Here are six properties we have to keep in mind.

1.   Meanings are linked to pronunciations

The first thing a meaning has to do is to be linked to a spoken (and/or written) form of the language. The form *this* has a meaning attached to it, while the form *thit* doesn't. What makes a word a word is that it is a pairing between a pronounceable piece of sound—a "phonetic" or "phonological structure"—and a meaning.

Let's call something a "phonological word" if it has a pronunciation—whether or not it's paired with a meaning. If a phonological word *is* paired with meaning, we'll call it a "meaningful word." The 19th- and early 20th-century linguist Ferdinand de Saussure called such a pairing a "sign." For instance, *thit* and *bliff* are simply phonological words—pronunciations that aren't linked to meanings. *This* is a meaningful word (or a sign). And *thqs* is just a string of letters that doesn't even spell a phonological word.

In the *Cratylus*, one of the crazier of Plato's dialogues, Socrates discovers with great delight that word after word he thinks about has a pronunciation that perfectly suits its meaning. When he comes across a word whose pronunciation doesn't match its meaning (by whatever weird criteria he's invented), he guesses that at one time it used to match, but that

43

sound changes over history have degraded the pronunciation from its original "perfect" form. De Saussure knew better. One of his lasting contributions is the notion of the "arbitrariness of the sign": the sound 'dog' bears no relation at all to what dogs are like. This is of course why words for the same thing, like *smoke* and *Rauch*, can be so different from language to language.

(Well, *usually* there's no relation between the sounds of words and what they mean. Some very small number of words, especially words for noises like *meow*, *whoosh*, and *hiccup*, are onomatopoeic—that is, to some degree they imitate the sounds they name. But only to some degree. For instance, in French dogs go *gnaf-gnaf*, not *bow-wow*. Words like *mama* and *papa* and *dada* are widespread in the languages of the world, but not because they sound like mothers and fathers. Rather, these are among the first sounds babies make, so mothers and fathers narcissistically think they themselves are what the babies are talking about.)

Some of the signs of signed languages do resemble what they refer to. But only to some degree. If someone tells you what the sign means, you can sometimes see the resemblance. If you just see the sign alone, though, you'd be hard put to guess what it's meant to resemble.

Where is the pairing between pronunciations and meanings located? In the ordinary view of language, where language is "out in the world," meanings are there too. The late 19th-century logician Gottlob Frege insisted on this perspective, and most modern Anglo-American philosophers of language have followed suit. I won't. From the cognitive perspective, if speakers are going to be able to *use* words and sentences, they have to have them in their heads. So meanings—as well as the links between pronunciations and meanings—have to be in the heads of speakers too.

Thinking in terms of paired pronunciations and meanings helps make our analysis of *smoke* in Chapter 6 clearer. The word *smoke* in *smoke a cigar* and the word *smoke* in *smoke a ham* have the same pronunciation, but it's attached to two different meanings. One component of each of these meanings is the meaning of the word *smoke* in *cigar smoke*. That's why the three words are related.

2. Meanings of sentences are built from the meanings of their parts

It seems obvious that the meaning of a sentence has something to do with the meanings of the words in it. The sentence *The lion chased the bear* involves a lion, a bear, and some chasing. But the meaning of the sentence is more than just the sum of the meanings of the words. After all, *The bear chased the lion* has the same words in it, but it doesn't mean the same thing. Here's why. Chasing is an action involving two characters with different roles: a chaser and someone being chased. The two sentences differ in which role is being played by the lion and which by the bear. The grammatical structure of the sentence tells us which is which: the subject of the sentence names the chaser, and the direct object names the character being chased.

Let's make the example just a little more elaborate: *The fat lion chased the sleepy bear*. Who's fat and who's sleepy? It depends where the words are: *The fat sleepy lion chased the bear*, *The sleepy lion chased the fat bear*, and so on. Again the difference comes from the grammatical structure: if an adjective precedes a noun (in English), the property named by the adjective belongs to the character named by the noun.

A passive sentence like *The bear was chased by the lion* contains a little grammatical marker *was*, followed by the verb in its past participle form. These tell us to reverse which character plays which role. So the bear ends up the character being chased, and the lion is the chaser. The result is that this sentence ends up attached to the same meaning as *The lion chased the bear* (or to something pretty close).

For a different case, the nonsensical string of words *The it appears war lost is that* has a pronunciation, but no grammatical structure at all. As a result, although its individual words can be paired with meanings, the pieces of meaning can't be combined, and so the string as a whole can't be paired with a meaning—it's not a meaningful sentence.

Examples like this lead to a general idea that has been called "compositionality" and is attributed to Frege:

45

"Fregean compositionality": The meaning of a compound expression (a phrase or sentence) is a function of the meanings of its parts and of the grammatical rules by which they are combined.

Traditionally, Fregean compositionality has been taken to imply that the meaning of a phrase or sentence is made up entirely of the meanings of its words, pasted together according to instructions given by the grammatical structure. The meanings of *fat* and *lion* are pasted together to form the meaning of *fat lion*, so a fat lion is something that's both fat and a lion. The meanings of *chase* and *the bear* are pasted together to form the meaning of *chase the bear*, so something is a chasing of the bear in case it is an act of chasing and the character being chased is the bear. And so on. But in reality it's not that simple.[1] In Chapter 12 we'll see some ways this traditional view has to be amplified in order to accommodate the wonderful richness of linguistic expression.

---

[1] For one thing, the words aren't the only "parts" that are combined into phrase and sentence meanings. There are other possibilities, for instance:

- IDIOMS such as *kick the bucket* and *cut and dried* are made up of ordinary words, but their meanings aren't made up from the meanings of their parts, except perhaps metaphorically. You have to learn these phrases as entire units.
- COMPOUNDS such as *snowman* and *hot dog* function as meaningful units. Sometimes the words that make up a compound contribute to its meaning, as in *snowman*, and sometimes they don't—a *hot dog* isn't a kind of canine, and a *honeymoon* doesn't have anything directly to do with honey and the moon. In some compounds such as *cranberry*, one of the parts (here, *cran*) is only a phonological word, not a meaningful word. And even when the words *do* contribute to the meaning of a compound, they don't always tell you the whole meaning. A *garbage man* isn't a man made of garbage, and a *snowman* isn't a man who takes away the snow.
- In idioms and compounds, a unit whose meaning combines with the rest of the sentence is larger than a single word. But there are also meaningful units that are smaller than words, for instance the underlined parts of these phrases:

a ketchup<u>less</u> hot dog	[= 'a hot dog <u>without</u> ketchup']
an <u>ex</u>-copilot	[= 'a <u>former</u> copilot']
an <u>unzippable</u> jacket	[='a jacket that <u>cannot</u> be zipped']

These prefixes and suffixes can be paraphrased by words, and so we can see that they're linked to their own independent meanings. The meaning of a prefix or suffix combines with the meaning of the word it's attached to, in much the same way as word meanings are combined into phrases.

3. Translations should preserve meaning

The third thing we want from meanings is that translations of words and sentences into a different language should preserve meaning—that's what a translation *is*. English *smoke* and German *Rauch* are phonological words from different languages that are linked to the same meaning. If you're translating a story from Yiddish into Japanese, you're creating a sequence of phonological words in Japanese that's linked to the same meaning as the Yiddish sequence. (This doesn't necessarily mean that every *word* of Yiddish has a direct Japanese translation. Sometimes it might take a whole phrase of Japanese to translate a single word of Yiddish.)

Someone in the audience always objects that you can't *fully* translate between languages. Well, sure, it's often hard to convey all the delicate nuances of something you're translating, especially if it's literature or poetry. But for lots of practical purposes, even important ones like diplomacy, we take it for granted that translation works pretty well at preserving meaning. And that degree of approximation is enough to make my point. (In Chapter 14 we'll talk about some of the potential barriers to more accurate translation.)

4. Meanings have to connect language to the world: the *referential* function

The fourth thing we want meanings to do is connect language to the world. Suppose I point at something and ask you, "Is this a dagger which I see before me?" In order to answer me, you have to pick out the object I have in mind and see whether it satisfies the meaning of *dagger*. More subtly, the word *this* signals you to pick out something that I'm pointing to. (Aha! That's roughly what *this* means, at least in this context.) This is the *referential* function of meanings.

If meanings are in the head, how can they connect to the world? I'll deal with this question in Parts Two and Three.

5. Meanings have to connect with each other: the *inferential* function

The fifth thing we want meanings to do is serve as a vehicle for reasoning (or inference). If I say *Amy is hungry and Tom is cooking*, you can infer that Amy is hungry. This follows from the standard logical axiom $P \& Q \rightarrow P$. For a less trivial example, one that doesn't follow automatically from standard logical axioms, suppose I tell you:

> Amy convinced Tom to go to New York for the weekend.

Then you ought to be able to infer that:

> Originally, Tom didn't plan to go to New York for the weekend. Now he does.

This is the *inferential* function of meanings: from one sentence, another follows.

A long tradition in philosophy attempts to mechanize the process of inference and make it explicit, starting with Aristotle's treatment of syllogisms, and running through Leibniz, Frege, and Russell to contemporary formal logic, with offshoots into artificial intelligence and heuristic reasoning (reasoning in terms of best guesses). This tradition has also led to theories of computation, giving rise eventually to the invention of digital computers, artificial intelligence, and (thanks to Noam Chomsky) formal theories of language.

The cognitive perspective demands an explicit account of inference too. It's different from the logicians' approach, though, because it's interested not just in formal systems of inference but in how people *make* inferences—how inference takes place in the head.

No matter which perspective we take, inference can't be derived from the phonological words. In the example above, for instance, the pronunciation of *didn't plan* has nothing to do with the pronunciation of *convince*. Rather, the connection has to do with something about their meanings.

Relationships among the meanings of words can often be spelled out in terms of inference. For instance, returning to *smoke*, from *Bill smoked* (#3) *the cigar*, we can infer that *Smoke* (#1) *came out of the cigar*. Similarly, from *The room was smoky* we can infer that *There was smoke* (#1) *in the room*. From these inferences we can see how *smoke* (#1) forms part of the meanings of *smoke* (#3) and *smoky*.

6. Meanings are hidden

Going back to the issue that started this chapter, a crucial property of meanings is that they're hidden. (Exactly the sense in which I mean "hidden" here will become clearer as we go along. I certainly don't have anything mystical in mind.) In the pairing of meaning with a pronunciation, say the phonological word *this*, we can hear the pronunciation (or see it, if it's written). And we have an immediate conviction that the phonological word is meaningful. But we can't explain its meaning, and we can't hear or see its meaning, despite the fact that it's in our head.

In other words, the meaning side of a sound–meaning pair is *unconscious*, except for producing the feeling that the attached piece of sound is meaningful. We'll work this part of the picture out in Part Two, including its rather startling consequences for a theory of consciousness.

You might protest that meanings don't *have* to be hidden or unconscious. After all, if I hear the word *dog*, I may well have a conscious visual image of a dog. Couldn't that picture in my mind do the work of a meaning? The short answer is No. I'll give a longer answer in the next chapter.

Let's sum up: In the cognitive perspective, the meaning of a word or sentence is something in the head of a language user—a speaker or hearer—that:

- links to or associates with the spoken or written form;
- combines with the meanings of other parts of the sentence;
- can link to translations of expressions into other languages;

- can connect with the world;
- serves as a vehicle for inference; and
- is hidden from awareness.

To work this story out, three big questions have to be answered eventually:

- How are meanings hidden from awareness?
- How do meanings connect with the world?
- And above all: How can meanings be in the head?

10
Meanings can't be visual images

One loose end in the last chapter was the possibility that meanings of words and sentences might be visual images rather than definitions in terms of words. Here are some reasons why this won't work.

The 18th-century philosopher George Berkeley's famous example is triangles. Suppose the meaning of the word *triangle* is a visual image of a triangle. Now an image of a triangle has to have a particular shape. So let's say your image of a triangle is like this one.

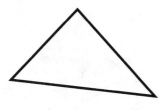

The problem is that triangles don't all have the same shape. Look at these next two. You might be tempted to say, "Well, these are close enough in shape to my triangle that they count as triangles."

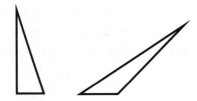

But now look at this next thing. I think it looks more like your triangle than the other two do.

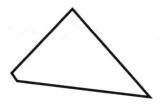

But this one isn't a triangle. "Well," you might say, "this last figure doesn't have three sides." Hold it, though: nothing in the visual image itself tells us that having three sides is what's important for trianglehood. Once you state that as the critical feature, you've gone outside of what visual images can do. If all we have is pictures, how do we know how to compare things to the "ideal"?

Similarly, dogs don't all look alike, and a German shepherd actually looks less like a toy poodle than like a wolf.

DOG   **DOG**   **WOLF**

So how can a single visual image of a dog be the meaning of the word? The conclusion is that a single image—whether you imagine it or actually draw it—is too particular to stand for all the different ways a triangle or a dog can look.

Or look at this picture.

Here's what Wittgenstein has to say:

> Imagine a picture representing a boxer in a particular stance. Now, this picture can be used to tell someone how he should stand, should hold himself; or how he should not hold himself; or how a particular man did stand in such-and-such a place; and so on.

Again, the visual image can't tell you what it's important to pay attention to—what meaning is supposed to be conveyed.

The famous example of another 18th-century philosopher, David Hume, is causation. What's the meaning of this sentence?

> The white ball hit the green ball, and that caused the green ball to move.

All you can visualize is the white ball hitting the green ball, followed by the green ball moving. But this is the same thing you would visualize for this sentence, which says nothing about causation:

> The white ball hit the green ball and then immediately the green ball moved.

Causation is a compelling aspect of the way we ordinarily understand the world, but it's not in the visual image as such—it's only in our *interpretation* of the image, the meaning we assign to it. (I return to this issue in Part Two.)

53

And what could you put in visual images that would convey the meanings of these sentences? Little arrows and other annotations aren't allowed! Our visual images don't have them.

> There's a bird in that tree.
> A bird was in that tree yesterday.
> Is there a bird in that tree?
> A bird might be in that tree.

Nothing visual can distinguish present time from past (first sentence vs. second), declaratives from questions (first sentence vs. third), or statements of fact from statements of possibility (first sentence vs. fourth).

Going further afield, consider these sentences:

> Birds like that tree.
> That tree looks like a bird.
> All birds sit in trees.
> I owe you $10.
> Millard Fillmore was the thirteenth President of the US.

Nothing in a visual image can describe the birds' state of mind, as conveyed by the first sentence. A visual image for the next sentence might be a drawing of a bird-shaped tree, but how does that make specific the tree's birdiness?

Similarly, visual imagery can't depict the meaning of *all* (third sentence), of social concepts and values like money and owing (fourth sentence), or any of the unvisualizable concepts in the last sentence, whose meaning doesn't depend on knowing what President Fillmore looked like. And finally, going back to our original puzzle, of course the word *this* can't be captured in a visual image.

In short, although the meanings of words and sentences sometimes evoke visual imagery, they can't *all* be visual images. So I stand by my assertion that meanings are hidden (or largely so).

Saying that meanings are hidden doesn't imply that they don't have effects. We see their effects in what we can do with them. We can identify and categorize objects in the world. We can follow instructions, draw inferences, draw pictures, and utter sentences that other people seem to understand. All of these depend on "grasping" meanings. The paradox is that we grasp meanings even though we have no awareness of their form. I'll make this clearer in Part Two.

11

Word meanings aren't cut and dried

(You can't avoid the slippery slope)

Let's explore a little more deeply what meanings are like. This chapter looks at what you might call the "texture" of word meanings.

In the ordinary perspective, words stand for categories with sharp boundaries. Something either is or is not snow, or gold, or a tiger, or a puddle—there's a fact of the matter. If we have a hard time making up our mind about it, this is because we're ignorant of the true nature of the category or the true definition of the word (remember Putnam on tigers and gold in Chapter 4?).

For many purposes, this perspective works fine. But in other cases, it leads us to expect sharp boundaries where there aren't any. A well-known old case is *bald*.

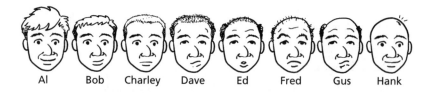

Al definitely isn't bald, and Hank definitely is. But no particular amount of hair divides bald from non-bald people. Is Dave bald or not?

How about Ed? How about Fred? We can't establish a definite fact of the matter, and I don't think it's because we don't know what *bald* means. No scientific or logical or mathematical theory of baldness is going to fix this. (The ancient philosophical version of this argument is called the "sorites paradox.")

Another familiar case is color terms. *Red* and *orange* have central (or basic) hues—the color of red and orange crayons, or of blood and oranges. But between them is a smooth transition of hues. There's no sharp dividing line where one side is definitely red and the other is definitely orange. And if we try to clear matters up by inserting a new category between them, say *red-orange*, we just end up with the same problem at the boundary between red and red-orange.

Suppose we set up an experiment: we show people various colors and ask them to name them. We find that our subjects are a little slower and a little less consistent with in-between colors than they are with basic colors. We also find that their responses to in-between colors depend more on context. For instance, if they've just been looking at colors in the orange range, they're more likely to call an in-between color "red." But if they've most recently been looking at reds, they're more likely to call the very same in-between color "orange."

It seems odd to say one of these answers is "right" and the other "wrong." And it's certainly funny to say our victims don't know what the words *red* and *orange* mean. Of course they do. A better scientific understanding of light won't change the situation either. In the physics of light, there's just a smooth transition of wavelengths with no dividing line.

A more cognitive way to think about this situation is that the word *red* in the speaker's head is linked strongly with basic red, and *orange* with basic orange, while non-basic shades are linked less strongly. So when a speaker is faced with in-between shades, the two links are about equally strong (or weak), and the brain is torn between the two choices. As a result, it responds more slowly, and its judgments are more fragile.

You experience the same sort of conflict, on a larger scale, any time you're making a tough decision. Should you order the duck?—or the halibut? They both look great. You end up deciding more slowly than if there's only one thing that appeals to you that night, and you may be more easily influenced by what someone else orders or what the waiter recommends. In naming in-between colors, we may not be so acutely conscious of our mental conflict, but our hesitation is still measurable by careful experiments.[1]

Another way that word meanings can smudge the boundaries involves so-called "family resemblance" concepts. What does the word *climb* mean? You might think of a sentence like this—

The bear climbed the tree.

—and you might conclude that climbing is defined as something like 'moving yourself upward by grabbing onto (or clambering on) a vertical surface.' But let's be linguists, and look at some other examples.

The bear climbed down the tree.
The bear climbed across the cliff.

Here, the bear is moving by grabbing onto a vertical surface, but he isn't moving upward. So going *upward* can't be essential to the definition of climbing. And now look at these examples:

The snake climbed the tree.
The airplane climbed to 30,000 feet.

Here, the snake and the airplane are moving upward all right, but they can't be clambering, since snakes and airplanes don't have arms and legs. In fact, the airplane isn't even contacting a vertical surface. So clambering and vertical surfaces aren't essential either.

Is anything *at all* essential? Well, if we get rid of both moving upward and clambering at the same time, we discover that the sentences are now odd.

---

[1] We'll get the same result no matter what collection of colors a particular language chooses to name. The boundaries between them are always fuzzy. We might get a different story if color *names* morphed smoothly into each other the way colors do—if every in-between shade had a name whose pronunciation sounded somewhere in between its neighbors, so that there was no discrete boundary between the pronunciations of *red* and *orange*. But human languages just don't work like that.

*The snake climbed down the tree.
*The airplane climbed down to 10,000 feet.

What's going on?

One possibility is that there are actually two different words pronounced *climb*, just like there are two words pronounced *bank*. One of them means 'move upward,' as in *The snake climbed the tree*, and the other means 'clamber,' as in *The bear climbed down the tree*. Fine. But now go back to our original example, *The bear climbed the tree*. Which kind of climbing do we mean? Is the bear going upward or is he clambering? On this story, it has to be one or the other.

This feels like a phony choice. The sentence really means both going upward and clambering, as we thought at the start, and it describes stereotypical climbing—the most normal or standard case. In contrast, climbing down and snakes climbing up are a little more unusual. They have a status rather like someone who is "kind of" bald.

So what we want to say about *climb* is that it really *is* a single word, not a pair of unrelated homonyms like the two *banks*. Its meaning involves two conditions—moving upward and clambering. If some action meets both conditions, we can call it climbing for sure. But on the other hand, an action doesn't need both conditions in order to qualify as climbing—just one will do the trick, though perhaps with not quite as much conviction.

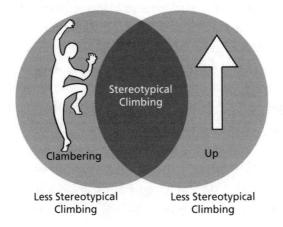

You might object: "Well, this crazy business with *climb* is just an exceptional case. Surely we don't have to worry about it too much." But in fact, cases like this are all over the place. Think about *books*. A stereotypical book is an object that consists of bound pages, with information inscribed on them in the form of pictures or written words. On the other hand, there are also blank books, with no words or pictures. And at the moment, the book I'm now writing consists only of information that isn't inscribed on bound pages. In the old days its physical form would be a pile of paper; now it's a bunch of electronic files. The electronic files and the bound blank pages have nothing at all in common. Yet they both count as books, because each is a facet of a stereotypical book. We might want to call them "honorary books" or "books by courtesy."

The most famous example of a family resemblance concept—the one that introduced the term—is Wittgenstein's analysis of the word *game*. He points out that for any factor you can think of—competition, having rules, being for amusement, and so on—you can find games that violate it, so there's no essential feature that all games have. (This is even clearer in the original German, where the word for *game*, *Spiel*, also translates as *play*.) The way Wittgenstein puts it is that games resemble each other the way members of a family do, each sharing different features with the others. And he makes it clear that this isn't peculiar to the word *game*: it's typical of all sorts of words.

Another example of a family resemblance concept, due to George Lakoff, is *mother*. A stereotypical mother has contributed genetic material to the child, has given birth to the child, and has raised the child. But surrogate mothers, adoptive mothers, and biological mothers who have given their child up for adoption each violate one or more of these conditions. Which one is the child's *real* mother? Often no single answer suits everyone's interests, because the ordinary meaning has fragmented.

What happens when the desire for cut-and-dried word meanings runs up against real life? A curious instance arose in 2006, when the International Astronomical Union wanted to deal with the discovery of more and more objects orbiting the sun at a great distance, many of them close to the size of Pluto. They didn't want to have to say there are more and more *planets* in the solar system—it might get out of hand. And scientific standards wouldn't allow them to talk about "sort of planets." So they decided to call these objects *dwarf planets*—an in-between category like *red-orange*—and they adopted a definition for *planet* that excluded dwarf planets. The unfortunate side effect was that they had to demote Pluto from its prestigious planetary status, to the annoyance of many astronomers and lay people. So the sentence *Pluto is a planet* changed from true to false.

One of the ringleaders of this coup is quoted as saying, "The debate about whether or not Pluto is a planet is critical to our understanding of the solar system. It is not semantics. It is fundamental classification." I beg to differ. It *is* semantics, and part of semantics *is* classification. After all, what changed about the solar system? Nothing—only more of its objects were discovered by astronomers. And what changed about Pluto? Only what astronomers decided to call it.

And their decision didn't really settle matters for good. Suppose that someday we discover, even further out from the sun, a lot of objects that are somewhere in size between Pluto and Mercury. Will they count as planets? Or as *dwarf* planets? We're back in the sorites paradox. So what difference does it really make what we call them? Only that if they're planets, their discoverers get more famous and schoolchildren have to memorize their names. (And notice: *planet* is a scientific term, the kind of thing that is supposed to be precise and objective!)

Sometimes the consequences are more serious. Suppose the government passes a law that says: "Bald people are exempt from military service." Then Dave and Ed will want to claim they're bald, and they'll try to find reasons to justify it. But suppose instead the law is: "All bald people must report for military service." Then Ed and Fred will want to claim they're *not* bald and find reasons to justify *that*—and Gus and Hank will try to get hair transplants! The government will have to issue a clarification to the effect: "For the purposes of this regulation, a person is bald if … etc." and will have to set up examination boards to rule on cases like Ed and Fred. And maybe academics of a certain school of thought will start arguing that baldness is not an inherent property but a social construct. This is a silly example, but if you change *bald* to *black* or *Jew* it isn't so silly any more.

Some other real cases (I'm sure you can think of more):

- How many people do you have to kill in order to call it *genocide*? Three, no; six million, yes. But what about a million and a half? Or half a million? Where do you draw the line?
- Is a fertilized human egg a person? Probably not. Is a nine-month fetus a person? Probably yes. Where in between does it change? This isn't entirely a matter of scientific fact. Hence the debate about abortion.
- How insane or mentally challenged does a criminal have to be before you can say that he didn't understand his crime, so we'll institutionalize him instead of imprisoning him?

The ordinary perspective usually presumes there are clear categories and abhors the prospect of the slippery slope. In practice, categories usually aren't so clear, and the slippery slope has to be accepted and carefully negotiated.

Dictionary definitions basically ignore all these facts of actual practice. This is why I distrust anyone who starts a discussion by citing Webster or some other dictionary, as though that makes controversial terms clear.

And, as Wittgenstein points out, if ordinary words like *bald* and *climb* and *book* are like this, there is no reason to expect *language* and *mean* and *true* to be any different.

12

Not all the meaning is
in the words

Let's now look at how word meanings (unruly as they are) are combined into the meanings of phrases and sentences. As I suggested in Chapter 9, the basic intuition is that the meaning of each grammatical chunk of the sentence is built by pasting together the meanings of the words in that chunk. This intuition is made explicit in the notion of Fregean compositionality, which says that the meaning of a phrase or sentence is made up of the meanings of its words, and that the grammatical structure tells how to paste the word meanings together.

Philosophers often seem to think of Fregean compositionality as almost sacred—as if without it, language would be completely out of control, unruly and unusable. Well, the news is that language is far from perfect. We keep discovering more and more things in it that violate Fregean compositionality (the dwarf planets of language). But it doesn't follow that language is unruly and unusable. Obviously we use it. I'd rephrase compositionality this way:

> "Enriched compositionality": The meaning of a compound expression (a phrase, sentence, or discourse) is a function of the meanings of its parts, of the grammatical rules by which are they combined—and of other stuff.

What's this "other stuff"? I'm going to sketch four places where Fregean compositionality faces a problem, and this will help us get a feel for what the "other stuff" is like. The message is that these things aren't blemishes on language, they're integral to its texture.

Implicature and discourse connection

Let's start with some examples of a sort made famous by the philosopher Paul Grice in the 1970s. As I'm going out the door, my wife says,

Will you be going near a mailbox?

What she *means*, of course, is 'Would you mail some letters for me?', but she's saying it politely. Or:

Amy: Hey, d'ya wanna get some lunch?
Tom: There's that nice Italian place around the corner.

Tom's meaning goes beyond the words he utters: implicitly, he's answering "Yes," and then he's going on to suggest *where* to get some lunch. We might also notice that *Italian place* is understood as meaning 'Italian restaurant'—it gets its full meaning not from the meanings of the words alone but also from the discourse context. So some of the "other stuff" comes from the need to understand a sentence in its social context: what would the reason be for saying *this* in *this* particular situation?

In these examples and many others to come, we can't paraphrase the understood material with precise and unique words. So we can't save Fregean compositionality by saying the words are there to compose the meaning, but you just haven't uttered them.

People often excuse cases like this by calling them "pragmatic" inferences (or, to use Grice's term, "implicatures") and taking them to be external to a theory of the meaning of sentences. But they're sure part of understanding each other, all the time.

Ellipsis

Here's an example from Chapter 9:

> Originally, Tom didn't plan to go to New York for the weekend. Now he does.

We understand the second sentence as saying 'Now he does plan to go to New York for the weekend.' How does it get that meaning?

One way to answer this question would be to say that, in a sense, this sentence "really is" *Now he does plan to go to New York for the weekend*—but the speaker has left out all the words that copy parts of the previous sentence. This is the approach of classical transformational grammar in the Chomskyan vein, as well as that of many philosophical theories: the fuller version of the sentence is its "deep structure" or "logical form," but much of it is erased before it's spoken. This answer would satisfy Fregean compositionality, because the words are there in the logical form. But it also requires us to say that your utterance includes words you don't pronounce, and that you don't pronounce them because they're the same as words in the previous sentence.

Alternatively, we could say that the meaning of the second sentence isn't just put together from the meanings of its words and the way they're grammatically combined. It also includes the meanings of parts of the *previous* sentences and the way *they* are combined. There are no hidden words, there's only a more complex way of building the meaning—through enriched compositionality.

How can we tell which way is better? Is it just a matter of taste? Well, no. For one thing, in some cases of ellipsis, the context has no words at all. Yet the speaker's meaning is still perfectly understandable, and in fact the very same utterance can have radically different meanings. Look at these situations.

Here, nobody has previously mentioned kissing or stepping off a roof. So the woman can't have left these words out because of some identical words in an earlier sentence. Rather, her meaning obviously depends on understanding the nonlinguistic context. So in this case the nonlinguistic context serves as the "other stuff" in enriched compositionality.

For a more complicated case, here are the lyrics of a 1930s Rodgers and Hart classic:

> It seems we stood and talked like this before. We looked at each other in the same way then. But I can't remember where or when.

We can't spell out the way we understand the last sentence just by copying words blindly from the previous two sentences. It takes a certain amount of ingenuity to construct a good paraphrase. This monster is about the closest I can get (maybe you can do better?):

> ...But I can't remember where or when we stood and talked like this before and looked at each other in the same way we're looking at each other now.

It seems funny to think of Rodgers and Hart's lyric as having a "logical form" that contains all these *words*, as Fregean composition would require. Enriched compositionality allows us to say that the lyric has no hidden words, and that its meaning comes partly from the meaning of the previous sentences. I don't think we should find this too far-fetched. After all, in the dialogue above, Tom's reply to Amy can't be derived from words in Amy's sentence either. (Although I do have to admit that right now, nobody has a detailed theory of how such indirect connections work.)

Reference transfer

Another case of enriched compositionality arises when we use the name of one thing to talk about something else.

> Plato is up there on the top shelf, next to Wittgenstein.
> ['Plato' = 'book by Plato']
> Let's check out the wax museum. They have the Beatles on display!
> ['the Beatles' = 'statues of the Beatles']
> Joe is parked out back. ['Joe' = 'Joe's car']
> [One waitress says to another:] The ham sandwich in the corner wants some coffee.
> ['ham sandwich' = 'person who ordered/who's eating a ham sandwich']

There are three possible strategies to account for the way we understand these sentences. One is to say that, although we never noticed it before, the name *Plato* is actually ambiguous. It can mean either the philosopher or a book he wrote, and it so happens that in the example above it means the book. This approach allows us to hang on to Fregean compositionality. But it has the odd consequence that every time you learn a person's name, you have to learn that it's also a name for books by that person and for statues of that person and for that person's car—they're completely separate meanings for that name. It doesn't make sense to think we learn this for every name, one by one. When you learn a name, you automatically know it can stand for these other things as well.

Another strategy for preserving Fregean compositionality is to say that *Plato* still means 'Plato' in the first example—it's not ambiguous—but the logical form of the sentence has the words *book by* in it. Then we conveniently delete *book by*. This approach is just like the deletion approach to ellipsis, which (as we've just seen) runs into uncomfortable problems.

But there's a simpler strategy. We can say that these examples have some pieces of meaning that just aren't expressed by words. As an English speaker, your system for relating meaning to pronunciation lets you take a short cut—you can leave these pieces of meaning out of what you actually say. (If you want to, you can express them as *book by*, *statue of*, and so on, but you don't have to.) Because your hearers have the same system, you can count on them to make out your meaning. Sure, this approach violates Fregean compositionality, because the words aren't there to express the meaning. But it doesn't endanger the coherence of language.[1]

Aspectual coercion

Here's a subtler case. Compare these sentences.

Joe jumped until the bell rang.
Joe jumped when the bell rang.
Joe slept until the bell rang.

In the first sentence, we understand Joe as jumping repeatedly. But if we change *until* to *when*, as in the second sentence, then Joe jumps only once. And if *jumped* is changed to *slept*, as in the third sentence, Joe is not understood as *sleeping* repeatedly. So where does the sense of repetition (so-called aspectual coercion) come from?

We have the same three possibilities as with reference transfer. First, we could save Frege by saying that *jump* and all the hundreds of other verbs that undergo aspectual coercion are actually two related verbs: *jump* means either 'make one jump' or 'make repeated jumps.' This approach, though, requires that every time you learn one of these verbs, you have to learn both meanings. Not so good.

Second, we could say that the logical form of *Joe jumped until the bell rang* contains the word *repeatedly*, but the speaker leaves it out. But exactly *what* is left out? It would be equally plausible for the logical form to contain the words *repeatedly*, or *over and over*, or *many times*. There's

---

[1] From this description, you might think the strategy of deleting words and the strategy of enriched compositionality are pretty much the same thing, and it's impossible to tell them apart. I assure you that once you start to work out the technical details, they do turn out to be different. For the courageous, Peter Culicover and I have worked out the arguments in our book *Simpler Syntax*. Suffice it to say here that enriched compositionality wins.

no definite way to say. What these choices have in common, of course, is their meaning—but not their pronunciation.

Third, we could say that in combining the meanings of *jump* and *until*, a piece of meaning has to be added in. If you want to, you *can* express this piece as *repeatedly* or *over and over*, but you don't have to say it at all. This violates Fregean compositionality, because the extra meaning doesn't come from the words. But as long as the principle for inducing the extra piece of meaning is well defined, everything works fine.

In each of these cases—discourse connections, ellipsis, reference transfer, and aspectual coercion—we've found pieces of meaning that go beyond just combining the individual word meanings with the grammatical structure. Some of these pieces come from the linguistic or nonlinguistic context, and some are special unexpressed pieces of meaning that help glue word meanings together in non-Fregean ways. I've shown you only the tiniest sample of these phenomena. They pervade the texture of the language. They are the "other stuff" in enriched composition. They're nothing to be afraid of, they aren't totally wild, they don't threaten language with chaos.

I haven't even touched here on literary devices such as metaphor, which go even further beyond what's present in the words and grammatical structure. My aim here has been to show that even the humblest everyday language use is shot through and through with enriched compositionality.

People sometimes say that language is a "mirror of thought" or a "window into human nature" (as in the subtitle of Steven Pinker's book *The Stuff of Thought*). These phrases raise the expectation that it's transparent: just look through language and you'll see what thought is like. That's what Frege thought. Faced with the kinds of things we've been talking about here, though, some of my students have decided language is actually more like a "cubist mirror" or a "funhouse mirror" or a "funnel for thought." It turns out that if you look at the details of Pinker's "window," language is more like a collection of small and oddly shaped peepholes with distorting lenses. If we squint through them all the right way, we can assemble the various perspectives into a sense of the larger schema behind them. And that's what we need linguistics for.

13

Meanings, concepts, and thoughts

We're now maneuvering into a position to begin to answer our original question from Chapter 1: What's the connection between language and thought?

From the cognitive perspective, the meaning of a word or sentence is something in a speaker's head that's linked to a pronunciation. It has all the interesting properties I listed in Chapter 9: sentence meanings are built from word meanings (and "other stuff"), meanings are preserved in translation, meanings serve as basis for reference and for inference— and meanings are hidden.

It's common to say that a word expresses a concept, where the concept is something in a speaker's head too. I'd like to pull meanings and concepts together, and say that the meaning of the word *is* the concept it expresses.

It's also common to say a sentence expresses a (complete) thought, which is supposed to be something in the speaker's head as well. So again, I'd like to connect these two notions, and say the meaning of a sentence *is* the thought that it expresses.

I have to make it clear, though, that not *all* concepts and thoughts are meanings of words or sentences. Plenty of concepts and thoughts can't be expressed very well in language, such as the thought of the exact pattern of light and shade on your desk or (to use Wittgenstein's example) the concept of what a clarinet sounds like. These sorts of concepts and thoughts can exist on their own in the head without being attached to words. But when a concept or thought *can be* attached to a pronunciation, I'd like to say that it serves as the meaning of that string of sounds.

We adult humans aren't the only ones that have thoughts we can't express. Apes and babies have concepts and thoughts without having any language at all. They find their way around in the world, they react in complicated yet consistent ways to what's going on around them, they solve problems. *Something* must be going on in their heads to direct their understanding of the world and their actions in it. Why not call these things in their heads concepts and thoughts?

Well, some people might insist that by definition, concepts and thoughts have to be attached to *words*, that something doesn't count as a concept or thought unless you can say it. Okay, then we'll need a different term for what I'm calling "concepts and thoughts that aren't attached to words." Suppose we call them "goncepts" and "shmoughts." If you prefer that terminology, then what I'm trying to say is that the meaning of a word is a "goncept," and it achieves the status of a "concept" simply by being linked to a pronunciation. On the other hand, the way we understand what a clarinet sounds like would only be a goncept, not a concept. And apes and babies would have no concepts, only goncepts, and they can't think, they can only shmink.

Using this terminology, we can ask what the difference is between the goncepts of apes and babies and those of adult humans, and we can ask what the difference is between goncepts that are also concepts, such as what triangles are, and goncepts that *aren't* also concepts, such as exactly what a clarinet sounds like. Whichever terminology we adopt, the issues that we have to sort out are exactly the same, as far as I can tell. So I'll stick to my original terminology. You're free to translate into whatever terminology you like.[1]

---

[1] There is a strain of philosophy of mind that asks if there could be such a thing as "nonconceptual content." As far as I understand it, the question is whether there could be such a thing as goncepts that aren't concepts, or whether there could be *parts* of concepts that are only goncepts. Of course there could.

You might be concerned that there's potentially a slippery slope here. If we attribute concepts to apes, what about pigs? lizards? paramecia, for goodness' sake? And how about computers? Thermostats, anyone? I'm not too worried. As we saw in the last chapter, lots of other concepts threaten a slippery slope without becoming incoherent. So why not the concept "concept"?

Instead of talking about "thoughts," philosophers often speak of "propositions," which are supposed to be what a sentence expresses regardless of how it's actually said. For instance, *My dog is dead* and the German sentence *Mein Hund ist tot* express the same proposition.[2] So far this sounds just like the way I've been using the phrase "meaning of a sentence." But there are at least two differences. For one thing, most philosophers seem to think of a proposition as something independent of the speaker, not as something in the speaker's head. For another, they often say: "A proposition is something that can be true or false." In ordinary language, a declarative sentence can be true or false, but it's odd to say *the meaning of this sentence* is true or false. And non-declarative sentences—questions, imperatives, and sentences like *Oh, if only it were Friday!*— certainly have meanings, but neither they nor their meanings can be true or false.

I think this has caused some confusion about what a proposition is meant to be. Like *differentiable* in Chapter 4, the word *proposition* is intended as a term of art. But is it supposed to correspond to the ordinary usage of the term *meaning of a sentence* or to the ordinary usage of the word *sentence*? The confusion is perpetuated by locutions like *Consider the proposition that snow is white*, which is often used as though the proposition *is* the sentence *Snow is white*. For this reason, I'm going to avoid the term *proposition* here.

---

[2] Just to be careful, technically a proposition is supposed to include parts of the meaning that need to come from the context. If I say *My dog is dead*, it refers to a different situation in the world than if *you* say the same thing. So the proposition I express when I say *My dog is dead* is something like 'Ray Jackendoff's dog is dead.' If I say *It's raining*, I express a proposition something like 'It's raining at Tufts University in Medford, Massachusetts, on October 15, 2010, at 2:46 p.m.'

Sometimes people say "thought is like a language," and this conception has been enshrined in the term "the language of thought."[3] I find this terminology misguided too. A language is a system that links concepts and thoughts with pronunciations. But concepts and thoughts themselves don't *have* pronunciations, they're *connected* to pronunciations. In other words, thoughts are not *like* a language, they function as a *part* of a language. Saying "thought is like a language" is as nonsensical as saying "wheels are like bicycles" or "peach pits are like peaches."

I suspect these locutions have arisen because people tend to think of pronunciation as *mere* pronunciation, an inessential and culturally dependent part of language. It's just a convenient way to get the 𝕽𝖊𝖆𝖑 𝕰𝖘𝖘𝖊𝖓𝖈𝖊, the thought, from one person to another. What possible philosophical interest could there be in sequences of speech sounds? By contrast, the truths of 𝕽𝖊𝖆𝖑 𝕸𝖊𝖆𝖓𝖎𝖓𝖌 are too profound to have to depend on mere people.

But if we adopt the cognitive perspective, and ask how language *works* for *people,* we find that the character of pronunciation is hugely important. It's an essential medium for the communication of thought. And, as we've seen in earlier chapters, the scientific investigation of the sound structure of language has yielded a rich and complex organization of patterns, well worth taking seriously.

(If you're wondering about the status of "private languages", please be patient till Chapter 36.)

---

[3] This term was made popular by philosopher/psychologist Jerry Fodor. It plays on the fact that in certain technical circles, the word *language* is like *smoke*—it's polysemous. One sense is the one we've been talking about here: a systematic mapping between thoughts and pronunciations in the heads of speakers. Another sense refers to any formal combinatorial system, whether it's a communication system or not. In this sense we can speak of musical and mathematical notation as formal languages. In fact, the sound structure of language in the first sense is itself a formal language in the second sense. In this second sense, thought *is* a language. But when people say "thought is like a language" they're usually thinking of the first sense, unfortunately.

14

Does your language determine your thought?

Here's another take on the connection between language and thought. People outside linguistics often ask me, "Don't you agree that the language we happen to speak affects the way we think?" This is a strong and widespread sentiment, and it seems at odds with the view I've been pushing here—that the same thought can be equally expressed in different languages. The most extreme version of this idea, often called "linguistic relativity," or "linguistic determinism," or the "Sapir–Whorf hypothesis" (after the early 20th-century linguists Edward Sapir and Benjamin Lee Whorf), is that your thought is deeply structured by the structure of your language, and that therefore speakers of different languages may not just *talk* in mutually incomprehensible fashion, but may also *think* in mutually incomprehensible fashion. It isn't that language is a mirror of thought, but rather that thought is a mirror of language.

A popular anecdote connected with linguistic relativity is that the Eskimos have lots of words for different kinds of snow, so presumably they think about snow differently than we do. But even if it's true, this doesn't show that their language determines the way they think. If anything, the influence goes the other way: they have to deal with snow more than we do, so they invent more words. Likewise, I would guess that we have more words than they do that have to do with software—and certainly more than we ourselves did fifty years ago. Our vocabulary is mostly shaped by human interests and needs, not the other way around.

I don't want to deny that vocabulary affects thought. Having a word for something can affect both what we notice and the way we divide objects and events into categories. Sometimes this is good: it might be important to recognize such a thing as genocide (remember Chapter 11). And sometimes it's bad, such as when it makes us insist on sharp lines where there aren't any—it's either genocide, in which case we apply sanctions, or it's not, in which case it's not so serious and we can ignore it.

Over the past decade some psycholinguists have done experiments exploring linguistic relativity in less obvious areas of language. Here's one fairly typical example. The Mayan language Tzeltal is spoken in a village on a mountainside, and it so happens that this language doesn't have words that translate as *left* and *right*. Rather, if you want to say where something is in relation to something else, you use the mountain-side: the object is "uphill" or "downhill" or "transverse" from the other object (a lot like *uptown*, *downtown*, and *crosstown* in Manhattan). So the question is: if you ask Tzeltal speakers to do a task that involves spatial relations but doesn't involve language, will they behave differently from speakers of a standard European language? If they do, it shows that the language makes them think differently, even when they're not speaking. And indeed some differences turn up, especially if the task is highly ambiguous (such as "Make this array of objects look the same as that one"). The significance of these results has been subject to a lot of dispute (I have friends on both sides), and there's no space here to go into more details. I just want you to notice: these are not Big Effects. It's not like Tzeltal speakers perceive the world hugely differently from us.

Some languages have a different collection of words for primary colors than English. For instance, Japanese has a single word that covers both green and blue, and Russian has completely different words for what we call light blue and dark blue. It turns out that even without using words, speakers of these languages classify colors differently, and

75

they show the sorts of in-between effects we talked about in Chapter 11, but at different points in the spectrum. Again, this is far from showing that their thought is incomprehensible to English speakers.

In French, German, and many other languages, nouns are sorted into "genders," which are marked by various grammatical devices. For instance, English *the* translates into French *le* when it precedes a masculine noun, and into *la* when it precedes a feminine noun. It so happens that *sun* translates into French as a masculine noun, and *moon* into a feminine noun, while German is just the opposite. Well, if you ask French speakers to free-associate characteristics that go with the sun vs. with the moon, it turns out that they give you more "masculine" characteristics for the sun and more "feminine" for the moon—and German speakers are just the opposite. So at some level they do think of them differently, and this may well show up in contexts like poetry, where free association motivates metaphors and the like. But again it's hardly a Big Effect.

le soleil   la lune   die Sonne   der Mond

An area of language that may make a more radical difference is numbers. Many languages have been reported to have number words that only go up to two or three at most. One of these is the Amazonian language Pirahã, which has received a lot of attention recently. The way children achieve the concept of numbers that go as high as you want seems to be first through learning the sequence of number words *one, two, three, four,....* After that, they figure out what the sequence is *for,* namely counting *things.* If you don't have words for counting, it's much harder—maybe impossible, but I'll leave that open—to engage in commerce, construct precise calendars, do science, and so on. So this is an area where a linguistic invention opens up huge domains of human endeavor.

But if we're looking for radical differences in the way people think, a much more fruitful place to look is culture, not language. We can even keep the language identical. Compare the thought processes of Americans on the liberal left and the religious right. We find *huge* differences on matters like morality, foreign policy, economics, and education. These differences are far more consequential than the subtle little things due to language that have been discovered experimentally.

Well, you might say (and we do sometimes), the left and the right speak different languages. That's why they can't understand each other. Um, yes, I suppose—the network of relations among the meanings of words like *marriage, liberty, freedom*, and *patriotic* is systematically different all over the place. And they choose buzzwords that favor their positions, like *pro-choice* vs. *pro-life*. But the structure of the language is identical, and the vocabulary is being manipulated to serve the culture, not the other way around.

The point is that it doesn't take differences in language to make radical differences in thought. Differences in culture—which may produce differences in language—do just fine. And these cultural differences can be much more striking than anything stemming from language itself. So why get excited about the minor linguistic biases on thought, when there are these huge cultural ones?

Coming attractions: In Chapter 38, we'll talk about how having language really does make certain kinds of thought possible. But it doesn't do this in a way that differs from language to language—all languages help in pretty much the same way.

Part Two
Consciousness and Perception

15
What's it like to be thinking?

I keep insisting that the meanings of words and phrases and sentences are hidden. It's time to explore this more carefully. It's going to take us surprisingly far afield.

As I mentioned in Chapter 9, Plato thought that the meanings of words are eternal essences that we mere humans have no access to. The meaning of *dog*, for instance, is an eternal essence of "dogginess." So in a way, Plato agrees that meanings are hidden.

If you think languages are out in the world, eternal essences make a kind of sense. But wait a minute. Do you think 21st-century American English is eternal? Will it still exist 23,000 years from now? Were there eternal essences of *carburetors* and *telephones* two thousand years ago, but people just hadn't made any actual ones yet? Were there eternal essences of *sentence* and *toenail* back when the only living things on earth were bacteria? Well, even if your answer to these weird questions is yes, Plato's eternal essences aren't much help in explaining how people *use* language—what people *do* have access to that enables them to understand other people's utterances about carburetors and toenails and to formulate their own.

Plato sort of thought meanings are "too far away from us"—they're in a part of the universe we can't access. I'd like to suggest instead that meanings are "too *close* to us," in a part of our *minds* we can't access. Put more baldly, *meanings are mostly unconscious*. To make clearer what I mean, I'd like you to do a little delicate introspection.

What are you aware of when you're thinking? I don't know about you, but I personally experience a lot of my thinking as talking to myself—verbal imagery, a Joycean stream of consciousness. For many of us, the running commentary hardly ever stops. Some people manage to shut it up for a while by meditating or doing yoga.

Of course we also experience other kinds of imagery, especially visual imagery. In fact, some people report that their imagery is mostly visual or kinesthetic. Good cooks probably have lively images of tastes and smells. And I have music running in my head almost all the time. But for most people, especially those of us who use words for a living, verbal imagery is what feels like Real Thinking.

Plato has this very impression (in the Sophist):

> Stranger: Are not thought and speech the same, with this exception, that what is called thought is the unuttered conversation of the soul with herself?
> Theaetetus: Quite true.
> Stranger: But the stream of thought which flows through the lips and is audible is called speech?
> Theaetetus: True.

A lot of more modern people from all different quarters come to the same conclusion. Here's John B. Watson, one of the fathers of behaviorism:[1]

> The hypothesis that all of the so-called "higher thought" processes go on in terms of faint reinstatements of the original muscular act (including speech here)...is, I believe, a tenable one.

Here's the philosopher Peter Carruthers:

---

[1] A central issue in psychology in the late 19th and early 20th centuries was whether there could be such a thing as "imageless thought." Those who thought there could be such a thing reported only the frailest of introspective evidence, and they were eventually discredited. But the proponents of thoughts as images didn't win either. Rather (at least in the received history of the field), the whole notion of a scientific study of thought as something in the head was discredited by the behaviorists. They were aided and abetted by the rising anti-psychologism of the philosophy of the time, e.g. Frege's. See also remarks on the behaviorists in Chapter 18.

It is images *of natural language sentences* which are the primary vehicles of our conscious thoughts. [Even my 4 1/2-year-old son said,] "I think in English... I can *hear* myself think."

Noam Chomsky also hints that thought is unspoken language:

Language is not properly regarded as a system of communication. It is a system for expressing thought, something quite different.... Language use is largely to oneself: "inner speech" for adults, monologue for children.

Wittgenstein has been here too:

When I think in language, there aren't "meanings" going through my mind in addition to the verbal expressions: the language is itself the vehicle of thought.

But he admits he's a bit uneasy:

"So you really wanted to say..." One is tempted to use the following picture: what he really "wanted to say", what he "meant" was already *present somewhere* in his mind even before we gave it expression.

—which implies that there's some sort of meaning independent of the language.

What's the voice in my head like? Above all, I *hear* it. My inner voice speaks *in English*, with English pronunciation, English word order, English verb agreement, and so on. Someone who speaks both English and French may say, "I speak both languages all right, but I *think* in French." Speaking of efforts to teach the Cherokee language to the younger generation, the superintendent of the tribe's schools is reported to have said "What makes you a Cherokee if you don't have Cherokee thoughts?" (Notice the presumption that the language both determines the character of thought and cements ethnic identity.)

This all seems very natural. But it doesn't sit very comfortably alongside some of the things about thought and meaning that came up in Chapter 9. Thinking is supposed to be pretty much independent of what language you think in. The thought or the meaning is supposed to be the *same* when we translate from one language to another. You can't ask, "What language are you *meaning* in?" or "What language are your *meanings* in?" Yet we, like all the folks quoted above, have the compelling conviction that these English (or Greek or Cherokee) phrases and sentences running through our heads are our thoughts.

I have to respectfully ask you to suspend this conviction for now. If we step into the cognitive perspective, a different story emerges. Pronunciation and meaning are both in our minds. The pronunciation of a word or sentence enters our awareness when someone actually says it, but also when the inner voice is "speaking." Some chunks of pronunciation, such as *this*, are meaningful—they're linked to a concept or a thought—and some, such as *thit*, are not.

But now the important part: When a chunk of pronunciation *is* meaningful, *we still can't directly perceive its meaning!* We're aware of the presence of the meaning only because the pronunciation acts as a perceivable "handle" attached to it. The meaning itself stays backstage. (Other images, especially visual images, can also serve as "handles" for thoughts, which is why people often think *they're* thoughts too. I'll come back to visual images in Chapter 25.)

There's a second part to the story. A piece of pronunciation that functions as a "handle" comes with a conscious feeling of "meaningfulness." This feeling is absent when we hear a chunk of pronunciation like *thit* or *fendle* that isn't a "handle" for anything. Through the feeling of meaningfulness, we get the conviction that the pronunciation *is* the thought, not just a symbol or vehicle for the thought.

An iconoclastic way of putting this would be to say there really are no such things as conscious thoughts (just as there really are no sunsets and no English language). Here's a more forgiving way of putting it. In the ordinary perspective, as we've seen, we have the conviction that our verbal images simply *are* our conscious thoughts. But from the cognitive perspective it's not so simple. What we *call* a "conscious thought" actually has three components. Two of them are conscious: the verbal imagery and the feeling of meaningfulness. The third is the meaning attached to the pronunciation. It does all the heavy lifting of establishing inference and reference—but it's unconscious.

In other words, we *experience* our verbal images as thoughts because their (imaged) pronunciation is accompanied by the feeling of meaningfulness. Our intuitive conviction is *sort of* right: the verbal images themselves aren't thoughts, but they're *connected* to thoughts.

Here's an approximation of what I have in mind. The ordinary perspective is the way it seems to us. The cognitive perspective is closer to the way it works.

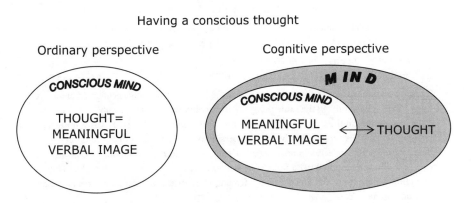

Having a conscious thought

A piece is still missing. How do we end up with this conviction that our verbal images are our thoughts? From the cognitive perspective, where we're asking how the mind works, it's very important to remember that convictions, no matter how strong, don't come by magic. *A conviction has to come from something going on in the head too.* So the cognitive perspective has to explain not only the pronunciation and the meaning of a sentence, but also the feeling of meaningfulness that goes with the pronunciation.

For convenience, I'll use the term "the Unconscious Meaning Hypothesis" to refer to this whole package:

- Pronunciation is conscious.
- It's accompanied by a conscious feeling of meaningfulness.
- It's linked to unconscious meaning—the thought or concept that the pronunciation expresses.

Discussions of consciousness often speak of "qualia," the components of experience such as the blueness of blue things, the painfulness of painful things, and so on. For readers who like qualia language, the Unconscious Meaning Hypothesis might be understood as saying that the qualia associated with so-called conscious thought are phonological rather than conceptual in character.[2]

---

[2] Here's a point of linguistics that picks up on our earlier discussion of different uses of *mean*. Two of the uses we've noticed are shown in these sentences.

"Ex-copilot" means *"former copilot."*	(Ch 7)
"Ex-copilot" means the same thing as *"former copilot."*	(Ch 9)

These two sentences mean about the same thing. This is grammatically peculiar. After all, *Pat hugged Sandy* doesn't mean the same thing as *Pat hugged the same thing as Sandy*.

Here's the reason the two sentences mean the same thing. In *X hugged Y*, X is supposed to be a person and Y is supposed to be another person, or perhaps a dog or a tree (in linguists' lingo, these are the "selectional restrictions" of *hug*). In *X means Y*, X is supposed to be a word or phrase and Y is supposed to be a meaning. You can cite words, so there's no problem filling in X. But, according to the Unconscious Meaning Hypothesis, you can't cite meanings. So how do you fill in Y?

One way to get around the problem is to fill in Y with words that are attached to the meaning you have in mind. That is, *former copilot* in the first example actually refers not to the words but to the meanings attached to the words. On this view, it's another example of reference transfer, like *The ham sandwich wants some coffee* in Chapter 12. Another way to get around the problem of filling in Y with meanings is by circumlocution, and that's what we're seeing in the second example: I'm not going to tell you directly what *ex-copilot* means, but whatever *former copilot* means, that's it.

The idea, then, is that these two sentences are both ways of dealing with the fact that you can't say meanings, you can only say phonology. And because we have the conviction that the phonology *is* the meaning, this all feels perfectly harmless, and both ways of saying it seem perfectly natural.

16

Some phenomena that test the Unconscious Meaning Hypothesis

You may find the Unconscious Meaning Hypothesis strange and counterintuitive, maybe even as weird as eternal essences of telephones. I want to spend the next few chapters sharpening it and helping you get used to it. First let's look at some things it explains about our experience of thought and meaning.

We first came to the idea that meanings are hidden in Chapter 9, when we looked at synonymous sentences like *The bear chased the lion* and *The lion was chased by the bear*. These sentences are linked to the same meaning (they express the same thought). But we're hard pressed to say what that shared meaning is, other than perhaps by pointing to a picture or offering more paraphrases. The Unconscious Meaning Hypothesis says that this is just what we should expect. The meaning is there in our heads, and we can use it to draw inferences and to pick out a picture the sentence describes. But since it's unconscious, we can't describe it except by means of more sentences. In other words, the two sentences are different "handles" for the same unconscious thought.

Translation offers the same story. The German sentence *Der Bär hat den Löwen gefangen* means the same thing as *The bear caught the lion*. But what's the same about them is something we can't hear. If you speak both German and English, you just know they're the same. Again the sentences are different "handles" for the same unconscious meaning, which can't be made palpable except by expression in a language or by pointing to a picture.

In Chapter 12, we found all sorts of bits of meaning that don't need to be expressed by words. Sometimes, of course, they *can* be expressed by words, but still, it's often hard to say exactly which words are the right ones. For instance, in aspectual coercion (*John jumped until the bell rang*), is the unexpressed meaning *repeatedly*, *over and over*, or *many times*? Any one of these could be used to express the hidden part of the meaning. So what is this hidden part, if it's not the words themselves?

The Unconscious Meaning Hypothesis says the meaning is an unconscious piece of mental structure that in this case happens not to have a "handle." We know it's there because of its effect on inferences. If you say *John slept until the bell rang*, I know he slept once. But if you say *John jumped until the bell rang*, I know he jumped many times. The extra jumps come from this part of the meaning that's hidden, that has no link to pronunciation.

Another perspective on the Unconscious Meaning Hypothesis comes from a well-known quote: "How can I know what I think until I see what I say?" This is usually cited to make the point that you don't have a thought until you actually say it. In other words, thought and language are the same. But all it *really* shows is that you aren't *aware* of the thought—you don't know what it is—until it comes out clothed in words. Before that, before it gets a phonological "handle," it's unconscious.

What about when you say: "The thought came to me in a flash"? Here you may have the sense of knowing what you want to say, but it may take a while to form all the sentences that express it. You know you have a thought, but you can only *perceive* it when it takes on phonological clothing as speech or verbal imagery—or when it comes to you as some other kind of image, say a visual image.

Next, think about what happens when you have a word or a name on the tip of your tongue. You know exactly what you mean, and you can

try out possibilities and reject them. "Um, is it *refrangible*? No. *Refractory*? No, dammit!" Or maybe you have some vague idea of what it sounds like: "I'm sure it starts with an *r* and goes 'di-DA-di-da.'" Or: "I know that guy over there, and I'm sure I know his name, but I can't come up with it." Or: "I'm sure I know the French word for *mushroom*, but what the hell is it?" What's happening is that you're failing to connect a piece of meaning with a piece of pronunciation. The result is that you have the conviction of meaningfulness, but it appears in your experience with only a vaguely perceivable form, or with a sense of a yawning gap—the absence of a perceivable form.[1]

In all these situations, meaning is formless unless it's connected to imaged pronunciation. Without a linked pronunciation, all that's left in awareness is the conviction of meaningfulness.

What's it like for speakers of signed languages to think? I'm told that instead of hearing sounds in their heads, they either feel hands moving or see hands moving—the signed language counterpart of pronunciation in spoken languages. And it turns out that when they have trouble remembering words or names, they experience a counterpart of the tip-of-the-tongue phenomenon that might be called a "tip-of-the-fingers" sensation. This is exactly what the Unconscious Meaning Hypothesis predicts.

What would it be like for people who speak *no* language? The Unconscious Meaning Hypothesis leads us to guess that they don't experience

---

[1] This account of what the tip-of-the-tongue sensation feels like is offered by the late 19th-century philosopher/psychologist William James. It's the most prominent case of what has been termed the "Feeling of Knowing." However, the research on Feeling of Knowing typically considers only the case where you can't recall something but feel you know it. I'd like to see this as a variation of the more usual situation where you *do* recall something and have the conviction that it's right.

A different situation occurs in the more massive word-finding difficulties (anomia) experienced by people who have certain kinds of strokes. I'm told that these people basically draw a blank—they have no idea of the appropriate words. And the blank doesn't come with a sense of meaningfulness, as though there *should* be a word for their thought. (Thanks to David Caplan for discussion of this issue.)

the verbal stream of consciousness that we normal speakers do, because they lack phonological "handles" to attach to their thoughts. Prelinguistic children would be a good example, except that we can't ask them how they experience their thought. And by the time they *can* talk, they can't remember what it was like back then.

A more promising source of evidence comes from congenitally deaf individuals who have had no exposure to a signed language. If they learn a signed language as adults, we can ask them what their thinking was like before. In a BBC documentary on the relatively new signed language of Nicaragua, one such person says (in the English translation), "I didn't even know what it meant to think. Thinking meant nothing to me." Of course he *must* have been able to think before he learned to speak—after all, he wasn't a robot or a zombie, he was functioning in society at least to some degree. But—as predicted by the Unconscious Meaning Hypothesis—he wasn't aware of it.[2]

In the last chapter, we saw Wittgenstein in a bind. His intuition is that if you erase the language that expresses his thought, there's nothing left going through his mind. But at at the same time, he realizes that it makes sense to say, "What I just said doesn't express what I was *trying* to say"—as if there is indeed something there besides the words.

The Unconscious Meaning Hypothesis resolves the puzzle. It says that we can only be aware of the content of our thoughts if they're linked

---

[2] Another report presents the experience of a deaf individual who had never put together an English sentence until he was 9 or 10 years old, and was not exposed to sign language until college. He has memories of wondering how the world worked, but having no way to ask the questions. He recalls having a sense that other people could communicate with each other, but that he wasn't able to. He describes saving up his questions until he had a way of asking them.

For example, he reports having wondered at 5 or 6 years old how people communicated on the telephone. One day he wanted his mother to stop talking on the phone. He knew from observation that a hose could be crimped to stop the flow of water, so he applied this reasoning to the telephone cord and tried to stop the sound by crimping the cord (to no avail, of course).

According to this report, then, this deaf boy had questions in his mind without having a language to think in. What's more, his story about the telephone shows that he was able to use analogical reasoning without talking his way through the logic in his head. (cont.)

with pronunciation. So if we haven't yet turned a thought into words, we're only aware at best of *thinking going on*, not of exactly what the thought *is*. If we then utter a sentence, we can unconsciously compare the thought it expresses with the thought we intended to express, and we can get the feeling that the utterance is inadequate. This is what keeps happening to me as I'm trying to write this book, and it's why it's taking me so long. (What's the "feeling that it's inadequate"? We'll get to that in Chapter 35.)[3]

The Unconscious Meaning Hypothesis leads us to ask: In what form did he experience these questions and this reasoning? Does this represent some form of "imageless thought"? From his description when asked about it, it sounds as though his experience was in terms of some kind of visual or kinesthetic imagery—the feel one has for "how things work"— accompanied by a feeling of connection or of questioning a connection between observed actions. As we'll see in Chapters 37 and 39, these intuitive feelings of connection and of questioning connections are also an essential part of thought carried on in inner language. (I am grateful to Naomi Berlove for this report.)

[3] A view close to the Unconscious Meaning Hypothesis is found in the work of the nineteenth-century philosopher, psychologist, and Judaic scholar Heymann Steinthal. I can't resist quoting him, because he's so obscure. In his 1881 *Abriss der Sprachwissenschaft* ("Sketch of Linguistics"), he spends many pages debunking the notion that thought and language are the same thing. As evidence, he points to the possibility of translation, to the intelligent behavior of animals and of deaf individuals with no exposure to language, to the nonlinguistic understanding of how machines work, and to the intelligence involved in the appreciation of art and music. He says that these phenomena are "only possible and understandable, if we recognize that *language creates its forms independently of logic, in fullest autonomy.*" He acknowledges that "Thinking is easier for us with the help of the word, because we are accustomed to this crutch." But in light of the evidence, he concludes "that the asserted *inseparability* of thought and speech is an exaggeration, and that man does not think in sounds and *through* sounds, but rather *with* and *in accompaniment* of sounds" [my translation, his emphasis]. In other words, he recognizes that thought is independent of language, and that the accompaniment of thought by conscious sounds is just that, an accompaniment.

The Unconscious Meaning Hypothesis actually goes a bit beyond Steinthal. It tries to explain *why* it's so seductive to identify thought with language—because of the feeling of meaningfulness that goes with inner speech. (Many thanks to Pim Levelt for bringing Steinthal to my attention.)

17

Conscious and unconscious

To work out the Unconscious Meaning Hypothesis further, we'd better think more carefully about what it means for something to be conscious or unconscious. This is always a perilous undertaking, but it has achieved (or re-achieved) some aura of respectability over the past twenty years.

I want to start by doing some more linguistic therapy, this time on the uses of *conscious, consciousness,* and related words. This will help us see how the ordinary perspective on consciousness works—what we normally take consciousness to be. Then we can start thinking about a cognitive perspective.

Here's one use of *conscious* and *unconscious*.

> Pat is conscious of the noises out in the street.
> Pat is conscious that there are noises out in the street.
> Pat was unconscious of the smell of gas in the kitchen.

Aware and *unaware* can be used the same way, with about the same meaning.

> Pat is aware of the noises out in the street.
> Pat is aware that there are noises out in the street.
> Pat was unaware of the smell of gas in the kitchen.

In this use, *conscious* and its relatives describe something going on in the head of an individual, who I'll call the "experiencer," that concerns something in the world, which I'll call the "stimulus." In these sentences, the experiencer is Pat, and the stimuli are the noises and the smell.

The stimulus can also be in the experiencer's body, as in the next two examples below, or even in the experiencer's head, as in the third and fourth examples.

Pat is conscious of the pain in her leg.
Pat is aware of her hunger.
Pat is conscious of a tune running through her head.[1]
Pat is aware of the nagging suspicion that she left her keys at home.

Another use of *conscious* and *unconscious* doesn't mention any stimulus.

Pat is conscious.
Pat is unconscious.

This use describes a general state of arousal, and it might be paraphrased as 'conscious of *things in general.*' *Unconscious* might be paraphrased just as 'knocked out,' or more specifically as 'unconscious of *things in general.*' Even though the stimulus isn't named, it's there in the meaning.[2]

A third use of *conscious* and *unconscious* leaves out the experiencer instead of the stimulus, as in this example.

The pronunciation and the feeling of meaningfulness are conscious.
But the attached meaning is unconscious.

---

[1] I occasionally have the experience of part of a symphony running through my head, then losing track of it. Then some minutes later, I notice it again, and I'm hearing a place later in the piece, as if it has continued playing in my head even though I was unconscious of it. Do we want to say that during the time in between, the music was still running through my head? Certainly not consciously. I'm not sure ordinary language gives us a good way to say this.

[2] This relation between *conscious of X* and just plain *conscious* isn't too unusual. Consider the word *polite.* You can't be polite without being polite *to someone.* So *Pat is polite* is best understood as 'Pat is polite to people in general,' and *Pat only said that to be polite* is understood as '...polite to the person she was talking to.' That is, one of the characters in the situation isn't mentioned, but it's still present in the meaning anyway, because of what *conscious* or *polite* means. Linguists call these unmentioned characters "implicit arguments." They're another sort of enriched composition in the sense of Chapter 12—parts of the meaning that don't get said.

Again, the experiencer is there in the way we understand it: 'the pronunciation is conscious to people' or 'people are conscious of the pronunciation.'

Now for the term *consciousness*. It has at least three uses. One is simply the noun form of *conscious*, and it appears in phrases entirely parallel to *conscious of the noises* in our original examples.

> Pat's consciousness of the noises out in the street grew more acute.
> Pat's consciousness of the tune running through her head drove her nuts.

The negative version of this is *unconsciousness*, as in *Pat's unconsciousness of the noises out in the street*.

The second use is quite different. It's like a place or a vessel in your mind where experiences of things occur. Things are "in it" and "out of it." Daniel Dennett calls this "place" the "Cartesian theater."

> The noises in the street intruded themselves into Pat's consciousness.
> The noises in the street don't reach Pat's consciousness.
> Pat tried to keep the pain in her leg out of her consciousness.
> The importance of this situation goes beyond Pat's consciousness.

The negative version of this isn't *unconsciousness*, but rather *unconscious* or *subconscious*.

> The influences of Pat's background in Imperialist Grammar are still lurking in her unconscious/in her subconscious. (*in her unconsciousness)

This suggests that the influences are in her mind "somewhere," but not in the "place" where things are conscious, where she experiences it.

The adverbs *consciously* and *unconsciously* also seem to pertain to these "places" in the mind.

> Pat is consciously trying to eat less.
> Pat unconsciously wants to fail the exams.

The first of these says that Pat is "keeping in mind" her attempts to eat less. The second says that Pat has a desire but doesn't (consciously) know it—it's working on her behind the scenes, outside the spotlight of consciousness.

And there's one more use of *consciousness*:

Pat drifted in and out of consciousness for days.

In this use, consciousness is again a like a "place." But this time it isn't stimuli that go in and out, it's the experiencer. When Pat drifts into consciousness, she's conscious of things in general. When she drifts out—or "falls into unconsciousness"—she's unconscious of things in general.

Here's a tricky question: Are you conscious when you're dreaming? On one hand, we want to say you're unconscious, because you're not experiencing things in the world. On the other hand, you're certainly having experiences: seeing things, talking to people, maybe even flying. So it's some funny way of being conscious, out on the fringes—sort of like when we talk about snakes and airplanes climbing, as we discussed in Chapter 11.

18

What does "What is consciousness?" mean?

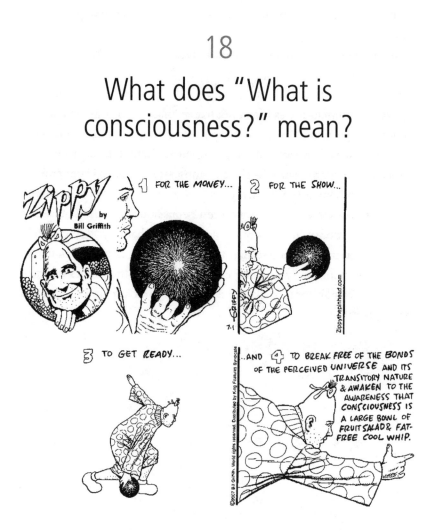

If we ask "What is consciousness?", what are we asking? I don't want to ask it in a deep portentous voice,

WHAT IS CONSCIOUSNESS?

I'm not interested in transcendental cosmic profundity, I'm interested in how the mind works. (We'll get to the profundity in Chapter 26.)

The first thing we have to settle is which sense of *consciousness* we're talking about. If we have in mind the "process" sense (*Pat is conscious of the noise*), the question could be rephrased as: "What's going on when someone is conscious of something?" If we're thinking of the "vessel" sense (*The noise entered Pat's consciousness*), the question could be: "When someone is conscious of something, where is the relevant action going on?"

There's a very traditional view, most prominently associated with Descartes, that the "vessel of consciousness" is the same thing as the mind. If someone isn't conscious of something, it simply hasn't "entered their mind." In this view, being conscious—or having a mind—is one of the Big Things that Make Us Human:

- Humans have souls.
- Humans are conscious.
- Humans are rational.
- Humans have language.
- Humans have moral responsibility.

Some people add an appealing fillip of 𝔭𝔯𝔬𝔣𝔲𝔫𝔡𝔦𝔱𝔶:

- 𝕳𝖚𝖒𝖆𝖓𝖘 𝖐𝖓𝖔𝖜 𝖙𝖍𝖊𝖞'𝖗𝖊 𝖌𝖔𝖎𝖓𝖌 𝖙𝖔 𝖉𝖎𝖊!

For Descartes, consciousness and the mind are part of the nonphysical soul, so they're outside the purview of physical investigation. (We'll get to souls in Chapter 31.)

According to this view, animals are mere machines (these days maybe we'd say they "only operate by instinct"). They lack souls, rationality, minds, language, and moral responsibility. They're *un*conscious. Instinct is *mere* instinct or *brute* instinct, something less than rational, something to be devalued.

Sometimes human emotions also go in this "lower" animal category— or at least negative and selfish emotions like lust, greed, and gluttony do. In order to achieve our true humanity, we're supposed to try to suppress these bad impulses, rise above them. On the other hand, certain other emotions like pure love of God and transcendental ecstasy are sometimes considered higher and more valuable than even reason. It depends who you talk to.

In the early 20th century, Freud proposed that beneath the "vessel" of consciousness is the deep, dark, roiling, scary domain of the unconscious, full of forbidden and threatening thoughts and motives. Freud's vision of the mind entailed a wrenching conceptual shift that took a long time to take hold. Even as late as the 1950s, the journalist Max Eastman could write of Freud's theory, "Brain action can be unconscious, and largely is, but to be mind and to be unconscious is, if words are to have genuine meaning, a contradiction in terms." Wittgenstein, writing around the same time, seems to equate "mental" and "conscious" too—at least he never talks about the "unconscious mind." Nowadays, though, anyone who does psychotherapy takes Freud's perspective for granted (even if the contents of the unconscious may be a lot different than Freud thought).

Around the same time, the behaviorists, led by John B. Watson and later B. F. Skinner, took a different tack, and proclaimed that science (that is to say, 𝔖𝔠𝔦𝔢𝔫𝔠𝔢) could and should only investigate the mechanical aspects of humans—their behavior. Talking about minds, they said, is all superstition. Look how much science gained when it stopped attributing desires and intentions to rocks. We could make even more progress if science would only stop attributing them to humans too. As for consciousness, forget it! A taboo subject.

The second half of the 20th century gave birth to the "cognitive revolution." The brain came to be thought of as an information-processing device, sort of like a computer. Older readers will remember that the early computers were nicknamed "electronic brains." And of course computer scientists borrowed the term "memory" from its counterpart in humans. (Then the computer term was borrowed *back* when we started talking about people "retrieving things from their memory *banks*"—computer memories in those days were huge racks of vacuum tubes—and about people's memories being "full.")

Since the beginning, computers have been routinely described from two perspectives. The "hardware" perspective describes what goes on in the physical device: the power supply, the layout of circuits, the changes of voltage in each circuit, and how each physical part of the computer contributes to the activity of other parts. The "software" perspective talks about the *logic* of what the computer is doing: the structure of programs and how they manipulate data structures (which may include other programs). These perspectives aren't independent. Everything going on in the software has to be physically supported by something going on in the hardware. Otherwise the computer couldn't do what it does from the software perspective—it doesn't work by magic. But usually we don't have to know how the hardware works—only the engineer and the repairman do. We can act as though the computer just carries out the software instructions, period. For all we care, as long as it works, it might as well *be* magic.

These two perspectives on computers made it attractive to think in a similar way about the brain and the mind. The brain plays a role like the physical computer, with neurons instead of transistors and blood vessels instead of a power supply. But we can also think of the brain as processing information or performing computations, and we can ask about the logical structure of this information and these computations. This is a version of the cognitive perspective, going back to pioneers such as John von Neumann.

Cognitive scientists often use the word *mind* (or *mind/brain*) for this perspective, but it's quite different from the Cartesian or even the Freudian notion of the mind. For instance, as we discussed earlier, in Chapter 2, the basic approach of modern linguistics is to think of language users as having a system of principles in their heads. But when we talk about the rules of grammar or of phonological structure being in the mind, we're not talking about anything conscious. Speakers can't tell you what the principles are, and no process like psychotherapy can uncover them. The principles are as inaccessible to introspection as the condition of your spleen. Speakers just use them intuitively—that is, unconsciously. This makes no sense in the traditional perspective that equates "mental" and "conscious."

This computational notion of the mind is an advance on the behaviorists—it does admit there's such a thing as a mind that's worth investigating scientifically. But it still looks at the mind/brain as a mechanical system, subject to the laws of physics, and it actually doesn't have much to say about consciousness. To be sure, it says that some of the information in the mind, such as the rules of grammar, are unconscious. But it doesn't say why any of the information in the mind should be *conscious*. Why isn't *everything* unconscious? Consciousness doesn't seem to play much of a role in this picture.

There's a more serious problem. In the ordinary perspective, a *person* is conscious of *something in the world*. It makes no sense to say a *brain* is conscious of its *neural firings*, or that a mind (in the computational sense) is conscious of information that it's processing. This is even true when we're talking about imagery. If you hear the Joycean stream of consciousness, or if you dream of a flying cow, it's not because there are words or a flying cow actually in your head. From the brain perspective, there are only neural firings in there, not too different from the neural firings when you hear spoken words or see real cows. From the computational perspective, there are only data structures (or "mental representations") in there, being manipulated by computational processes.

But the computational perspective on brain and mind can still help us make sense of the question "What is consciousness?" Your experiences depend on what's going on in your brain. If you take drugs that alter the operation of your brain, or if you suffer brain damage, it affects not only your behavior but your experience. When you're recognizing a face, different parts of your brain are active than when you're recognizing buildings. If your skull is opened for brain surgery and different parts of your brain are electrically stimulated, you may report various experiences: tingles in parts of your body, hearing tunes, nostalgic memories, and so on.

To understand the connection between stuff going on in your brain and your having an experience, we need to ask: How can *anything* in the mind/brain, whether we regard it as neural firings or as information manipulation, add up to *experience*? This is the traditional mind–body problem, where "mind" is understood in the traditional sense, not the computational sense.

In answering this question, it's important to remember that we're not just asking about your ability to respond to stimuli intelligently. That's a question about what determines your physical behavior. We can account for *that* with a mechanistic solution (at least in principle). No, we're asking about having *experiences*. I'm writing this while sitting out on my patio on a beautiful late June day, experiencing the sight of the screen of my laptop, the stone wall, and the bushes; the sounds of kids playing and birds singing and traffic going by and my computer's little whine; the feel of the keyboard under my fingers. How do we get to any of that from neural firing or information processing?

David Chalmers has called this the "Hard Problem," the real sticking point in a physical explanation of consciousness. Many philosophers and neuroscientists concur with Chalmers (for example John Searle and William Robinson). Many others, such as Daniel Dennett and Paul and Patricia Churchland, contend that the problem actually isn't so hard, and maybe if we look closely enough we'll find that we've already solved it. I personally don't think this question is tractable at this point in the sciences of the mind and brain, so I'd just as soon set it aside for now. (On the other hand, I'm not one of those guys who says "We'll have it solved in fifteen years!" or "We'll never solve it!" or "It's beyond human capacities to solve it!" Let's just keep our eyes open for the right opportunity.)

Meanwhile, we don't have to give up hope. There's a second important question we can ask about the connection between the brain and experience: What *particular* patterns of neural firing and information manipulation are correlated with which particular aspects of experience? This question, I think, *is* tractable, and in fact it's the subject of vigorous research. We can break it down: Is being conscious of things a special property of neurons? Of certain kinds of neurons? Of big enough collections of neurons? Of big enough collections of neurons with some particular organization? Or from the computational perspective: Is being conscious of things a special property of certain forms of data structures and information manipulation? Are certain brain activities (from one perspective) and certain data structures (from the other) more responsible for the sight of the stone wall, and others for the sound of the birds?

Within the brain perspective, Francis Crick and Christof Koch have called this the question of the "neural correlates of consciousness," and along with many others they have investigated it primarily in terms of visual experience. Thinking in terms of the "vessel" sense of consciousness, they ask: What areas of the brain are most directly correlated with what aspects of experience? In terms of the "process" sense, they ask: When we're having such-and-such kinds of experience, what are these areas doing (in concert with the rest of the brain, of course)?

From the computational perspective, we can pose a parallel question about the "cognitive correlates of consciousness." In the "vessel" sense of consciousness, we can ask: Among the different sorts of data structures the mind processes, which sorts correlate best with the character of various aspects of experience? In the "process" sense, we can ask: Exactly what is happening to these data structures when the relevant aspects of experience are present?

To sum up this chapter: "What is consciousness?" is best answered in terms of both brain and computational (or cognitive) perspectives. From either perspective, we can ask which parts of the mind/brain correlate with which aspects of experience, and exactly what is going on in these parts when a particular experience is taking place. In addition, though, we face the Hard Problem of how anything going on in the brain could add up to experience. Along with Crick, Koch, and many others, I suggest we can make a lot of progress on the question of correlation without first answering the Hard Problem.

19

Three cognitive correlates of conscious thought

Let's now go back to the Unconscious Meaning Hypothesis—the idea that what we experience as conscious thought gets its form not from meaning, but from the inner voice, the verbal images of pronunciation. We can now think of this as a hypothesis about the cognitive correlates of consciousness.

From the cognitive perspective, a linguistic expression consists of three linked data structures in the mind: phonology (pronunciation), syntax (grammar), and semantics (meaning). Phonology organizes the expression as a pattern of speech sounds grouped into syllables, words, and phrases, and overlaid with intonation (the rises and falls in the pitch of the voice). Syntax organizes the expression in terms of grammatical units: nouns, verbs, and so on, grouped into phrases, clauses, and sentences. Semantics organizes the meaning in terms of conceptual units: conceptualized objects and persons (such as lions and bears) play roles in conceptualized situations and events (such as events of chasing). Semantics is the data structure involved in thinking—it links to the rest of our understanding of the world.

The Unconscious Meaning Hypothesis says that among these three data structures, the one that most resembles the experience of thought is phonology. We hear phonological words in our heads, words from a particular language—"I think in English." In other words, imaged pronunciation rather than meaning is the main cognitive correlate of conscious thought. If you still find this hypothesis unsettling, please continue to bear with me. And you may want to review the reasons that led us to it in Chapters 15 and 16.

In Chapter 15, we talked about a second component in the experience of your inner voice: the feeling of meaningfulness that's associated with the pronunciation. What's the cognitive correlate of this component of the experience? Could it be the thought? If so, that would disprove the Unconscious Meaning Hypothesis, because then thought *would* be conscious.

But I don't think this is the right answer. Here's why. When you hear something like *thit* that isn't linked to a meaning, no feeling of meaningfulness comes along with it—it's just a noise. When you *do* have the feeling of meaningfulness, it actually doesn't much matter exactly *what* the meaning is. All that matters is that the pronunciation has a link to *some* meaning or another. So the feeling of meaningfulness really only depends on the *existence* of a link, not on the thought the link is attached *to*.

There's one more important thing we still have to account for. When you hear other people (or yourself) actually speaking, you recognize it as a real sound, out there in the world. When you're hearing the inner voice in your head, you recognize it as a voice in your head, as a verbal image. In either case, your mind/brain has to link up phonological, grammatical, and semantic structures, so the sound goes with the meaning. But if they're the same in this respect, what makes having a verbal image different from hearing actual speech?

Remember: The difference can't just be that you simply *know* where the sound is coming from. The mind/brain can't achieve this understanding by magic—it has to *create* it. In fact, the mind doesn't always get it right. When people talk to us in our dreams, we experience the speech as their real voices, not as voices in our own heads. And schizophrenics experience unbidden voices not as inner speech, but as someone (such as God or the devil) speaking to them. "So what?" you may say; "These are abnormal situations. They don't count. After all, we get it right when things are normal." Well, the thing is, these less normal cases show that our experience isn't hooked up directly to reality. Our sense of reality has to be generated by the mind/brain—even when what's out there really *is* real. (And by the way, what's so abnormal about dreaming?)

Just to make life a bit more uncomfortable: As we noticed in Chapters 5 and 6, pronunciation isn't exactly "out in the world" anyway. All there is out in the world is sound waves. It's an incredible computational feat for the brain to divide these waves into sounds and words, a feat that we've had a hell of a time getting computers to duplicate. When you experience real speech in terms of words made of speech sounds, are you *right* (even though it's "really" sound waves")? Or are you having an illusion? A funny question. I guess we could say you're right if you manage to decode the words that the speaker had in mind. But that goes way beyond the physical signal "out in the world." It's talking about what's in the speaker's mind, which we can't observe directly. And is it *wrong* if you hear a parrot or a computer as speaking, rather than just making noises? Well, only kind of. All in all, right and wrong seem to me the wrong categories here.

Here's a better way to think about it: When you're hearing external speech (others' or your own), your mind is receiving auditory signals from the ears and constructing patterns of pronunciation linked to them. When you're *imagining* speech or just hearing it in your head, your mind is constructing a pronunciation *without* a link to auditory signals. So the presence or absence of this link can act as a normal cognitive correlate of the distinction between the experiences of "really hearing" and "imagining hearing."

I say a "normal" cognitive correlate in order to take into account the experience of dreamers and schizophrenics. In these cases, something else must be responsible for the sense of externally heard speech. One possibility is that the correlate isn't the link itself, but a "monitor" that checks for the presence of a link between pronunciation and auditory signals. Normally it signals "external" when it finds a link, and "image" when the link is absent. But when you're dreaming, it signals "external" no matter what (and not just to speech but to objects too—you *see* things out there, as if they were real, as we'll discuss in Chapter 21). In schizophrenia, perhaps the monitor signals unsystematically, accounting for the schizophrenic's blurred sense of reality. It's sort of like when something is wrong with your car's engine, but the "check engine" light fails to go on, because something is wrong with the circuit for the light itself. You go driving merrily along, thinking everything is okay. The same sort of thing is happening with the sense of reality in dreaming and schizophrenia. The idea, then, is that we experience verbal images when we have a pronunciation in mind that isn't linked to an auditory signal—and the monitor is working normally.

Of course there are other auditory signals that don't link to pronunciations, such as music and the sound of the traffic. These aren't heard as speech—they acquire their cognitive significance through other routes in the mind. Also, signed languages replace auditory input with visual, and replace verbal pronunciation with linguistically structured hand and face configurations.

Here's a diagram that sums up where we've gotten so far with the Unconscious Meaning Hypothesis. It's an elaboration of the way I laid out the cognitive perspective in Chapter 15.

Having a conscious thought

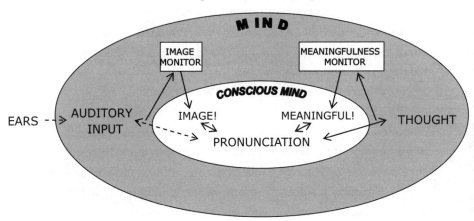

As in the previous diagram, an unconscious thought is linked to a pronunciation that's a cognitive correlate of consciousness. The pronunciation contributes the *form* of the experience—hearing the thought in English.

This diagram has two new parts. The first is the "meaningfulness monitor," which checks to see if there is a link between the pronunciation and a thought. In this case there is a link, so the monitor registers the feeling "meaningful" linked to the pronunciation, as a cognitive correlate of consciousness. I'm going to call this feeling of meaningfulness a "character tag"—it signals the overall character of the experience.

The second new part is the "image monitor," which checks to see if there is a link between the pronunciation and auditory input delivered from the ears. In this case there isn't a link (as I've indicated by the dashed line), so the monitor registers the feeling "image" as another character tag linked to the pronunciation, again as a cognitive correlate of consciousness.

The pronunciation is a rich data structure in the mind that correlates with a rich aspect of experience. The other two cognitive correlates, the character tags, are relatively simple data structures—the presence or absence of links between different data structures in the mind. They correlate with simple yet profound distinctions in the "feel" of the experience. In Chapters 25 and 26 we'll return to these sorts of distinctions of "feel" and lay out a few more.

20

Some prestigious theories of consciousness

Before pushing on farther, I'd like to pause a moment and see what the Unconscious Meaning Hypothesis has to say about some other approaches to consciousness. As I mentioned in Chapter 18, there's a long tradition of thinking that our intelligence and our consciousness are the highest, most noble, most awe-inspiring aspects of being human. And because intelligence and consciousness are both awe-inspiring, people often infer (or take for granted!) that they must be the same thing. For instance, the neuroscientist Antonio Damasio says that conscious images are "the highest level of biological phenomena." Another neuroscientist, Bernard Baars, says that consciousness "is king of the hill: all active mental processes make use of it."

According to the Unconscious Meaning Hypothesis, this is a big mistake. For one thing, we now know that other animals, especially higher primates like chimpanzees and gorillas, *can* think. In the laboratory, they solve complicated problems set by clever experimenters, and in real life they navigate the world, find food, avoid predators, and even create tools. Most impressively, they deal with a sophisticated social environment in a fashion that has been termed "Machiavellian intelligence." Maybe they don't think with the precision and scope we do—they don't invent plows and televisions and theories of consciousness—but neither are they just "driven by instinct" like machines, as Aristotle and Descartes thought.

Of course, there are major differences between us and our primate cousins. One difference is that we have language—the ability to convert our thoughts into communicable form by linking them to pronunciation. According to the Unconscious Meaning Hypothesis, this linking bestows on us a second difference: language enables us to be conscious of our thoughts in a way that animals can't be. But it's not through awareness of the thoughts themselves. Rather, it's through awareness of the phonological "handles" linked to the thoughts, which other animals lack. (This is not to say that if other animals had language, they'd be as smart as us. There are lots of other important cognitive differences.)

In short, beings without language can have thoughts, and *our* consciousness derives its form from the pronunciation of the inner voice, not directly from our thoughts themselves. So thought and consciousness aren't the same thing at all.

From the standpoint of the traditional view of consciousness, this conclusion seems crazy. How can the contents of consciousness be nothing but a string of sounds? That's way too trivial, not nearly awe-inspiring enough. Nevertheless, the Unconscious Meaning Hypothesis is based on really *paying attention to the experience of thinking,* not by starting with a preconception that consciousness must somehow be Profound.

The Unconscious Meaning Hypothesis also calls into question many views of consciousness that have been popular among recent philosophers and neuroscientists. I can't go through them all, but I'll mention some of the more prominent ones. Readers who have a favorite I don't mention are invited to see how it fares in light of the Unconscious Meaning Hypothesis.

Some theories of consciousness from a neural perspective attribute it to some general property of neurons, such as some particular quantum activity, the activity of certain receptors on neurons, or some "proto-awareness" connected to the receptive fields of neurons. I certainly agree that certain neural activities must be necessary for you to be conscious rather than out cold. But why do the neural activities responsible for *pronunciation* correlate closely with the form of your experience, yet those responsible for *thought* don't? In fact, even if you think that thought *is* a cognitive correlate of consciousness, everybody knows that the neural activities connected with producing eye movements and regulating heart rate aren't correlates of consciousness. So why some neural activities and not others? As far as I know, these theories never even ask these questions.

A more promising theory is that consciousness is a sort of "executive" capacity that oversees the activity of the mind when it gets into difficulty. The idea is that as an activity becomes more automatic, it fades from consciousness. For instance, as you're learning to drive, you gradually stop thinking about where the brake pedal is, and you don't need to consciously put your foot there—it just goes there automatically. This view is espoused by people as different as the philosopher/psychologist William James, the developmental psychologist Jerome Bruner, the computer scientist Marvin Minsky, and the neurophysiologist John Eccles.

In the same vein, the neuroscientist Christof Koch proposes that the contents of consciousness are "potent symbolic representations of a fiendish amount of simultaneous information associated with any one percept—its meaning." He views consciousness as providing an "executive summary" of the current situation, which can be "sent off to the planning stages of the brain to help decide a future course of action." "The function of consciousness, therefore, is to handle those special situations for which no automatic procedures are available." In other words, consciousness is the best, highest, and most important part of thinking.

The proponents of this "executive" view never seem to notice that plenty of conscious activities don't present any difficulties at all. Think of lying on the beach on a beautiful day. You're perfectly relaxed, there's no stress. You hear the waves, watch people, listen to the seagulls, and so on. The "executive" theory predicts that since there are no problems to be solved here, the environment should fade from your awareness. But it doesn't—unless you doze off, of course.

My guess is that executive activity is actually more a function of *attention* than of *consciousness*. After you learn to drive, you don't have to pay attention to where your foot is going, and when you're conscious of all the stuff at the beach, you may or may not pay attention to it.[1]

Even if this view of consciousness as an "executive" manages to deal somehow with the experience of the beach, it's still in serious trouble. According to the Unconscious Meaning Hypothesis, the main cognitive correlate of the experience of thinking is pronunciation. But pronunciation—a string of sounds—isn't any use at all to the "executive" or planning part of the brain, which, as Koch notices, needs the *meaning*. Meaning is *unconscious*, aside from the simple feeling of meaningfulness. This means that the contents of consciousness can't be what the brain needs in order to cope with difficult situations.

According to another popular view of consciousness, espoused by Douglas Hofstadter among many others, consciousness somehow arises when the mind creates a reflexive representation of itself—consciousness consists of (or is produced by) "higher-order" thoughts about thinking, so-called "metacognition." This sounds appropriately profound, and Hofstadter even manages to make it sound awe-inspiring.

The Unconscious Meaning Hypothesis does recognize two components that sort of look like the mind representing itself. One is the feeling of meaningfulness, which comes from the mind keeping track of whether it has linked pronunciation with meaning. The other is the sense that a chunk of language is an image in the head rather than someone speaking, which comes from the mind keeping track of whether it has linked pronunciation to an auditory input. These two components are indeed

---

[1] The philosopher Ned Block distinguishes "phenomenal consciousness"—the full contents of your field of awareness—from "access consciousness"—the contents of consciousness that you can actually report verbally. Access consciousness might be identified with the focus of attention, and hence with the parts of experience that can be linked to elements of thought involved in conscious planning. In Block's terms, I'm interested here in phenomenal consciousness, which seems to be a good deal broader.

mental representations of what's going on in the mind, and they do contribute an important part to the character of our experience.

But these factors don't contribute the *form* of our experience. They're much too crude—they can't distinguish one thought from another. The main thing that differentiates the experience of one word or phrase from another is its pronunciation. And pronunciation as such is completely useless for representing thoughts about your own mind or your own thoughts. It's only a coding of sounds that are linked with thought— something way more humble than this "metacognitive" view expects. (In Chapter 38 we'll see how having phonological "handles" for thought does help us reflect on our thoughts. We still have a lot of ground to cover first, though.)

Another influential theory of consciousness is Bernard Baars's view of the conscious field as a "global workspace":

> ...conscious contents become "globally available" to many unconscious systems. The reader's consciousness of *this phrase*, for example, makes *this phrase* available to interpretive systems that analyze its syntax and meaning, its emotional and motivational import, and its implications for thought and action.

David Chalmers puts it like this:

> ...the contents of awareness are to be understood as those information contents that are accessible to central systems, and brought to bear in a widespread way in the control of behavior.

Stanislas Dehaene and Lionel Naccache say:

> ...dynamic mobilization makes [information available within one faculty of mind] directly available in its original format to all other workspace processes.

This view again treats consciousness as closely linked with thought— consciousness broadcasts thoughts to the whole mind. It's easy to see that this approach has the same problem as the "executive" and "meta-cognitive" approaches. The "central systems" of the mind are concerned with making inferences, integrating knowledge, and planning a course of action. They have to work with *meaning* or *thought*, which is not a cognitive correlate of consciousness. The data structure or "format" that does correlate with consciousness is *pronunciation*—patterns of sounds, which are of absolutely no use to the central systems! So again, the form of thought and the form of consciousness aren't the same.[2]

I think all of these views suffer from the fact that they don't pay attention to the experience of "hearing thoughts" as language in the head. And when they do mention language, they fail to distinguish between the two entirely different data structures involved in meaning and in pronunciation. It's meaning that does the work the "executive" and "global workspace" theories want consciousness to do. But it's the other data structure, pronunciation, that's actually conscious.

[2] A reader has suggested that the quotes above are speaking of access consciousness in Ned Block's sense (note 1). If so, (a) they leave the nature of phenomenal consciousness completely open, and (b) they still fall to the objection that the form of consciousness is determined by pronunciation.

21

What's it like to see things?

So far I've been talking about thought and consciousness in terms of language. But we can't stop there. We also have to look at nonverbal kinds of thought and consciousness, the sorts we might share with babies and apes. So I want to look a bit at the experience of seeing.

We take seeing for granted. The world out there is full of all these things, and our eyes tell our brains about them. Seeing the world seems totally transparent, even more so than using language. Well, it turns out it's not that simple. What comes to the eyes isn't enough to explain what we see.

In Chapter 10, we looked at why visual imagery alone can't serve as the form of thought. The same examples I used there also show why understanding the things we see in the world involves more than what comes to the eyes. For instance, seeing that something is a triangle involves comparing it not just to some particular triangle we might have in memory, but to the abstract definition of a triangle—having three sides and three angles. And when we see an action causing something to happen, all our eyes provide is the action taking place, followed by the other thing happening immediately after. To understand that this adds up to causation, our minds have to make additional connections that aren't present in the visual input. Our minds make these connections even when we watch cartoons, where all that reaches our eyes is a sequence of pictures created by an animator.

It turns out that visual perception has many properties reminiscent of language perception, and it's interesting to explore the parallels. Let's start with *ambiguous* sentences, whose pronunciation can be linked with more than one meaning.

Visiting relatives can be boring.
You have no idea how good meat tastes.
The man in the chair with a broken leg is drooling.

In just the same way, visual displays like these can be understood in more than one way.

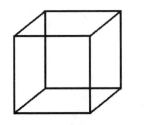

Necker cube

duck - rabbit

Wittgenstein has a long passage about the duck-rabbit and related displays. He ruminates about seeing it under different "aspects," and he senses a "close kinship" between seeing something in a particular aspect and "experiencing the meaning of a word." I don't know of a convenient term for the duck-rabbit figure *without* any interpretation. Let's call it a "visual surface." This is the most we can get from the eyes alone. I'd like to think of the experience of the "duck-rabbit as duck" as linking the visual surface to one meaning, and "duck-rabbit as rabbit" as linking it to another—different ways of achieving a "visual understanding" of the visual surface. The fact that the same visual surface can be linked to two ways of understanding it shows that the mind is adding something to what the eyes alone provide.

115

I'm going to try to show you that just as the meaning of a sentence is unconscious, visual understanding is too. That is, there is a counterpart of the Unconscious Meaning Hypothesis for vision. For example, let's go back to our example of "reference transfer" from Chapter 12.

The ham sandwich in the corner wants some coffee.

In order for this sentence to make sense, its subject has to be understood not as 'the ham sandwich' but as 'the person with the ham sandwich', even though the words *the person with* aren't there in the pronunciation.

A sort of visual counterpart of reference transfer is so-called "amodal completion" in examples like the "Kanizsa triangle" below. You can't help but see an upright triangle in front of three circles and an upside-down triangle, even though the visual surface doesn't give you the complete borders of any of these shapes.

Kanizsa triangle

So your visual understanding goes beyond what's presented to the eyes, in much the same way as linguistic understanding goes beyond what's presented in the pronunciation.

Another case we discussed in Chapter 12 was ellipsis:

Amy doesn't want to go to New York, but I do.

This is interpreted as '...but I do want to go to New York.' It can't be interpreted as, say, '...but I do like cheese.' A counterpart in vision is so-called "modal completion," or occlusion. In the left-hand figure below, you can't help but see a horizontal bar passing behind the vertical bar. That is, you see it as the middle figure below. Of course, if the left-hand figure had a real vertical bar that you could remove, it just might turn out that behind the vertical bar was some weird shape, as in the right-hand figure. But it's real hard to see the left-hand figure that way.

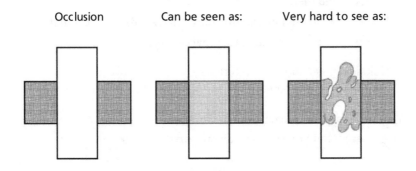

Occlusion   Can be seen as: Very hard to see as:

Actually, if you think about it, *all* visual perception involves occlusion. You don't see the backs of objects, but you assume they're there. You'd be freaked out if the person you're looking at turned around and what you saw was a hollow shell like the back of a mask. When I've spoken of meanings in *language* being "hidden," I've basically been drawing on the analogy to seeing. At least half of *every* object we see is hidden.

Another example: what's the difference between seeing a bookcase and a bookcase with a cat behind it?

They *look* the same—they present the same visual surface—but they feel different. The difference is in your visual understanding. This case is sort of parallel to the difference between *Plato is on the top shelf* when you mean the real guy Plato and when you mean the book by Plato. They sound the same but feel different, because of the difference in the way you understand them.

In the next two sentences, the individual words are meaningful, but they don't add up to anything that makes sense.[1]

Colorless green ideas sleep furiously.
I've forgotten the score of the sonata I hope to compose someday.

Visual displays like the next two have the same problem. Any small part makes sense, but you can't put all the parts together.

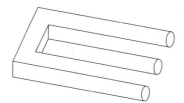

"trident"

M. C. Escher, "Waterfall"

---

[1] These are famous examples of Chomsky's, the first from his *Syntactic Structures*, the second from *Aspects of the Theory of Syntax*. The first sentence *might* be understood with a very heavy application of metaphor; the second sentence might be understood as ironic. In either case, they only make a sort of sense because lots of meaning has been added through enriched composition.

What would be the visual analogue of a *meaningless* utterance—an utterance that can't be linked to a meaning at all? Consider the way the display below looks if you haven't yet had the experience of "seeing it": "Oh, *that*'s what it is!"

Perhaps a linguistic parallel to this figure would be this mock-French expression, which is made of real French words that make no sense together, but which "pops" into English if you read it out loud.

Pas de lieu Rhône que nous.

In both cases, the perception comes with the "aspect" of meaningless-ness, and then suddenly, when it "pops," it becomes linked to a meaning that makes the experience altogether different.[2]

There's a huge number of phenomena like these, many far more strik-ing (but they often involve color and/or videos so I can't show them to you here). They're the stock in trade of psychologists and neuroscien-tists studying visual perception, just as odd sentences are the stock in trade of linguists. Here's why I'm showing them to you: From the ordi-nary perspective, "seeing the world" is perfectly straightforward, and

---

[2] In case you don't get it: The picture is a Dalmatian seen from the left and behind, and the sentence is *Paddle your own canoe.*

these phenomena are somewhat mysterious and (to at least some people) titillating. From the cognitive and neural perspectives, though, we want go beyond mystery and titillation to know how these things work.

Why is it interesting to study illusions? The reason is that when we experience illusions like the ones I've shown you, the visual system is just doing its job in the normal way. But it so happens that in these cases it comes up with unexpected results. So these phenomena help reveal the tricks that the visual system uses to come up with visual understanding.

It turns out that "seeing the world as it is," that is, achieving visual understanding, involves a phenomenal amount of mental computation. Somehow, the brain converts the patterns of light arriving on the retina into perceptions of a rich three-dimensional external world—which, as we've just seen, includes lots of things that aren't in the patterns of light at all. As Kant guessed, and as the gestalt psychologists of the early 20th century really demonstrated, our mind/brains have to *construct* the world that we see. The prominent psychologist George Miller put it like this:

> The crowning intellectual accomplishment of the brain is the real world... all the fundamental aspects of the real world of our experience are adaptive interpretations of the really real world of physics.

A lot is understood about how this is accomplished, but far from everything.

One thing becomes clear right away in this research: How the mind arrives at visual understanding is completely hidden from consciousness. We can't figure out how it works by just reflecting on our experience, as the philosophers of the past tried to. Above all, we have absolutely no sense that our view of the world is generated inside our heads. Visual understanding comes with an unshakable conviction of objective reality—awareness of "the world out there." You never think to question this conviction, unless you're an artist or you're studying visual perception, in which case it breaks down pretty fast.

22

Two components of thought and meaning

When I used the term "meaning" in the last chapter in reference to visual perception, was I talking about the same thing as when I talk about the meaning of a word, phrase, or sentence? Let's sum up the things they have in common.

- Linguistic meaning is hidden from awareness, but much of it is linked to pronunciation. Similarly, the last chapter suggested that visual meaning (or visual understanding) is hidden from awareness, but some parts of it are linked to a visual surface.
- A pronunciation feels meaningful when it's linked to a meaning. It then serves as a conscious "handle" for the meaning. Similarly, a visual surface feels meaningful when it's linked to a visual meaning. It then serves as a conscious "handle" for the visual meaning.
- An ambiguous phrase or sentence is linked to two different meanings. An ambiguous visual surface like the Necker cube or the duck-rabbit is linked to two different visual meanings.
- Linguistic meanings are what make inference possible. Visual meanings are what make "spatial inference" possible. For example, they lead us to anticipate what we'll see when we remove an occlusion or move around to the back of something. And if we a see a car heading for a tree, we expect a crash.

Still, this doesn't mean that linguistic and visual meaning are the same thing. In fact, there are lots of reasons to believe they're not. In Chapter 10, we saw many aspects of thought that can be expressed in language but not in pictures: causation, states of mind, possibility, social relations, and even simple things like triangles in general. By the same token, many aspects of visual understanding can't be expressed in language. As they say, a picture is worth a thousand words. Try to describe in words *exactly* what the duck-rabbit looks like.

But there has to be some connection between the two kinds of meaning. If there weren't, how could we talk about what we see—however imperfectly? How do we connect one way of seeing the duck-rabbit with the word *duck*, and the other way with the word *rabbit*?

From the ordinary perspective, of course, this question hardly bears asking. We just talk about what we see in the world, and that's all there is to it. It's as natural and obvious as anything. It's only when we enter the cognitive perspective, and ask how we *do* it, how our *brains* do it, that suddenly there's a big puzzle. After all, speech sounds don't *resemble* visual appearances at all. What connects and *duck*?

Here's a sketch of how we make this connection. Thought and meaning draw on two complementary kinds of mental representation (or data structures). One kind, which I'll call "spatial structure," is more closely related to visual perception and visual imagery. The other kind, which I'll call "conceptual structure," is more closely related to language. Each has its own virtues for encoding thoughts.

Spatial structure deals with matters like the detailed shape of objects, how they're laid out in space, and how they move around. But it's more than a picture or a video, because it encodes everything you understand about the size, shape, and position of objects. For instance, even though two objects may be different sizes in the visual surface, you may understand them as the same size, because spatial structure encodes them as the same size but at different distances.

And spatial structure encodes not just the parts of objects you see at the moment, but their *full* shapes, even things like a balloon being hollow. When the cat goes behind the bookcase, you don't see it, because it's not encoded in the visual surface. But you still know it's there, because it's encoded in spatial structure.

Conceptual structure encodes different sorts of things. It deals with matters like keeping track of the individuals you know, assigning objects to categories (such as 'dog'), and decomposing events into the actions of their characters (such as bears chasing lions). In addition to the parts of meaning linked to words, it encodes all the parts that *aren't* linked to words, such as those I talked about in Chapter 12.

There's an important difference between the two structures. The relation between spatial structure and a visual surface is based on the geometric principles that relate three-dimensional shapes to how they look from a particular point of view. In contrast, as we saw in Chapter 9, the relation between a conceptual structure and a phonological word is completely arbitrary (Saussure's "arbitrariness of the sign"). Nothing in the sound *dog* gives any clue that its meaning has anything to do with those animals that people keep as pets. We have to learn these associations one by one. Still, once we learn the associations, they're as automatic as seeing.

Now we add a new piece: Spatial structure and conceptual structure are also linked to each other. The totality of thought and meaning is an amalgam of the two.

Here's a way to think about the relation between the two structures. Have you ever used Google Maps? The 2008 version (it keeps changing) offered three ways to look at the area you've selected: a regular map, a satellite photo, and a "hybrid," which superimposes the regular map on the satellite photo. What you get from the satellite photo is sort of like spatial structure. You can see all the details of shape and color, all the surfaces of the streets (complete with cars), all the tops of the buildings, all the trees, and so on. So if there are particular visual details you're looking for, the satellite photo is great. But—it can't tell you the names of the streets, whether any of them are one-way, where the subway stop is, and so on. The regular map is perfect for this. Sort of like conceptual structure, it provides you with a lot of precise, discrete details that can't emerge from a picture. But it doesn't tell you anything about colors, buildings, trees, and so on. In other words, each of these formats has its own strengths and weaknesses. We can draw from the best of both by using the hybrid map, which links the two together.

We can now see the beginning of an answer to how we manage to talk about what we see. Light striking the eyes leads the mind/brain to compute a visual surface. The mind/brain links this to a visual meaning, encoded in terms of spatial structure. The spatial structure in turn can link to a conceptual structure, which can link to pronunciation, which then can be converted into motor instructions to the vocal tract so you say something. In other words, there's a multi-step linkage from the eyes' view on the world to motions of the vocal tract. But the only parts of this that are present to experience are the visual surface and the pronunciation—conscious seeing and conscious talking. The rest is hidden.

Talking about what you see

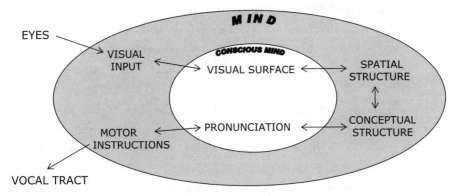

So far I may have given the impression that language is only linked to conceptual structure and vision to spatial structure. It's actually more interesting than that. Think about the meaning of a word like *mosquito*. Its conceptual structure might say that it's a kind of insect, that it bites people and sucks blood, that it spreads disease, and so on. But this information wouldn't help you identify a mosquito if you saw one ("Oh, look out, there's a mosquito on your neck!"). So the word also has to include a link in memory to what mosquitos look like, which is exactly what spatial structure is good at. You probably also know what mosquitos sound like, which would presumably be encoded in a link to some sort of "auditory structure" (which I haven't shown in the diagram). And you know what a mosquito bite feels like, which might be encoded by a link to some sort of data structure that concerns body sensations (also not shown). So a word meaning and the knowledge associated with it may include several sorts of structures, all linked together.

Here I have to pause for a little sermon. This question of how we talk about what we see hasn't been a concern to most theories of meaning, if it's mentioned at all.[1] Linguists and philosophers often seem to treat the

---

[1] I am forever grateful to my late friend, the psychologist and philosopher John Macnamara, for posing this question so clearly, and providing hints about the linkage between spatial structure and conceptual structure.

meanings of words and sentences as though they're sealed in their own little box, isolated from more general understanding. The word *mosquito* is just taken to refer to mosquitos, with little or no discussion of how this connection comes about. Sometimes the connection is said to come through a mysterious notion of "intentionality" that constitutes the "aboutness" of words and connects them to the world. This way of thinking about word meanings arises from taking the ordinary perspective on language and on seeing. Words are just out there in the world (and maybe in the head too), and they refer to what's out there in the world. The mystery is how they could do this.

The cognitive perspective gives us a way to unravel the mystery. In this approach, the relation of linguistic meaning to perception is absolutely central. Meaning draws deeply on all sorts of perceptual understanding, and this is what enables us to use language in the context of our real lives (not just in a semantics text).

At this point, you might be asking: "If we have this rich spatial structure, why do we need conceptual structure too? Wouldn't it be simpler if there were only one form for thought?"

The answer is that there are lots of things that conceptual structure is good at encoding that can't be done with spatial structure—in the same way as maps are good at encoding things that satellite photos can't show. Let's go back again to our examples in Chapter 10. Nothing in a visual surface or a spatial structure can tell us things like:

- The relationships among different categories, for example that dogs and worms are both kinds of living things;
- The names of individuals—nothing about what this guy looks like can tell you that his name is Humphrey Bogart;
- The time at which something is thought to be taking place—past, present, or future;
- Relationships other than spatial relationships, such as two people being cousins, my cousin owning a dog, your liking ice cream, and Wittgenstein being a famous philosopher;

126

- Whether we think something is actually the case or we're wondering whether it's the case (the difference between a declarative sentence and a question);
- Whether some property pertains to the object I'm looking at (*THAT swan is white*) or to all objects of the same sort (*ALL swans are white*).

"Fine," you might reply, "I'll agree that conceptual structure is necessary for the meanings of linguistic expressions. But why couldn't it be *just* for language, a special kind of thought that language gives us?" The answer is that monkeys and apes also make use of some conceptual relations that can't be encoded in spatial structure. The primatologists Dorothy Cheney and Robert Seyfarth demonstrate that "baboon metaphysics"—the relations that baboons and other monkey species recognize in their world include social relations such as 'X is kin to Y,' 'X is dominant to Y,' and 'X is allied with Y.' None of these can be encoded just as part of the way other baboons look. The baboon world is full of these annotations that specify social relations among individuals. They have a huge influence on baboon behavior—as it were, baboons have a complex social map overlaid on the perceptual map.

It's worth mentioning that these baboon social relations are prototypes for human relations as well. The notion of kinship is basic to concepts like 'brother,' 'cousin,' and 'family.' The notion of one person being dominant over another is basic to things like 'boss,' 'sergeant,' and 'command.' The notion of two people in an alliance underlies 'friend,' 'buddy,' 'ally,' and 'collaborate.' Again, these relations can't be represented in terms of how people and their actions *look*, so they must be encoded in conceptual structure.

To sum up, thought and meaning are shared between two linked data structures in the mind, conceptual structure and spatial structure (and perhaps others). If you're coming to thought from hearing language, conceptual structure is dominant, but spatial structure and other structures such as auditory structure are easily engaged. If you're coming to thought from vision, spatial structure is dominant, but conceptual structure plays an essential role in encoding the abstract relations among the objects you're looking at. The linkage between the two structures is what permits us to talk about what we see.

But remember: Neither of these structures is a cognitive correlate of consciousness. Rather, the relevant structures are pronunciation in language and the visual surface in vision.

23
Seeing something as a fork

Among the aspects of our understanding that belong to conceptual structure, a very basic one is the "type/token distinction." Suppose you have a particular spatial structure, say of a fork, stored in memory. There's nothing in the way it looks (the visual surface it's linked to) that tells you whether this is a representation of a particular fork, say the one I just put in the sink, or of forks in general, or maybe of forks of the same design as the one I just put in the sink. If it's meant to be a particular fork, the conceptual structure linked to it marks it as a "token." If it's meant to be a category of forks, the conceptual structure marks it as a "type."

Now the interesting thing is that everything you *perceive* is a particular individual (a token)—you can't perceive categories (types). And you can only *imagine* particular individuals—you can't *imagine* categories. If you try to imagine a type, say forks in general, your image is still a particular fork, a particular token. This was the problem we encountered in Chapter 10, when we asked if a visual image of a triangle could be the meaning of the word *triangle*—it was too specific.

When you recognize something in your visual environment (a token) as an instance of a particular type you know (*Ah, a fork!*), what happens?

- In the act of perceiving the object, your mind generates a visual surface and a spatial structure in response to the environment.
- The spatial structure in turn is linked to a conceptual structure that says this is a particular object—a token.[1]
- This combination of a spatial structure and conceptual structure is matched up with the concept of forks in general, stored in your

---

[1] Linking a spatial structure to a token isn't an entirely trivial matter. Through various experimental techniques, it is possible to present a stimulus (say a printed word) in such a way that experimental subjects aren't conscious of it—they claim they haven't seen it. But it still has effects on what they do next, such as how fast they identify another related word. It turns out that when they *are* conscious of the stimulus, there is longer-lasting and more broad-based activation in the brain than when they don't see the stimulus. This long-lived resonance is usually interpreted as evidence for the Global Workspace theory of consciousness mentioned in Chapter 20. Within the present story, though, it seems to indicate a broad linking of different data structures concerned with different aspects of understanding, such as spatial and conceptual structures. And when this linking is achieved, the stimulus acquires a "thatness"—it is encoded as *something* rather than, say, a fluctuation in ambient noise. It is its "thatness" that makes a mental representation available for attention and therefore for being noticed. In the context of the present discussion, we can identify "thatness" with the linking to a token feature.

long-term memory. This concept consists of a spatial structure, which encodes what forks look like, linked to a conceptual structure that says this is a type of object, that you use it to eat with, that it has a number of parallel points, that it's usually made of metal or plastic, and so on.

- The conceptual structure in turn is linked to the phonological word *fork*, also in long-term memory.

The diagram below shows all these linkages. The dotted arrows are the links that are established as part of this particular situation of seeing the fork. The solid arrows are the links that are stored in long-term memory—what you know about forks.

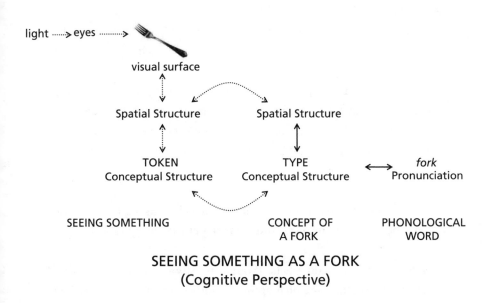

SEEING SOMETHING AS A FORK
(Cognitive Perspective)

The only parts of this that reach consciousness, though, are the visual surface and the phonological word (or pronunciation). So as far as we're aware, seeing something as a fork is much simpler:

131

WORLD   WORD

SEEING SOMETHING AS A FORK
(Ordinary Perspective)

And this is indeed the way the ordinary perspective understands the process—as a direct connection between ![fork icon] and *fork*.

I haven't yet said why you see the object in the world rather than in your head. We'll get to that in Chapter 25.

Token concepts can come about because of what you perceive. But since you can't perceive types—category concepts—where do *they* come from?

From the ordinary perspective, you learn that various things go together in a category of dogs or forks or triangles. But from the cognitive perspective, "learning" a category amounts to your mind constructing a type concept in response to sample tokens. This leads to an important conclusion:

We can understand things in the world as belonging to categories only because we (or our minds) construct the categories.

What your mind constructs, though, mostly consists of spatial and conceptual structures—which aren't cognitive correlates of consciousness. This has an interesting consequence for what it's like to learn a type. You may just notice that you "get it"—you can tell whether things belong to the category or not, without knowing exactly how you do it. This is because the concept you've constructed is unconscious. Only its effects in judging tokens are conscious.

The type concept may also be linked to some examples you're familiar with. These tokens may be associated with visual images, which you can be conscious of. This sort of experience may lead you to think that learning a type just amounts to collecting a lot of examples (the so-called "exemplar" theory of category learning). This won't work, for much the same reason that a single visual image won't work: you still have to specify what you have to pay attention to in each example, and you also have to work out what all the examples have in common—which amounts to constructing the type concept. Showing in detail why this approach to types won't work would be too long a digression, though, so if you don't mind, I'll drop this line of investigation and move on.

24

Other modalities of spatial perception

So far I've been talking about spatial structure as though it's a sort of souped-up visual image. But you can also use your sense of touch (or "haptic" perception) to determine the shapes and arrangements of objects, turning them over in your hands or running your hands over them. You can even use your tongue to tell the shapes of things like nuts and pills, by rolling them around in your mouth. (When my granddaughter was 8 months old, she seemed to think you could learn at least as much about objects by mouthing them as by handling them.)

The sense of shape you get haptically has to line up somehow with the sense of shape you get visually. If an object you're handling in the dark feels like a cube, you'll sure be surprised if the lights are turned on and it looks like a sphere.

From the ordinary perspective, this seems perfectly obvious. (Is this line getting predictable?) But from the cognitive perspective, there's the usual question of how the brain does it. The sensation of taking in a shape with your eyes is totally different from the sensation of taking in a shape by moving your hand across it. Yet these two sensations add up to the same understanding: it's an object of such-and-such a size and shape. The smallish experimental literature suggests that we're pretty good at correlating the two—though not entirely perfect, especially when shapes get complex and subtle.

Within the story we're working out here, we can sort of see how it has to work. Using touch and pressure sensations from your hand, your mind/brain has to compute the way an object feels at each moment. We might call this sort of mental representation a "haptic view." The way objects feel is another cognitive correlate of consciousness. That is, the haptic view is yet another possible "handle" on what we're encountering in the world.

The way an object feels on a particular haptic view usually isn't enough to understand its overall shape. Most of the time, we have to integrate a sequence of haptic views as we move our hands over the surface of the object. If the object is large, say an elephant or a room, we have to walk around it, feeling it all the while.[1] What are the haptic views integrated *into*? Well, if they're going to be compared with what you see, somehow they have to be linked to a spatial structure that encodes the overall shape of the object. And eventually, through spatial structure and conceptual structure, you can link your haptic perception to language: "Aha—it's an elephant."

Of course you can't find out everything about an object through haptic perception—its color, for instance. In fact you can't find out *anything* about it if it's not within reach. On the other hand, vision can't tell us much about the weight or the temperature of objects, but haptic perception can. Haptic perception is also better for determining texture—slippery, smooth, rough, hard, soft—for finding out what parts can be wiggled, and sometimes for detecting vibration that can't be seen. Haptic perception can't read ordinary print, which depends on color contrast. But letters carved into a gravestone aren't too hard to make out by touch, and people do learn to read Braille. So just as language and vision are good at encoding different things—with some overlap—so are vision and haptic perception. In the end it can all get integrated into a hybrid understanding.

[1] Actually, if you're looking at a large object, you have to take it all in with a series of eye fixations. So in some cases seeing actually is a bit like handling. But it still doesn't feel that way.

This all suggests that the congenitally blind ought to have a pretty good understanding of shape and spatial layout for things they can reach and touch. And this seems to be correct. For instance, when Barbara Landau and Lila Gleitman led blind children along two sides of a room and asked them to go back directly to where they started, the children had no trouble cutting across the diagonal.

Another modality of perception (or possibly a collection of modalities) is "proprioception," perception of your own body configuration. When you're climbing stairs, you have a pretty good idea of how high to lift your feet, without looking. You don't have to watch your hand every moment while you're reaching for something—you know how to get your hand there. When I'm playing the clarinet, I can't see my fingers or my mouth, but I have a pretty good idea of what they're doing by how they feel. A more impressive example of this sort is the blind Art Tatum playing stride piano at lightning speed. And try watching the gymnastics of a violinist's bow arm, which is guided only through proprioception. For that matter, try watching gymnastics. Like other things we've talked about, at least the simple cases of this coordination seem so straightforward and transparent that they require no explanation. But they do require one!

Some further phenomena help show how complex proprioceptive perception can be. When you're using a tool, say a hammer or a tennis racket, have you noticed that you seem to know where the head of the tool is? You temporarily experience the tool as part of your arm—you *feel* the contact of the hammer on the nail or the racket on the ball, not the pressure on your hand and the torque on your arm. This shows that your mind/brain can compute the position and trajectory of your body in an adaptable fashion, creating what might be considered a useful illusion.

For an entirely different sort of case, Oliver Sacks describes the case of a woman who through brain damage lost proprioceptive sensation. She wasn't paralyzed, but she had no idea where her limbs were—unless she looked at them. She was gradually able to train herself to get around with great effort, by watching all her limb movements. Again, this shows that your own body position doesn't come for free—the brain has to figure it out.

Since proprioception typically coordinates with vision and touch, it must be linked to them via spatial structure. Unlike vision and touch, proprioception only yields information about a single object in the environment, but it's a very important one: your own body. This information is especially crucial for guiding action.[2]

Here's a diagram of how all these parts link up.

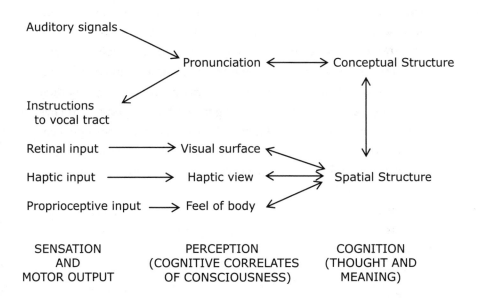

SENSATION AND MOTOR OUTPUT   PERCEPTION (COGNITIVE CORRELATES OF CONSCIOUSNESS)   COGNITION (THOUGHT AND MEANING)

[2] Hearing can also be a source of spatial information, such as when you're biking and hear a car coming up behind you. Bats have a much more sophisticated system of this sort: they use echolocation to identify objects and navigate through complicated environments. In the end, this too has to converge on the bat's counterpart of spatial structure, so that it can be coordinated with vision, proprioception, and the guidance of motion. To the extent that bats are conscious, the present story leads us to guess that somewhere in the bat's stream of computation starting with the auditory signal and culminating in spatial structure, there ought to be a kind of mental representation associated with echolocation that is a cognitive correlate of consciousness. Of course there's probably no way of ever knowing, since we can't ask the bats about it.

I'd better add that not all thought goes on in terms of spatial and conceptual structure. When a composer is writing music, the work of imagining and evaluating creative alternatives isn't going on in conceptual structure. Rather, the goal is to create some sort of satisfying auditory structure that has nothing to do with pronunciation. In the case of Beethoven, who wrote down a lot of his preliminary ideas in his sketchbooks, we can actually follow the course of his musical thought—he often begins with rather banal scraps of melody and gradually molds them into familiar masterworks.

Similarly, when a cook is deciding how to season the soup, the work of imagination and evaluation is going on in the modalities of taste and smell, whatever cognitive structures are responsible for them.

Another very important part of cognition is left out of this diagram. People often forget that the main reason for having a brain is to work the body. It doesn't do an organism any good to find out about the world if it can't put its knowledge to use in doing things. So the system also needs an action component whose input is spatial structure and proprioception—the spatial arrangement of the world and one's own body within it—and which culminates in instructions to the muscles.

25

How do we see the world as "out there"?

Now I need to pick up a point that I left hanging a little way back. The diagram in the previous chapter labels pronunciation and visual surfaces as cognitive correlates of consciousness. These provide experience with its form. Chapter 19 talked about two other cognitive correlates of consciousness in language, the "character tags" that contribute the "feel" of meaningfulness and the "feel" of reality versus imagery. In contrast to the complexity of pronunciation and visual surfaces, these "feels" are simple binary distinctions: Is what I'm hearing meaningful or not? Is it a sentence that someone uttered, or is it "in my head"?

I'd like to look more closely at these "character tags," which mark the overall character of the experience.[1] I'll contrast them with the "content features" of conceptual structure and spatial structure—such as that this object belongs to the category 'fork,' it's heavy and smooth, it has points, you use it to eat with, it belongs to you, it's 17 years old, and so on.

It's not hard to extend these character tags to vision. Here's an example from Chapter 21 again.

---

[1] It's hard to think of an appropriate name for these things. In *Consciousness and the Computational Mind* I called them "affects," and in *Language, Consciousness, Culture* I called them "valuation features." Call them whatever you'd like.

The first time you saw this, it may have looked to you like just a bunch of spots—maybe a black and white Jackson Pollock or something. At some point the dalmatian "popped out," and suddenly the picture was meaningful to you (or it never popped out and you were frustrated). By analogy with our analysis of language, we might say that a visual surface is experienced as meaningful if it can be linked with a spatial structure. The cognitive correlate of the experience is a character tag that marks the presence or absence of this link.

The other character tag—external reality vs. imagery—has more startling effects. When you look at something out in the world, light strikes your eyes, and in response your brain constructs a visual surface. The visual surface encoded in your brain is the cognitive correlate of your visual consciousness—but *you experience something real out in the world*.

Why do you experience it out in the world and not in your head? From the ordinary perspective, this seems like another silly question. It's out there, so naturally that's where you see it. But from the cognitive perspective, as always, we have to ask how the brain makes this happen.

Here's one reason you experience an object out there. Among the object's content features—its representation in spatial and conceptual structure—is its location, there in front of your eyes, outside your head. That fork is located over there in the sink, not stuck inside your brain. So you can't help but understand it as being external to you.

That might seem to settle the matter. But actually it's not quite enough. To see why, let's think about visual imagery. Say you imagine an ostrich (or if you prefer, Big Bird). You have a visual experience, but it's not linked to anything coming in through your eyes. Rather, it's just a visual surface that's linked to some visual understanding in spatial and conceptual structures. And because it's a visual surface, you experience it—it's conscious.

Now, where is this ostrich you imagine? You may experience it as being inside your head, even though you can't *look* there. But you can also imagine the ostrich walking through the door into the room you're in right now—out there in the world. From the cognitive perspective, even though it's an image, you've endowed it with content features that give it an external location, just like objects you perceive.

In other words, experiencing something as *out there in the world* isn't the same as experiencing it as *real*. So what makes the difference between vividly imagining the ostrich walking in and seeing one *really* walk in? One possibility is that an imagined ostrich, no matter how vivid it might be, still isn't as vivid as a real ostrich—that is, the content features of an image are vaguer than those of a real perception. This may be a difference between them most of the time. But not always. You may be able to imagine something so vividly that it's almost like seeing it. And you may only be able to see some real things very vaguely, say through a fog—so vaguely that you're not even quite sure you're seeing them. So vagueness isn't the criterion we're looking for to tell images and real things apart.

There's another difference between perception and imagery, though. When you experience something as real, there's a link between the visual surface and input from the eyes. By contrast, when you experience an image, there's no such link. So this link—or, alternatively, the detection of this link by a monitor—can serve as a character tag, a cognitive correlate of this "feel" of reality in visual consciousness. It works in exactly the same way as the character tag I discussed in Chapter 19, which gives us the difference between the experience of hearing someone speak and the experience of a verbal image.

As with verbal imagery, there are two important exceptions to this story. First, when you're dreaming, the eyes aren't providing any input, but still you have the experience of interacting with real things and real people. Second, people who have hallucinations may experience them as completely real—that's one reason they can be so frightening.

The account we gave for verbal imagery works the same way here. These are situations where the monitor that checks for a link between input from the eyes and the visual surface isn't functioning normally. During dreams, it seems to be simply turned off.[2] And during hallucinations, it's behaving erratically, like a malfunctioning "check engine" light.

We've now arrived at another surprising conclusion:

The presence of a link between input from the eyes and the visual surface is (normally) what makes the world look real.

Ouch. This conclusion is so alien to the ordinary perspective that it may be hard to stomach. On the other hand, it *is* an answer to the question of how we manage to experience the world. The ordinary perspective either doesn't ask the question at all, or is forced to answer it by appeals to mystery or, in the old days, God.

Does this conclusion mean that our experience of the world out there is an illusion? I don't think that's the right way to think about it. It only makes sense to talk about an illusion in comparison to some standard of what's *not* an illusion. And seeing the world out there under normal conditions is about the best example we have of something that's not an illusion.

---

[2] If the monitor is turned off, you shouldn't be able to have dreams of having imagery. I've never heard a report of such a thing. But if people *do* have such experiences, I guess I'll have to make my story more complicated.

26

Other "feels" in experience

We now have two character tags that play a role in the "feel" of both language and vision: *meaningful* vs. *meaningless*, and *real* vs. *image*. I'd now like to look at some more of these "feels."

Familiarity and novelty

Think about the feeling of familiarity that comes with some things you perceive. You see a face in a crowd and say to yourself, "Who *is* that? I'm sure I know him!—Oh yeah, of course: he used to run that deli in Kendall Square!" Or you hear some music on the radio and after awhile you say to yourself, "What *is* that? I'm sure I know it!" (and in my own case, "I'm sure I've played it!"). How does the sound of the tune change as the feeling of familiarity dawns? There's nothing in the *notes* that's different. Sometimes you have this response first, and then it takes you a while to remember the name of the person or tune, or where you encountered them before. (You may find this paragraph a Wittgensteinian sort of observation. The *Investigations* are full of this sort of thing.)

The feeling of familiarity doesn't come for free. Just having seen something before doesn't make it look familiar. As with everything else we've discussed, the mind/brain has to *create* or *construct* this feeling and link it to the thing being perceived. Presumably, like the previous two "feels" we've talked about, it arises from a monitor that detects a connection between two different things going on in the brain, and assigns a character tag to the experience. This monitor checks whether what's being perceived or imagined connects or resonates with something stored in long-term memory. When there isn't any such resonance, the object you're seeing feels novel or unfamiliar.

To help see that the sense of familiarity is constructed, think about the experience of *déjà vu*. This is a feeling of familiarity attached to something that you "rationally" know is unfamiliar. You may also have had the experience of *jamais vu*, of seeing something familiar "as if altogether new."

Or think about what happens in memory experiments. One day the psychologists show you a bunch of pictures. Then the next day you come back for another bunch, and they ask you which ones you've seen before. Some just look familiar to you and others just don't—what else do you have to go on? The experimenters then compare your responses to what they showed you the previous day, in the hope that they'll learn something about how the mind/brain works from your pattern of answers. They may be trying to find out things like: Has your brain actually not stored the ones you don't recognize, or has it stored them but failed to produce the feeling of familiarity? When you say you've seen a picture that they actually didn't show you, what accounts for it? And so on.

People with a sort of brain damage called "proposagnosia" find all people's faces unfamiliar—sometimes even their own. They can see other things perfectly well, and they can often recognize people by their voices. Certain experimental manipulations show that at some unconscious level of processing, they are actually reacting differently to familiar and unfamiliar faces. So it's not as though their memory is wiped out. Still, they tell you quite sincerely that they have no idea who any of these people you're showing them are. Their impairment is evidently in the part of the mind/brain that registers familiarity: they can see the form of faces, but faces all *feel* novel. Oliver Sacks's famous *Man Who Mistook His Wife for a Hat* suffers from a more general "visual agnosia"—he fails to recognize not only faces but all sorts of objects. The feeling of familiarity or novelty doesn't just pertain to things we see and hear. It also comes along with images or ideas that flit through our minds. If an image has the feeling of familiarity, we experience it as a *memory*. If it has the feeling of novelty, we experience it as a *new idea*. This version of the character tag—memory vs. new idea—is notoriously error-prone (from the ordinary perspective). Here's a familiar clash that depends on it: "I'm sure I asked you to take out the trash!" "Well, it's news to me!"

More serious (for academics, anyway) is when we discover that something we've published as a new and original idea later turns out to be something we read years before and forgot about. Still more serious for real life is the problem of the reliability of eyewitness testimony. It's not too hard to coax people into experiencing memories of things that never happened to them, sometimes with unfortunate legal consequences for other individuals involved in the alleged events.

Does it matter? Positive or negative?

Another important character tag is the sense that something *matters*— it's *important*, worth paying attention to. Things can matter either in a positive or a negative way. We find ourselves attracted to positive things (we *like* them, we *desire* them) and aversive toward negative things (we *dislike* them, we *shun* them, we *fear* them). We might think of this as a link between the percept and an emotional response. (I think this is what Antonio Damasio means by "somatic markers" attached to memories, in his *Descartes' Error*.)

A lot of the time you can't say exactly what makes something attractive or yummy or ugly or yucky, or why *you* care even though evidently *I* don't. Your primary reaction is an immediate, intuitive gut feeling. Explanations come later, and they're often after the fact and not entirely comprehensible. Just *why* do you like the way Landowska plays Bach? Just what *is* it about the wine that makes it taste so good? And although the difference is in your response to it, it feels like the attractiveness or ugliness is a property of the object itself, just like its shape, color, and size. It's definitely not in the eye of the beholder, or at least the beholder doesn't experience it that way.

As with meaningfulness and familiarity, this feeling can apply to images as well as objects. I can imagine an encounter with my nemesis and experience him in imagination just as negatively as in real life (or even more so). I can imagine a party I'm dreading and get all uptight. I can imagine playing a passage of Brahms in a way that I've never heard before—or a way of phrasing this sentence that I've never heard before—and experience it as pleasing or not.

Sacred and taboo

A related character tag is the feeling of something being *sacred*—you experience it as being charged with this very special luminosity or intensity (well, there's really no good word for it…). The negative counterpart is *taboo*, where you experience the object with this very special darkness.

This feeling is central to religious experience. People attach a sense of the sacred to God, to houses of worship, and to ritual objects and ritual practices. But it isn't restricted to religious stuff. We may experience it in the presence of great mountains, or the ocean, or a stunning sunset. We may experience it under the influence of certain drugs. Some epileptics (such as Dostoevsky, apparently) experience it before a seizure. Some scientists, especially (it seems to me) mathematicians and cosmologists, experience it in the presence of a great theory—and describe it as a religious experience (such as when Stephen Hawking closes *A Brief History of Time* with: "For then we will have seen the mind of God"). Less consequential things can be invested with this feeling too. Some people feel that, say, Descartes' birthplace is sacred. For other people it might be Earl Scruggs's banjo or the baseball that Barry Bonds hit for his record-breaking home run. Some people even experience it when thinking about the mysteries of consciousness—this is why consciousness feels so PROFOUND.

From the neural perspective, this feeling evidently has something to do with activity in the right temporal lobe. But the feeling isn't of something in the *brain*. Again, we experience it as a property of things in the *world*.

Self-controlled vs. non-self-controlled

Next think about images—they could be verbal or visual, or for that matter proprioceptive (say, remembering what it felt like when you twisted your ankle). Some of them have the feel of just "popping into your head." Others feel like you deliberately made them up: "I'm now imagining an ostrich walking in the door," "I'm now imagining how I'm going to repaint the kitchen." Of course, even when they *do* pop into your head, your mind/brain has made them up, so from a cognitive perspective the difference is hugely phony. But there's no question the distinction is part of your experience, so a theory of consciousness and understanding has to explain where it comes from. Let's call this distinction the feeling of "non-self-controlled" vs. "self-controlled" images.

We can apply this character tag to perception as well. Visual perception always has the feel of being non-self-controlled—the world is imposing itself on you, you have no choice. In the language domain, though, you have a feeling for when you're listening to your own voice (self-controlled) vs. someone else's (non-self-controlled)—and maybe you occasionally have the feeling of hearing your own voice as though it's someone else's (as I do). The sound of my clarinet as I play it has the feel of being self-controlled; when my duet partner Steve plays *his* clarinet, I experience the sound as non-self-controlled.

The domain where this character feature really comes to the fore is in *action*. It feels different when you deliberately move your leg and when you twitch involuntarily. "In the first case, *I* did it." That is, you experience a self-controlled action as willed, deliberate, intentional. And there's also: "The grief just welled out of me, I couldn't help sobbing"—*non*-self-controlled. Again, from a cognitive point of view there's no question that your brain generates the twitch and the sobbing just as much as the deliberate movement of your leg. It's just that you don't experience them as coming from *you*, from your will.

Oddly enough, you don't necessarily have to *actually* perform an action in order to get the feeling you've done it intentionally. In dreams, we experience ourselves doing all kinds of things on purpose that we don't actually do at all—we're still lying in bed.

If this way of thinking about deliberate action is at all on the right track, it has a terribly disturbing consequence:

Our sense of free will doesn't come out of nowhere. Our mind/ brain has to construct it. It is just another one of these "feels" that our minds build into conscious experience.

Well, maybe this shouldn't be a surprise. For centuries people have been arguing whether or not we have free will, and they have recoiled from the taboo conclusion that we don't.

Fuel has been added to the fire by recent evidence from cognitive neuroscience. According to some experiments, it looks like our sense of willing an action may arise in consciousness some hundreds of milliseconds *after* the brain has initiated the performance of the action. And, with the proper experimental setup, you can trick people into thinking they did things on purpose that they couldn't have done (their "intention" monitor lights up). Reviewing lots of evidence of this sort, Daniel Wegner reveals his view on the matter in the title of his book, *The Illusion of Conscious Will*.

By now this line of reasoning should have a familiar ring to it. If we're willing to say that free will is an illusion, we ought to also accept the argument that there's no such thing as the English language (Chapter 3), that there's no such thing as words (Chapter 5), that there's no such thing as baldness (Chapter 11), that there's no such thing as causation (Chapters 10 and 21), and even that our experience of a real visual world is an illusion (Chapter 25). This is nuts. All discourse breaks down. There *has* to be a better way to talk about this stuff.

In line with the approach in the previous situations, I think it helps to keep track of what perspective we're operating in. In the ordinary perspective, yes Virginia, we have free will. And sometimes we think we're acting out of free will when we aren't, and vice versa. If we take the cognitive and neuroscientific perspectives, we approach the issue differently: The mind/brain must be doing something that gives us the feeling of free will, and our job as scientists is to figure out what it is. We can ask, as Daniel Dennett has, why evolution would equip us with the experience of free will—why it might be adaptive to have such a sort of experience, and why our human experience of free will came out the way it did. But in this perspective it's kind of funny to ask whether free will is *really* free. It just is what it is.

What's new in the approach I'm proposing here is that the experience of volition has a specific cognitive correlate, namely the character tag 'self-controlled' vs. 'non-self-controlled.' This character tag belongs to a small family of character tags in human cognition, each of which contributes one of these profound but elusive "feels" in experience. So our sense of free will isn't a splendidly isolated puzzle here—it fits in with the equally puzzling issues of our sense of reality, our sense of meaningfulness, our sense of familiarity, and our sense of the sacred.

I'm imagining that some readers won't find this rhetorical tack very satisfying. I submit that no other approaches—aside from complacently throwing science and philosophy out the window—are very satisfying either.

* * *

If you haven't given up on me by now, let me see if I can put this all together. Our understanding of the world has to be created by our mind/brain. It's encoded in terms of a combination of conceptual structure

149

and spatial structure, which aren't specific to a single modality of perception, as well as other representations that I've had less to say about, such as auditory structure.

Our *experience* of the world also has to be created by the brain, but it draws more directly on perceptual representations that are grounded in particular sensory modalities, such as pronunciation in language, the visual surface in vision, and the haptic view in haptic perception. These provide the content features of experience, which give experience its form. You're seeing, hearing, or touching something in the world, and sensing the position and motion of your body. And you know which of these kinds of sensation you're having.[1]

But there's more to our awareness of the world. It also partakes of "metacognitive" character tags that contribute a *feel* to the entities we experience. They cut across all modalities.

- The distinction between perception and imagery can be found in vision, hearing, language, the haptic sense, and proprioception.
- Percepts and images in any modality can be either familiar or novel.
- The distinction between meaningful and meaningless percepts can be found in both vision and language.
- The distinction between positively important (attractive), negatively important (aversive), and neutral can be found in percepts of every modality, as can the distinction between sacred, taboo, and neutral.
- And the distinction between self-controlled and non-self-controlled percepts is available in a range of modalities, especially in imagery.

---

[1] Some of these sensations may originate from input in other sensory modalities. Tastes contain a large admixture of smell information, but the experience is still of *taste*. More surprisingly, you can alter a video of a speaker's lip movements, leaving the audio the same, and viewers will *hear* the sound as different—it *sounds* like a *b* instead of a *d*. So visual input can be interpreted by the brain as a sound. This is called the McGurk effect, after its discoverer.

The fact that content features *are* modality-dependent suggests that their *neural* correlates ought to be found in perceptual areas of the brain. And indeed that's where the people working on visual consciousness look for them. But the character tags don't belong to any perceptual modality—they cut across all of them. This suggests that their neural correlates might have quite a different configuration.

All of this is by way of expanding the Unconscious Meaning Hypothesis, showing that it's not simply a hypothesis about language and thought, but part of a more comprehensive view of how we understand the world and how we experience it. The relation between language and thought is just a special case of how the mind works in general.

Part Three
Reference and Truth

27

How do we use language to talk about the world?

It's time to get back to meaning and see what kind of progress we've made. Let's review the properties we want meanings to have (from Chapter 9):

(a) Meanings are in the heads of language users.

(b) Meanings are linked to or associated with the spoken or written form.

(c) Word and phrase meanings combine with the meanings of other parts of the sentence.

(d) Synonymous expressions, either within or across languages, are linked to the same meaning.

(e) The referential function of meaning: (at least some) meanings can be connected with the world.

(f) The inferential function of meaning: meanings serve as a vehicle for reasoning (making inferences).

(g) Aside from a feeling of meaningfulness, meanings are hidden from awareness.

Here's what we've found so far. Meanings consist of conceptual structures and spatial structures linked together in the heads of language users (check off a). They can be linked to spoken or written forms of language (check off b). If a linkage of a conceptual structure and a spatial structure is connected to different pronunciations in the same language, or in different languages, the expressions mean the same thing (check off *d*). Conceptual structures and spatial structures can also exist without links to linguistic expression, in which case they serve as (part of) nonlinguistic thought.

We experience spoken language in the form of pronunciation. We experience thought as a voice in the head—also in the form provided by pronunciation. Conceptual and spatial structures don't contribute directly to the form of our experience, except for the character tags that give consciousness its "feel"—that is, they're almost entirely hidden (check off *g*).

I can't say much in this book about (*c*), the way word and phrase meanings combine—beyond the fact that much of meaning isn't found in the meanings of the words (Chapter 12). Nor can I say much about (*f*), the inferential function of meaning. That would require a detailed study of the properties of conceptual and spatial structures. Much of my research over the years has been about making conceptual structure rich and explicit enough for a formal theory of compositionality and inference, and a lot of work in formal semantics and cognitive grammar is also directed toward this goal. Unfortunately there's been far less research on a theory of spatial structure.

In the next few chapters, I'd like to look at (*e*), the referential function of meaning—how we use language to talk about the world.

One thing conceptual structure has to do is keep track of the individuals you know something about. Each of these individuals is encoded in conceptual structure with a token feature (to use the term of Chapter 23), which is linked to everything you know about the individual—both its content features and its character tags. Let's call the combination of a token feature with this other material a "reference file."

When you first notice something in your visual field, your mind/brain has to link up the spatial structure created by your visual system with a token feature. If your mind can locate a compatible reference file to link to, you experience the sight as familiar. If no such file can be found, you have to set up a new token feature that's linked to the new spatial structure, and you experience the sight as novel.

Seeing something isn't the only way to invoke a reference file. Language gives us another way. Suppose I say something to you about my cousin Beth's dog Buddy. In doing so, I've mentioned three individuals: Buddy, Beth, and myself. What happens in your mind?

- On the strength of my mentioning them, your mind will provide each of these individuals with a reference file. You presumably have a file for me already, and you may or may not have to set up new ones for Beth and Buddy.
- Each of these files specifies that the individual in question has a name, linked to a pronunciation (*Buddy, Beth, Ray*).
- Buddy's file is linked to the type 'dog.'
- If you know what Beth and Buddy and I look like, our files contain spatial structures that encode that knowledge.
- The files are linked to each other by relations that specify that Beth is my cousin and that Beth owns Buddy. These linking relations can be considered part of *both* reference files, since you know of Beth that she owns Buddy, and you know of Buddy that Beth owns her.

The figure below shows all the linkages (I've substituted ordinary pictures for the much more abstract spatial structure).[1]

Spatial Structure				
Conceptual Structure	Token ← 'cousin'→	Token → 'owns' →	Token →	'instance-of'→ Type
	Name	Name	Name	Name
Pronunciation	*Ray*	*Beth*	*Buddy*	*dog*

---

[1] For the fastidious: I've notated the arrows linking me and Beth pointing in both directions, because the relation 'cousin of' is symmetrical—each of us is the cousin of the other. But the other arrows are unidirectional, because ownership and being an instance of a type are not symmetrical.

If you know a person by appearance but not by name (say a familiar bit actor in a film), their reference file contains only spatial structure features plus a token feature. If you know a person by name but not by appearance (say Julius Caesar), their reference file contains linguistic features such as their name, but not visual features. If you know both the person's appearance and name (the way I know my cousin Beth), the file contains both kinds of features.

The two halves of a partially occluded object, such as the horizontal bar here,

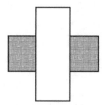

are linked to a unified entity in spatial structure, and from there to a single token feature and a single reference file. That's what makes you understand them as a single object. And when you pay attention to parts of an object—say the handle on a cup—the handle gets its own reference file, linked by the 'part-of' relation to the file for the whole object.

When information about an object comes in from multiple modalities, say a person's appearance and voice, they're unified into an understanding of "this object" by being integrated into a single reference file. When characters in a film speak, their voices come from speakers that aren't usually in the same place as the visual image. Yet because our minds unify the sound with the visual image, we hear the voices coming from the characters' mouths.

Objects we perceive "out in the world" aren't the only things that have reference files. Mental images have reference files too, just with different character tags. When I see a unicorn in my dream, it comes with the character tag of objective externality. But when I wake up and think about it, it has a different character tag, which I'll call "virtual."

Like "virtual reality," entities with this character tag are pure constructions that mimic reality. This character tag also shows up in our concepts of individuals like Santa Claus and Sherlock Holmes (to whom we'll return in Chapter 30).

Normally, once a reference file is established, it remains there in your conceptual structure. That's why you think the cat is still there even when it's run behind the bookcase. The psychologist Karen Wynn has shown that even young infants keep track of hidden objects. For instance, if they watch you put two toys behind a curtain one after another, they're surprised if you open the curtain and there's only one toy there. Somewhat stranger is Fei Xu and Susan Carey's finding: if you put a duck behind the curtain, and then open the curtain to reveal a truck instead, infants under about 10 months old *aren't* surprised. In our terms, they're keeping track of the hidden objects as tokens, but they aren't keeping track of their visual appearance. (They start getting it right at about 12 months.)

But reference files aren't forever. When you break a lump of clay in half, you now have two files: the previous file has been split. At the same time, you keep track of their history, associating with each file the memory that they stem from a single individual. So altogether three reference files are involved in understanding the situation—the original lump and its two descendants.

Here's a more surprising situation: You've been seeing this woman from time to time around the neighborhood, but one day you see *two* of her at the town pool, and you realize that they're actually identical twins. Or: For a long time I vaguely knew about a literary/cultural theorist named Bloom. I thought he had died a few years back. Then one day, I was surprised to come across a new book by him, and suddenly had the embarrassing realization "Ohhh! There's *Harold* Bloom, who wrote the book, and then there's *Allan* Bloom, who died!" Achieving this realization required me to split the "Bloom" file into two, each with its own token feature.

You can also merge two files, when you stick two lumps of clay together and mold them into a sphere (and again you keep track of its history as originally two individuals). Or you may discover that those streams running through different parts of town are actually parts of the same stream. We also merge files when we discover that the individuals we've identified under two names or descriptions are actually the same individual—the reverse of the twins case. Classic examples are Frege's *The morning star is the evening star* and the more widely known *Clark Kent is Superman*.

Now it's easy to provide an account of the referential function of meanings. A linguistic expression refers to something if it's linked to a reference file. That's all there is to it.

"Wait!"—I hear you saying—"It can't be that simple. How do linguistic expressions refer to things *in the world?*" The answer is that they refer to the things that we *conceptualize* as being in the world. If the character tags that go with a reference file mark this as something that's objective and external, then the expression refers to something that's experienced or thought of as objective and external. If the character tags mark this as "virtual"—as an image or as imaginary—then the expression refers to something that's experienced and understood as an image or imaginary.

If this is right, the puzzle about how linguistic expressions manage to be "about the world" isn't exactly a puzzle about *language*. It's more a puzzle about *cognition*: how do conceptual structures and spatial structures and pronunciation and visual surfaces and character tags in someone's head add up to the experience of a world out there full of words and objects? Once we figure out the mental structures that lead us to experience the world—as we discussed in Part Two—it's not too hard to link language up to *them*.

Of course, this account of reference only works if we're operating in the cognitive perspective. From the ordinary perspective, the linguistic expression is out there in the world, and so is the thing it refers to. Exotica like reference files and character tags simply aren't part of the picture. From the cognitive perspective, though, the question is how people *use* linguistic expressions to refer. People can only refer to things that they've conceptualized. If you haven't thought of it, or if you haven't noticed it,

how can you refer to it? In turn, for there to be an "it" for you to think of
or notice, you have to have a conceptual structure that includes a token
feature. And for you to experience or understand the "it" as "out in the
world," its conceptual structure has to come with a certain configuration
of character tags.

"But what about all the things in the world that we *haven't* conceptualized yet? How does language refer to *them*?" This question again falls
back into the ordinary perspective. From the cognitive perspective, the
world we conceptualize just *is* the world as far as we are concerned. We
have nothing to say about things we haven't conceptualized in one way
or another, so why should we worry how our language refers to them?
If someone else *has* conceptualized them, then fine, *they* can refer to
them. (And just to be careful: "Things we haven't conceptualized" is
itself a conceptualization!)

28

Mismatching reference in conversation

Let's look a little closer at what happens when somebody refers to something. Suppose you and I are talking and I say, "Hey, look at that funny cloud!" and point. You look where I'm pointing and figure out what cloud I'm talking about. How does this work?

In the ordinary perspective, the phrase *that funny cloud* refers to an object in the environment. In the cognitive perspective, it's a little more complicated. I *use* the phrase to refer to the cloud, and you figure out what I'm referring to.

Let's unpack this some more: My mind registers the cloud in the environment by constructing a spatial structure. It links this spatial structure to a token feature and to character tags that give me the experience of something out there. Then I decide to say something about it, so I link the pronunciation *that funny cloud* to this reference file, and say it. When you hear the phrase, you take it that I'm referring to something we can both see. So you (or your mind) set up a token feature, and with the help of your observation of my pointing, you try to link it with something in your visual field that meets the description of a *funny cloud*. When you succeed, you may say: "Oh yeah, *that*!" By using this phrase, you tell me that you've achieved conceptual and spatial structures that (you think) match mine—that is, you've understood the message.

But suppose we're talking on the phone and I say "Hey, look at that funny cloud!" You're baffled. The meaning of my expression tells you to set up a token feature, but you can't link it with anything we can both see. As a result, the expression refers for me, but it doesn't for you. I've failed my responsibility in the conversation, which is to enable you to achieve conceptual and spatial structures that match mine—that is, to pass my thought on to you.

The demonstratives *this* and *that* are among a number of grammatical devices that help the hearer manage reference files. Some others are underlined in the following little narrative.

A centaur galloped by.
There was <u>this</u> unicorn standing there singing.   [unstressed *this*]
<u>The</u> centaur stopped and stared.
<u>She</u> couldn't believe her eyes.

In the first sentence, the indefinite article *a* signals the hearer to set up a new token feature—to introduce a new individual of the type 'centaur' into the understanding of the situation. In informal speech, unstressed *this* has the same effect, as we see in the second sentence. In the third sentence, though, the definite article *the* signals that the centaur in question should already have a reference file in the hearer's collection. A definite pronoun like *she* can have the same effect, as we see in the fourth sentence.[1]

A thoughtful speaker chooses expressions that guide the hearer through the cast of characters. Not everyone is so considerate. I bet you can think of people who litter their conversation with definite expressions and pronouns that you have no idea how to identify. When

[1] Just to be cautious: these aren't the only uses of indefinite and definite articles and pronouns—just the ones relevant to what I'm talking about here.

By the way, this narrative contains some hidden referents. In the first sentence, the centaur has to have galloped by *some particular place*, and this place serves as the understood point of view of the narration. And in the context of the first two sentences, you probably understand the third sentence as saying the centaur stared *at the unicorn*, even though it doesn't say so. More enriched compositionality.

children do it, we're tolerant and make an extra effort to understand. When adults do it, it's just annoying.

Philosophy of language situated in the ordinary perspective sometimes gets tied in knots about reference because it doesn't take account of the possibility that different people's reference files might not match. One well-known case comes from Keith Donnellan: Gina says something to Phil about *the guy drinking a martini over there* and gestures toward Bob. In Donnellan's telling, Bob is actually drinking water. So, Donnellan asks, does Gina's phrase refer to Bob, even though he's not a guy drinking a martini? And the answer proves controversial, in ways I won't bother going into.

From the cognitive perspective, the story has to be told a little differently. I want to be very careful here. The issue isn't Gina's description of Bob vs. the Truth About Bob. Rather, it's Gina's description of Bob vs. *the Narrator's* description of Bob. If Gina has used her phrase sincerely, she must think Bob is drinking a martini. From *her* point of view, then, she *has* referred to Bob—her expression is properly linked to her reference file for Bob. But the Narrator's reference file for Bob has Bob drinking water. If we went and tasted Bob's drink, we might find we agree with Gina, or we might agree with the Narrator. If we agree with Gina, then it's the Narrator whose description is out of touch.

Now, what about Phil? Suppose Phil has no idea what the guy is drinking. Then he'll accept Gina's description. Gina's reference to Bob goes through without a hitch, and Phil ends up adding to *his* reference file for Bob that he's drinking a martini. On the other hand, suppose Phil thinks Bob is drinking water. Then he takes Gina's description of Bob to be inaccurate, and he has to deal with the discrepancy. There are various ways he can do this. He may guess who Gina has in mind, and charitably ignore what he takes to be her misdescription. Or he can ask her for clarification: "Do you mean Bob over there?" Or if he doesn't mind being a little rude, he might say "You mean the guy with the *water*, don't you?"

The goal in any case is for Phil and Gina to achieve a mutual impression that they're on the same page. As long as they're satisfied, that's all that matters for the moment. Of course, they may discover later that they weren't actually on the same page, in which case they have to undertake some sort of repair.

This description of the situation seems to me altogether true to life. It begins to show us how people's language use works when communication isn't entirely pristine. It seems a pointless diversion to ask if Gina really referred to Bob, or if the phrase *the guy drinking a martini* really referred to Bob. What matters is whether Gina and Phil end up understanding each other. You can't demand a clean answer when the situation is dirty.

29

What kinds of things can we refer to? (Cognitive metaphysics, Lesson 1)

The basic question of metaphysics, a major branch of philosophy, is what sorts of very fundamental things exist. Are there objects? times? properties? events? numbers? types? Recently a subfield has developed called metametaphysics, whose question is: When we ask metaphysical questions, what are we talking about? Are we talking about reality (the "realist stance")? Or just about how we *talk* about reality (the "deflationary stance")?

As far as I know, metametaphysicians haven't explored a third possibility: a cognitive stance. In these terms, metaphysical questions are about how people understand the world—about what sorts of entities people's minds populate the world with. We talk about reality a certain way because of the way we take reality to be.[1] To see what I mean, let's do a little linguistics again.

Demonstrative pronouns like *this* or *that* are the simplest expressions we use to refer to entities in the world we conceptualize. If I say the

---

[1] In his book *Individuals*, P. F. Strawson calls this enterprise "descriptive metaphysics." He says (p. 10), "Metaphysics has a long and distinguished history, and it is consequently unlikely that there are any new truths to be discovered in descriptive metaphysics." The present chapter and the next two suggest that there actually are some.

sentence below, my pronunciation *that* is linked to a token feature that is also linked to something I experience in the world and am pointing to.

Would you pick <u>that</u> up, please? [*pointing*]

What I'm asking you to pick up in this example is some unspecified sort of physical object. Physical objects are mostly what the philosophical literature on reference talks about—things like tables, chairs, forks, dogs, Socrates, that guy over there drinking a martini, and the present king of France (who we take up in the next chapter). Reference to objects is all I've talked about so far too. But we can actually use demonstrative pronouns to refer to a much richer range of things. Let's look at some examples.

I'd sure like one of <u>those</u>! [*pointing to a Porsche driving by*]

Here the speaker points to the Porsche, but, oddly enough, uses a plural pronoun. This sentence expresses the speaker's desire not to have *that car*, but rather to have something of the *type* (or category) the car belongs to. So the demonstrative pronoun is being used to refer to a *type* rather than to a token. The world looks the same, but the sentence guides the hearer to attend to it differently. The moral for a cognitive metaphysics: If we can understand something as an instance of a type, then we must understand the world to contain types.

In pointing to the Porsche, we're still talking about *objects*. We can go farther afield:

Did you hear <u>that</u>?
Listen to <u>this</u>.

The verbs *hear* and *listen* describe auditory experiences. The phrase following them refers to what's being experienced: either a sound (*Did you hear some honking just now?*) or an object making a sound (*Did you hear an ambulance just now?*). As usual, *this* and *that* are linked to reference files. But the meaning of the verb tells us that the contents of the files have to describe sounds, not objects. Since speakers can refer to sounds this way, they must understand the world to contain sounds. Big surprise.

(People in metaphysics rarely talk about sounds. But they're interesting. Remember the metaphysical puzzle that sounds such as words and songs posed back in chapter 5? In present terms, the question is this: Is the word *puddle* a token that we experience every time we say or hear it? Or is it a type, of which we create a new token every time we say or hear it? There seems no way to decide. The type/token distinction seems fuzzier for these sorts of entities than for physical objects.)

How about this example?

> Please put your coat <u>right here</u> [*pointing*] and your hat <u>over there</u>. [*pointing*]

Right here and *over there* are used to refer not to objects but to *places*. What's a place? Places are often described in relation to an object, as in *under the bed, along the beach, inside the box*. But the place isn't the same as the object. We can use the same object to define many different places: *in the box, on the box, next to the box, behind the box, five feet away from the box*, and so on. And some places aren't defined in terms of an object, such as *in outer space* or *I'd like the chandelier to hang down to <u>here</u>* [pointing to a place in the air in the middle of an empty room]. So the demonstratives *here* and *there* in the example are linked to reference files, but the contents of the files describe a place rather than an object.

Even though we can point to places, they're not "visible" as such—they aren't present in the visual surface. But they *are* present in visual understanding, that is, in spatial structure. So they're part of our conceptualized world.

Next:

> Can you do <u>this</u>? [*demonstrating*]
> 'Osculating' means doing <u>this</u>. [*demonstrating*] (an example from Chapter 7)

When a demonstrative pronoun occurs with the verb *do*, it turns out to refer to an action rather than an object—something you can *do*. There's an interesting wrinkle. If I demonstrate an action and say *Can you do this?*, I'm asking *you* to perform the action that *I* performed. If I say *'Osculating' means doing this* and I demonstrate, I'm showing not what *I* do, but what *anyone* does in performing the action. That is, these expressions abstract the action away from the person performing it—it counts as the same (type of) action no matter who does it.

(It's beginning to look like the ability to understand this kind of abstraction has a brain basis in the so-called mirror neurons. Monkeys' mirror neurons fire either if they're performing a certain action or if they're watching someone else do it. So their brains seem to be sensitive to the same action, no matter who's doing it. It's still a big mystery how the inputs to these neurons are set up so this happens!)

Please indulge me for one more case.

> I'd like you to make the shelf about this long. [*holding the hands a certain distance apart*]
> There were only this many people at the party last night. [*holding up four fingers*]

In the first example, the speaker isn't using *this* to refer to an object. Rather, it refers to a *length* or a *distance* that the not-yet-existing shelf is supposed to satisfy. And in the second example, *this* is being used to refer not to fingers, but rather to the *number* of fingers. Now a two-foot long shelf doesn't look like a two-foot space between your hands, and four people don't look like four of your fingers. In fact, in *I heard this many honks* [holding up four fingers], the number isn't even used to count something you can see. So lengths and numbers abstract really far away from the way the world looks. You might say we don't *see* them, but we *read* them into what we see. This might make a standard metaphysician rather uneasy. Still, we refer to them, so they must be part of the world as we understand it.

Summing up these examples: By using demonstratives in different grammatical contexts, a speaker can invite a hearer to derive a whole variety of interpretations from the very same visual surface. The differences among these interpretations are encoded only in spatial structure and/or conceptual structure. Yet in each case the speaker points to something or demonstrates something that the demonstrative refers to. So these examples show that we can refer to types, sounds, places, directions, actions, lengths, and amounts in the external world as we understand it, using the very same basic mechanism of language that we use to refer to objects. They all can get reference files in conceptual structure.

Here's some more evidence that we recognize all these sorts of entities. We can ask a question that requests the hearer to identify a physical object. The hearer can reply either with a linguistic expression or by pointing to something "out in the world."

| What did you see? | A unicorn. | [or *point to something*] |

And it turns out that we can also also ask about all these other sorts of entities. The answer to the question can be either a linguistic expression, a nonlinguistic point to something, or a demonstration.

What kind do you want?	A Porsche.	[or *pointing*]
What did you hear?	Some honking.	[or *imitation of sound*]
Where's my hat?	In the kitchen.	[or *pointing*]
What did you do?	Stuck out my tongue.	[or *demonstrating*]
How long was the fish?	Two feet long.	[or *holding hands apart*]
How many people came?	Four.	[or *holding up four fingers*]

And we can use *the same* to compare either two physical objects or two of any of these other sorts of entities.

He wore the same hat he always wears.
He ate the same sandwich he always eats.
   [It had *better* be the same type, not the same token!]
The car is making the same scary noise it always makes.

Your hat is in the same place as your coat.
You can do the same thing you always do. Anything you can do, I can
    do better!
The fish was the same length (or just as long) as my arm.
There were the same number of people (or just as many people) at the
    party as in the class.

We *talk* and *act* as though this whole menagerie of entities is "out there in the world" for us to refer to, point to, and demonstrate. So, within the ordinary perspective, they all exist. From the cognitive perspective, though, these examples show us not what there is in the world, but what's involved in forming *our understanding* of the world. Our way of talking about the world isn't "in error" or "misguided" or "just language." If we didn't understand the world this way, there wouldn't be anything in our minds to link linguistic expressions like these examples to. As for what's really *really* in the world, maybe that's the business of theoretical physics, but an answer that *we humans* can formulate and understand still has to be filtered through the human cognitive apparatus.

These examples far from exhaust the entities we understand the world to have in it. They're just the relatively concrete ones. There are lots of more abstract ones too, like values and relationships and mortgages. For our purposes here, one very important one is *sentences*. We can point to sentences with demonstratives:

Did he really say *that*?

We can ask questions whose answers are quoted sentences.

What did he say? "The stock market is collapsing."

And we can make statements of identity:

I think Bill just said the same thing you said.

As we saw in Chapter 5, words and sentences are strange kinds of entities. But whatever their weird properties from the point of view of

171

traditional metaphysics, we talk and act as though they're right out there along with cars and stars.

More technically, when you speak, hear, or imagine a sentence, it gets a reference file so you can refer back to it and compare it with other sentences. This is going to be important in a few minutes.

30

Reference files for pictures and thoughts

René Magritte entitled this painting *La trahison des images* ('The treachery of images'). The caption says "This isn't a pipe." Of *course* it isn't a pipe, silly—it's only an *image* of a pipe. Let's figure out how we understand this.

The painting is something we perceive out in the world. So our mind gives it a reference file whose character tag is 'real.' Its content features say that it's a token object and that it's a two-dimensional pattern on the page. Since we pick out the pipe-image as part of the painting (the same way we pick out a handle as part of a cup), it gets its own reference file. It too has the character tag 'real,' and its content features also say it's a token object that's a two-dimensional pattern. In addition, the two reference files are linked by a 'part-of' relation—the pipe-image is part of the painting. So far, so good.

But why is this particular part of the painting understood as an image of a pipe? The reason is that it *represents* or *depicts* a pipe.[1] Now comes the tricky part. What's the status of the pipe that the image depicts? We understand it not as a two-dimensional pattern on the page, but as a three-dimensional free-standing object. Since we understand the depicted pipe this way, it must have its own reference file! So we end up with not two but three reference files: one for the painting, one for the pipe-image, and one for the depicted pipe.

"Wait! Where did this extra entity come from? There's no real pipe around!" That's right. By understanding the painting as a depiction, we've *constructed* what might be called a "virtual pipe," which forms part of our conceptualization of the painting. The conceptualization of a virtual pipe does differ from the conceptualization of a real pipe, but not in its content features—its shape, color, and so forth. Rather, the difference is in its character tags—it carries the feature 'virtual' rather than 'real.' The figure on the next page sketches the conceptualization of the picture. (As in Chapter 27, I have to let actual images stand in for spatial structure. And since the images are all two-dimensional, I have to add annotations to indicate that the image is two-dimensional but the virtual pipe is three-dimensional.)

---

[1] Exactly what does it take for an image to represent or depict something? This is pretty complicated and I don't want to get into it here. A hint: Representations don't have to be "realistic." Cartoons are representations, and in a way, so are the notches that a hunter puts on his gun to commemorate the animals he's killed.

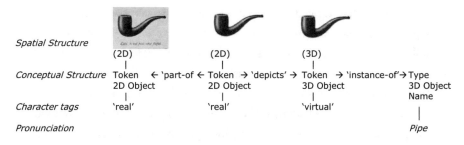

Spatial Structure	(2D)	(2D)	(3D)	
	│	│	│	
Conceptual Structure	Token ← 'part-of' ←	Token → 'depicts' →	Token → 'instance-of'→	Type
	2D Object	2D Object	3D Object	3D Object
	│	│	│	Name
Character tags	'real'	'real'	'virtual'	│
Pronunciation				Pipe

Now, suppose I ignore Magritte's warning and talk about the picture the way we normally do:

Gosh, that pipe looks like one my Dad used to smoke.

Am I referring to the pipe-image, or to the virtual pipe? Well, it's kind of hard to tell. In this sentence—

That pipe is a sort that isn't very expensive.

—I'm talking about the cost of that sort of real pipe, not the cost of paintings of pipes. On the other hand, in this sentence—

That pipe is painted in lush realistic colors.

—I'm talking about the image. So it looks as though in the context of the picture, the expression *that pipe* can refer either to the pipe-image *or* the virtual pipe.

Usually this ambiguity is harmless, and the context makes it clear when necessary. But not always. Here's a context where the ambiguity makes a difference.

There's a scratch on the pipe in the painting.

On one meaning, the painting has gotten scratched in the area of the pipe-image. On the other, the virtual pipe is depicted as having a virtual scratch on it.

When we use the words *pipe* and *scratch* to talk about images this way, nothing has changed in the meanings of the words themselves. Rather, a general principle of language lets us talk about depictions by using the

175

words for what they depict. We encountered this principle back in Chapter 12, when we used the sentence *They have the Beatles on display* to talk about statues of the Beatles in a wax museum. There, it seemed odd to say that the name *the Beatles* has two meanings, the actual guys and their statues. In the same way here, it would be funny to say that the word *pipe* has two meanings, the thing you smoke tobacco in and an image—as if the two uses are like smoking a cigar vs. smoking a herring. It makes more sense to say that the word *always* names the object but that, thanks to enriched compositionality, we can also use the word to talk about an image that *depicts* the object.

In addition, when we talk about an image or a statue as a depiction of something, we've set up this double reference to the image and what it depicts. This too is a case of enriched compositionality, where the meaning of the sentence contains parts that don't come from the meanings of the words.

Here's a related case. What are we doing when we use a banana as a pretend telephone? We're performing a real action, speaking a certain way while holding a banana a certain way, and this action depicts another action, a virtual action. One of the characters in the real action is a banana, which depicts a virtual telephone that is a character in the virtual action. Because the banana depicts a telephone, we're entitled to *call* it a telephone.

That's not all. Since the virtual action is a phone call, there has to be another character on the other end of the conversation. So we understand there to be a virtual character we're "talking to," and we set up a reference file for *him* so we can talk about him as part of the pretense: "Uncle Harold wants to know when you're coming to visit."

Not all pictures depict virtual objects, of course. How do we conceptualize Johann Georg Edlinger's portrait of Mozart?

Again there's a reference file for the painting as a whole, and one for the figure itself. This time, though, the figure is linked to a reference file for a real individual, not a virtual one (assuming you know who Mozart was).

Here's where it gets interesting. Nothing in the picture itself tells you whether the depicted individual is to be understood as real or virtual. Only the name attached to the picture can tell you that. If the painting were called *18th-century Viennese gentleman*, we would have no way of knowing whether the guy was an actual person or a figment of the artist's imagination.

When a picture depicts a real person, we may be able to compare the depiction with the person. One of Mozart's friends might have said to the artist,

> That's quite a portrait! You've made Mozart handsomer than Mozart really is.

What he's conveying is that the person as depicted doesn't match the actual person—the depiction relation isn't quite accurate. Let's look a little more closely at how this works. The second *Mozart* in the sentence clearly is meant to refer to the real guy. But the first *Mozart* is meant to refer to the image—the Mozart that Edlinger *made*. So the sentence

177

compares real-Mozart's handsomeness to the depicted handsomeness of image-Mozart.

Pictures aren't the only thing that leads us to construct reference files for virtual individuals. Chapter 27 mentioned fictional people like Sherlock Holmes. Holmes came into virtual existence by way of language rather than pictures (though pictures soon followed). He's conceptualized as a virtual person who has virtual adventures. Most of the language we use to talk about such folks is exactly the language we use to talk about real people. At best we rely on little cues like the _mythical_ Santa Claus or *Once upon a time* to determine that they're meant as virtual. Sometimes the cover of a book says "A novel." Often, though, it's just a matter of understanding the context.[2]

A case I find especially fascinating is the status of legends and myths. These present themselves as history, depicting real characters in real events. We may have the sense that they've originated as figments of someone's imagination, but still we sometimes kind of like to believe (or pretend) they depict real events. This presents a quandary: Does the reference file for *Achilles* have the character tag 'real' or 'virtual'? Well, it may not matter for enjoying the story, so maybe we just leave the question open. But it's not always that easy. Kids who are beginning to suspect Santa Claus is virtual sometimes still *want* to believe in him. And exactly what are the character tags for *Moses* and *Jesus*? For lots of people, the choice is hugely important!

It's not just pictures and stories that we understand as depicting things. Here's a famous example from Bertrand Russell:

I thought your yacht was larger than it is.

A curious thing about this sentence is that if you take off *I thought*, the remainder means something completely different—that the yacht has

---

[2] In his book *Frame Analysis*, the sociologist Erving Goffman discusses in exhaustive detail these sorts of contexts that alter the way we understand objects and actions. Prime among his examples is our understanding of theater, in which the actors depict virtual characters. He calls such a systematic alteration or amplification of understanding a "keying," and the context in which a virtual world is depicted a "frame," evoking an analogy to a picture frame.

gotten smaller. This isn't the way we understand the full sentence, though. Rather, it describes an inaccurate depiction, just like what we imagined Mozart's friend saying. So here's the analysis.

- Parallel to the reference file for the painting, there's a reference file for my thought, with the character tag 'real.' I'm saying I had a real thought.
- Parallel to the reference file for the image, there's a reference file for my yacht-concept, with the character tag 'real,' which forms part of the thought. I'm saying I had a real concept of your yacht.
- Parallel to the reference file for the real Mozart, there's a reference file for your actual yacht. My yacht-concept depicted your yacht.
- However, my yacht-concept failed to depict your actual yacht correctly.
- The phrase *your yacht* refers to my yacht-concept. The pronoun *it* refers to your actual yacht.
- The context that leads us to this enriched interpretation of the sentence is the phrase *I thought*, which has an effect parallel to the presentation of a picture or the phrase *In this picture*...

From this example, we learn that we ordinarily think and talk about thoughts in much the same way as we think and talk about pictures. We conceptualize thoughts as entities in people's heads. They can depict either actual objects and actions or virtual objects and actions (in which case we call them "imaginary"), and sometimes mixtures of the two. When they depict actual objects and actions, they may be inaccurate, in which case we call them something like "false beliefs."[3]

[3] This approach, then, is an account of the naïve Theory of Mind, our ability to understand others' thoughts and perceptions. There is a rich experimental literature on when Theory of Mind develops in children, whether apes ever achieve it, and whether autistic individuals lack it.

I think this account can be extended to all the standard examples of *de dicto* vs. *de re* (also known as referential opacity vs. transparency) in the philosophical literature. My *Semantics and Cognition* goes through the examples in a framework a little different from the one developed here, but similarly drawing out the relevant parallels with descriptions of pictures. None of the philosophical accounts I am familiar with notices these parallels, which I think are crucial to understanding what's going on in these phenomena.

Let's go back to the last chapter's theme of "cognitive metaphysics"—what sorts of things do we act as though the world has in it? We now see that in order to talk about people's thoughts, we have to accord the thoughts their own reference files. We also have to construct reference files for the parts of a thought—the image-characters and image-actions that make up the thought. In addition, we understand thoughts, like pictures, as depicting or representing objects and actions, sometimes real and sometimes virtual.

It doesn't matter if that's not the way thoughts really work, on the cognitive and neural perspectives. But that's the way the cognitive perspective says that the ordinary perspective treats them.

31
More cognitive metaphysics: Persons

In Chapter 18 I talked about a traditional view of "what makes us human," going back at least to Descartes: Humans have souls, are conscious, are rational, have language, and have moral responsibility. I want to look at this view a little more closely. Its intuitive appeal tells us something about the ordinary perspective on people.

Here's the idea. We understand the world to contain physical objects like rocks, trees, bicycles, and tables. Among the physical objects, certain kinds, such as ants, worms, rats, and tigers, can move around under their own power. And among these "animate" entities is the very special class of *persons*. Unlike animals and inanimate objects, persons have social relations, social roles, rights, obligations, and moral responsibility.

As with all the other concepts we've looked at (especially in Chapter 11), the notion of 'person' isn't cut and dried. We're happy to think of some non-humans as "honorary" persons, particularly pets and personified animals like Brer Rabbit and Bugs Bunny.[1] Still, we do draw the line somewhere: the mosquito buzzing in your ear isn't a person by any stretch of the imagination, at least in our culture. Much more noxious is

[1] Another "honorary" case is the modern American legal treatment of corporations as persons. This has the salutary result that one can sue a corporation and hold it legally responsible for its actions. On the other hand, as many have pointed out, you can't put a corporation in jail. And, as a person, a corporation has the right to free speech, leading to the legality of massive corporate influence on elections and legislation.

when things go in the other direction—when people treat humans as non-persons. It's all too common for people to declare that their enemies or members of lower-status social groups are dogs, pigs, or monkeys, and to use that to justify treating them without compassion.

The conceptual twist here is that persons, unlike animals, are taken to have a special part that's separate from the body—an entity we might call "mind" or "soul" or "spirit" or "self," take your choice. To see how this might work, let's return to our discussion of *book* back in Chapter 11. We saw there that a stereotypical book has a physical aspect—a collection of bound pages with writing on them—plus an "informational" aspect—the ideas conveyed by the writing. But these two aspects can be detached from each other, since there are physical books consisting of blank pages, and there are pageless "informational" books on a computer.

The idea is that persons have the same sort of dual aspect. We think of a normal person as having both a body and a soul, but we can also conceive of the two coming apart. A dead body is one "from which the soul has departed." But all cultures seem to think of it still as a kind of person, treating it with a kind of respect we don't accord to other inanimate objects. And on the other hand, all cultures seem to have concepts of souls existing independently of bodies: souls ascending to heaven after death, spirits of departed ancestors watching people's lives, and pure disembodied spirits like angels, ghosts, gods, and devils.

We can also conceive of a soul detaching from a body and attaching to a different one, in at least four different ways. The first is reincarnation, where the soul of someone who has died is implanted in a new body. (And if it's a culture where they think you can be reincarnated as an animal, then they think animals have souls too.) The second is metamorphosis: the prince is changed into a frog—but he's still the prince! The third is body-switching, as in the movie *Freaky Friday*, where mother and daughter wake up in each other's bodies. The fourth is spirit possession, where a spirit gets into someone's head or body and takes over control of their actions. Ideas like these are completely straightforward to understand, and lots of cultures come up with one or another of them in their folktales, legends, or religion.

In dreams, we sometimes "know" a person is different from the one he or she looks like: "I dreamt I was talking to Uncle Sol, but for some reason he was young and blond, not old and bald." And people with an affliction called Capgras Syndrome will swear that their spouse (or some other socially significant person) has been replaced by an impostor—who looks just the same![2] In these cases too, the person's identity is somehow conceived of as separate from their physical features.

We can only imagine these sorts of switches because we conceive of the body and the soul as separate. It's hard to imagine ordinary "soulless" objects undergoing this kind of change. Try to think of your coffee mug and frying pan becoming each other, or two ordinary non-anthropomorphized frogs in the pond trading identities. It's simply weird.

---

[2] The protagonist of the novel *Atmospheric Disturbances*, by Rivka Galchen (Picador, 2008) apparently suffers from Capgras Syndrome, as does a character in *The Echo Maker*, by Richard Powers (MacMillan Picador, 2006). During an illness, my wife's aunt showed these symptoms intermittently, at various times declaring that her husband, her daughter, or her nurse were impostors.

Who you are, your personal identity, goes with your soul, not with your body. When Descartes wanted to prove that he existed (*Cogito, ergo sum*), it was the existence of his mind, not his body, that mattered. And the mom and the daughter wake up with their minds in each other's bodies—they don't wake up in their own bodies but with each other's *minds*.

Religions all incorporate this conception of persons, and it feels perfectly natural. One of the central issues that religions deal with is what happens to you—your soul, your identity—when you die. Notice, they don't question *whether* you have a self or a soul. They only differ in what they say happens to it. Religions also populate the world with all sorts of supernatural beings like spirits and gods, who interact with people in one way or another. They display human characteristics like jealousy, forgiveness, benevolence, malevolence, justice, and revenge, and they're often taken to be responsible for preserving the natural and moral order.

In Descartes' version of the cognitive perspective, this was perfectly okay. In fact, right after proving that he himself exists, he sets himself the task of proving that God exists too.

A modern cognitive perspective will have none of this. Some people take a hard line: "There's no soul. Everything in the world of our experience and thought has a physical cause." Others take a less hard line that adds up to the same thing: "*I bet* there's no soul, and *I bet* we can explain everything in the world of our experience and thought in physical terms." For instance, the title of Antonio Damasio's book *Descartes' Error* refers to the philosopher's belief in a soul. And Francis Crick's *Astonishing Hypothesis* is a bet that there isn't such a thing. Except for some niggling doubts (well, some people see them as overwhelming) about the "Hard Problem of Consciousness" (Chapter 18), the case against the soul seems pretty strong these days.

The modern cognitive perspective joins forces with biological and evolutionary perspectives, and claims that the human mind came to be the way it is through mindless processes of genetic mutation and natural selection. The explanation doesn't require a God who thought us up and created us. And humans have moral codes, not because some God decreed the moral order, but because natural selection happened to favor groups of people who were biased to take care of each other over groups where everyone was biased to just look out for themselves.[3] That is, moral codes, like languages, are a product of the human mind.

This is all very well and good, but when we get down to brass tacks, look what it says: There's nothing special about you. You're just a chance product of a mindless evolutionary process operating in an insignificant corner of the vast universe. Your life has no meaning. In fact, there's not even a You, there's just a clump of neurons interacting with each other that happen to converge on a convenient computation of "Selfhood."

Well. Between this picture and one in which you not only exist but are important, where your life is meaningful and even sacred, where it matters what you do, where there's a God out there who cares about you, which would *you* choose? I think a lot of people would say, "If science tells me I don't exist, and that there's no right and wrong, then the hell with science." And I think this is one reason we see such widespread public resistance to teaching evolution in the schools.

The scientists have countered with attacks on religion, specifically on the existence of God. My sense is that the existence of God isn't the real issue here. The real crisis is in the subtext: the existence and importance of Me. One thing I miss in this literature is any discussion of the sense of the sacred, which, as pointed out in Chapter 26, is a vital aspect of religious experience. Another thing I miss is a possible way to resolve the

---

[3] A little more careful formulation for readers who might be concerned that I'm inappropriately invoking group selection: Natural selection favored people who formed groups, and who were inclined to take a bit of care for people in their group, over people who either shunned groups or, when in a group, still only looked out for themselves. And why, you might ask, did natural selection favor such groups? The answer I find most satisfying, if also most distressing, is that looking out for each other *within* the group was an advantage in fighting and defeating *other* groups. A modern manifestation of this is the increase in patriotism and national cohesion in the time of war.

crisis, suggested by movements as different as existentialism, Chasidism, and Buddhism, at least as I understand them: your life becomes meaningful and sacred by your making it so, through the way you live it.

The disconnect here should look familiar. It's just a more drastic version of "There's no such thing as English, sunsets, words, colors, free will, etc. etc." And again, the way to resolve it is to recognize that it arises from not keeping track of which perspective we're in. The ordinary perspective is insistent on people having something "soulular" in addition to their bodies, something that gives them their identity. The cognitive perspective tries to do without—though it still has to explain why we *understand* or *conceptualize* people in terms of souls. Is one of these perspectives *wrong*? As in all the other cases, it depends what your purpose is.

Getting back to our main theme here, a cognitive metaphysics has to treat persons the same way it treats books. There's a single reference file for a person, but if necessary we can split the reference file into two. One part, the body, has content features that situate it in the physical domain. The other part, the mind/soul/spirit/self, has content features that situate it in this other mysterious "personal" domain. That seems to be the way we conceptualize ourselves and each other.

32
What's truth?

It's time to tackle that most sacred of philosophical topics, Truth. Right from the start, we have to remember that *true* and *truth* are just words. If *bald* and *smoke* and *climb* are full of complexity and indeterminacy, we should expect no less from *true* and *truth*. We can't let ourselves succumb to the temptation of assuming 𝕿𝖗𝖚𝖙𝖍 has some underlying pure 𝕰𝖘𝖘𝖊𝖓𝖈𝖊.

First, some linguistics, to get a better idea of what we're talking about. The use of *true* that philosophers are most interested in, and the one I'll concentrate on here, ascribes a property to a declarative sentence. The sentence in question may be quoted, or it may be referred to by a phrase like *that sentence.*

> *"Snow is white"* is true.
> It's true that snow is white.
> The preceding sentence is true.
> That statement/claim/assertion/proposition is true.

Here's a traditional description of the meaning of *true*: A sentence is true if it corresponds to the way the world is. Alternatively, using the terms of Chapter 30, a sentence is true if it depicts the world accurately—in the same way that a picture or a thought may depict the world accurately.

Less often remarked is that this same use of *true* can be ascribed to a string of sentences that form a narrative, as in these three sentences.

What you say is true.   [a sentence or a narrative]
What the newspaper says about the president is true.   [a narrative]
This story can't be true.   [a narrative]

Questions, imperatives, proposals, and performatives (sentences that establish a fact by being uttered) can't be characterized as true. And jokes are made up of declarative sentences, but they can't be characterized as true either.

*"*Is snow white?*" is true.   [question]
*"*Eat your dinner*" is true.   [imperative]
*"*Let's get some lunch*" is true.   [proposal]
*"*I now pronounce you husband and wife*" is true.   [performative]
*"*A priest, a minister, and a rabbi walk into a bar…*" is true.   [joke]

Here are two grammatical variants of this use.

a true sentence/story/statement/claim/assertion/proposition
the truth of that sentence/story/claim/assertion/proposition

The opposite of *true* in this use is of course *false*, and the opposite of *truth* is *falsity*.

"*Snow is green*" is false.
What you say/what the newspaper says is false.
a false sentence/statement/story/claim/assertion/proposition
the falsity of that sentence/statement/story/claim/assertion/proposition

Another use of *truth* appears in the next example. Its counterpart is *falsehood* rather than *falsity*.

the truth about 9/11
*the falsity about 9/11
a falsehood about 9/11

The next examples contain a grammatical variant on this use.

He's telling the truth.
I want to find out the truth.

These have a hidden piece of meaning—*the truth* means something like 'the truth *about X,*' where *X* is some character or situation we understand from the context.[1] Still another use in this subfamily is:

> We take these truths to be self-evident: That all men are created equal...

Here *truth* means 'true sentence' or 'true proposition.'

A slightly more distant use of *true* turns up in phrases like these.

> a true copy of the document
> a true belief about the war
> a true picture of Mozart[2]

These too are used to describe accurate depictions, except that this time the entity that is doing the depicting isn't a sentence.

And here's a still more distant use:

> the true cause of the smell in the attic
> the true solution to our problems
> a true lover of opera
> a true friend

Again, the thing that's *true* isn't a sentence. But in this case it's not even an object that depicts something:

> *This* is the true cause of that smell in the attic! [holding up a dead squirrel]

False doesn't work in this context either.

> *the false cause of the smell in the attic
> *the false solution to our problems

---

[1] We've seen this sort of thing before, in examples like *be polite*, which has to mean 'being polite to so-and-so' or 'be polite to people in general,' and *be unconscious*, which means 'be unconscious of things in general.'

[2] Actually, this phrase is as likely to be applied to a verbal description as to an actual picture, as in *The biography of Mozart by Einstein doesn't give a true picture of his love life.*

*a false lover of opera
(*although* a false friend)

This use can often be paraphrased by *genuine* or *real*—

the genuine/real cause of the smell
a genuine/real lover of opera
a genuine/real friend

—whereas the "sentential" use of *true* can't.

* "Snow is white" is genuine/real.
"Snow is white" is a genuine/real sentence. ≠ "Snow is white" is a
true sentence.

In addition, there are some uses in idioms like *true to life*, which describes an accurate depiction, and the somewhat archaic *his aim was true*, which describes an accurate shot (in a different though related use of *accurate*).

All these uses show a family resemblance, not unlike the uses of *smoke* in Chapter 6 and *conscious* in Chapter 17.

33

Problems for an ordinary perspective on truth

Now let's go back to the first use of *true*, where it expresses a property of a sentence or narrative. How do you tell whether a particular sentence is true? One well-known explication was proposed by the logician Alfred Tarski:

"Snow is white" is true if and only if snow is white.

This is rescued from silliness by saying that the second *snow is white* is intended as a temporary stand-in for a set of conditions stated in a "metalanguage" such as logic or mathematics. Tarski's goal is a "theory of truth" that states "truth-conditions" for all sentences of natural languages. If the world satisfies the truth-conditions for a sentence, the sentence is true; if it doesn't, the sentence is false. This is all within the ordinary perspective, of course.

This sort of theory of truth runs into various sorts of problems. I'll go through a few. First, remember our bald guys in Chapter 11? Here are three of them.

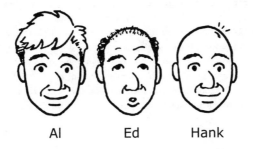

Al   Ed   Hank

Our friend Ed is bald compared to Al, but not bald compared to Hank. Is the sentence *Ed is bald* true or false? It's not clear.

Here's a related case.

The distance from Boston to New York is 200 miles.

Is it true? It does the job if you're trying to figure out whether you can drive from Boston to New York in an hour (no) or in a day (yes). On the other hand, if you need to be more accurate, how do you measure the distance? From the center of Boston to the center of New York? From the nearest border to the nearest border? Or from your actual starting point in Boston to your actual endpoint in New York? Do you measure by the fastest road, or the shortest, or the one you're actually going to take? The absolute truth of the sentence seems less the issue than its suitability for your current purpose.[1]

Speaking of baldness, another much-discussed example goes back to Russell: *The present king of France is bald*. Russell thought it must be false, because there's no present king of France. The problem is that if it's false, then its negation, *The present king of France isn't bald*, must be true. But it can't be, because there's no present king of France. So some people conclude the sentence is neither true nor false. A similar issue comes up with our example in Chapter 28, where Gina says of Bob, *The guy with a martini is talking to Heather*, but (according to the Narrator) Bob is drinking water. Is the sentence true or false?

For a last example, how can both these sentences be true?

---

[1] The philosopher Jerrold Katz once asserted that this sentence is either true or false, and that's the end of the story. The problems I've posed here come from my response.

This example is also interesting because, like some examples in Chapter 29, it seems to refer to a distance. The philosopher Jim Higginbotham thinks it doesn't. He proposes that the logical form of this sentence is really something like 'The number of miles from Boston to New York is 200', so the sentence is really about numbers, not distances. However, (a) he doesn't show how to relate this proposed logical form to the actual sentence, and (b) he neglects to notice that a mile is a distance—and if you're counting miles, you're referring to them.

Sherlock Holmes was British.
Sherlock Holmes didn't exist.

Since there was no Holmes, *Sherlock Holmes was British* ought to have the same funny status as *The present king of France is bald*, whatever we want to say that status is. But actually, we automatically understand the sentence within another (unmentioned) context—the virtual world depicted in the story. Within *this* world, Sherlock Holmes was indeed British, not, say, Romanian. So *Sherlock Holmes was British* is true—within this virtual world. (William James gives this account too.)

How about *Sherlock Holmes didn't exist*? This one's obviously false within the virtual world of the story. But in the ordinary world, there was no Holmes, so the sentence is true. In other words, both these sentences are ambiguous as to what world they depict, and we interpret them whichever way is most informative, without any sense of conscious choice. From this we see that our original intuitive definition—a sentence is true if it corresponds to the way the world is—leaves open a crucial question: the way *which* world is?

These sorts of examples reinforce my admonition at the beginning of the last chapter that *true* is a word just like any other, full of unclear and indeterminate cases. The philosophical problems with truth arise for four interrelated reasons.

- They take for granted the ordinary perspective, in which sentences in the world are connected directly to states of affairs in the world.
- They take for granted that truth must be totally clear and totally sharp-edged.
- They insist that a theory of meaning has to begin with a theory of truth.
- They act as though all we need to do in the face of these sorts of problematic examples is sharpen this perspective.

As usual, the cognitive perspective makes the problem quite different: What are people *doing* when they *judge* sentences to be true?

Immediately I hear the usual suspects piping up: *"Judgments* of truth may be all well and good, but what about the real thing—*truth*, plain and simple? What about the eternal truths of mathematics? *They* aren't a matter of someone's judgment. *Two plus two equals four* was already true when only bacteria roamed the earth." Well, if you want to insist on the ordinary perspective, on 𝕽𝖊𝖆𝖑 𝕿𝖗𝖚𝖙𝖍, then yes, that's what you have to say. From the cognitive perspective, though, the issue is rather: How do we humans come to *grasp* mathematical statements as true, and why do they *seem* to us to be eternal? And that's an interesting question for psychology and neuroscience, not a matter of pure philosophy.

This is not to say the ordinary perspective on truth is *wrong*. As with sunsets, in some circumstances the ordinary perspective works best, and in other circumstances, a sun-centered or a brain-centered perspective is more suitable. I'm proposing that if our goal is to understand how thought and meaning work, part of that is to understand how people judge sentences to be true, and for this the cognitive perspective is going to be more suitable. But you'll have to judge for yourself.

34

What's it like to judge a sentence true?

The ordinary view of truth does get one thing right. Truth does require a correspondence between a sentence and the world (or at least *some* world). But it doesn't tell us how there can be a correspondence between two things in the world as different as bald heads and sentences.

The cognitive perspective lets us do better. Let's look at the act of judging a sentence true. So imagine: You're looking at a visual scene like this one:

and I say *There's a cat on the mat*. What are you experiencing?

The linguistic part of the experience has the form of a string of words out there in the world, accompanied by the feeling that they're meaningful. The visual part of the experience has the form of a visual surface out there accompanied by the feeling that it's meaningful. What else? Well, suppose instead my sentence were *There are two cats on the mat*. You would still find it meaningful. How would the experience be different?

The first sentence might come with a feeling of a sort of silent "Uh-huh," and the second with a silent "Nope." Or you might have a proprioceptive image of nodding or shaking your head—or you might *actually* nod or shake your head. The words and the head gestures on their own don't mean much, but they're conscious "handles" for feelings associated with the sentences. We might describe one feeling as assent (or conviction, or congruence), and the other as dissent (or opposition, or incongruence). That is, judging a sentence true or false is marked in experience by a feeling associated with the sentence. We can express this feeling of conviction about the sentence by saying *"There's a cat on the mat* is true." (What does it feel like to judge *"There's a cat on the mat* is true" as true? Well, it comes with the same feeling of conviction.)

Shrieks erupt: "Truth is a *feeling*? For heaven's sake, my *feelings* have *nothing* to do with whether a sentence is true!" Well, so far this is just a description of the *experience* of judging a sentence true. Now we go behind the scenes and review what your mind is doing to create that experience.

In response to light reflected off the picture, your mind constructs a visual surface, which is a cognitive correlate of consciousness. It also constructs a spatial structure and a conceptual structure, which are *not* cognitive correlates of consciousness. The presence of the link between visual input and the visual surface leads to a character tag of 'real.' The presence of the link between the visual surface and the spatial structure leads to a character tag of 'meaningful.' So you experience the visual surface as a real meaningful object out there.[1]

---

[1] Actually, in the situation here, the sentence matches a picture, not reality. Within the virtual world depicted by the picture, there's a token cat. But whether it's supposed to depict any particular real cat isn't an issue. So your understanding the picture and assenting to the truth of *There's a cat on the mat* depends on your "entering the virtual world," just like your judgment of Sherlock Holmes being British.

In response to the sounds I make in saying the sentence, your mind constructs a pronunciation, which is a cognitive correlate of consciousness. It also constructs a conceptual structure and (in this case) a spatial structure, which are not cognitive correlates of consciousness. The link between the auditory input and the pronunciation leads to a character tag of 'external sound.' The link between the pronunciation and the conceptual structure leads to a character tag of 'meaningful.' So you experience the pronunciation as a real and meaningful utterance.

So far, your mind has an understanding of a picture and an understanding of a sentence. But now, because both are couched in terms of conceptual and spatial structures, your mind can compare them and look for a match. And unlike the ordinary perspective, your mind is in the fortunate position of comparing apples and apples. You end up judging the sentence true if there's a match—or, at the next degree of approximation, if there's a good enough match for the present context. (What's good enough for the corner bar may not work so well in court or the operating room.)

How do we get from a match to a conscious judgment? As usual, this can't happen by magic. Remember, all the structures your mind is comparing are unconscious, so you don't have any experience of *them*. But suppose there's a mechanism in the mind that *detects* a match or its absence. We encountered a number of mechanisms like this in Chapters 19, 25, and 26. We said there that each of these mechanisms assigns a character tag that's a cognitive correlate of a feeling associated with things you perceive—'real,' 'meaningful,' 'familiar,' 'sacred,' and so on. In the case of truth-judgments we're dealing with a three-way distinction: you may judge a sentence true or false, or you may just be turning it over in your mind, in which case you're noncommittal or neutral.

The hypothesis, then, is that, from the cognitive perspective, assenting to a sentence—judging it's true—amounts to assigning it a character tag that we might call 'commitment' or 'conviction.' The conscious feeling correlated with this feature is that the sentence out there in the world depicts reality accurately—the sentence is "objective." Disagreeing with a sentence (finding it false) amounts to assigning it the opposite value of this feature, 'dissent' or 'opposition'; and not making a judgment assigns it the neutral value of the tag.

There's a kind of paradox here, in that truth is understood as an objective property of the sentence, despite the fact that it's the result of a subjective judgment. The paradox is resolved by the fact that the experience of objectivity is constructed by the mind, as part of making the judgment. As we saw in Chapter 25, "seeing the world" as objectively "out there" is a construction on the part of the mind. We also encountered this sort of situation way back in Chapter 8, in connection with words like *enjoyable* and *interesting*. We talk about someone *enjoying* an activity. But we also talk about the activity being simply *enjoyable*, as though that's an objective property of the activity, independent of there being anyone around to enjoy it. Similarly, even further back in chapter 2, we talked about how we think of a language as an "objective" thing in the world, independent of a community of speakers. These other examples show us that the ordinary understanding of truth as "objective" isn't a peculiarity of truth. From the cognitive perspective, it's quite undistinguished in this respect.

Let's go back to the cat on the mat. When you judge the sentence true, you're matching the sentence's meaning with spatial and conceptual structures that come from what you see. But the spatial and conceptual structures could also come from your pre-existing understanding—your memory. Where did your pre-existing understanding come from? Three possibilities: from your own perceptual experience in the past, from things you figured out from *other* pre-existing understanding, or from things people told you.

Think about this last situation. When someone tells you something, your mind constructs a meaning for the utterance (which, if all goes well, matches the meaning they had in mind). If this meaning jibes with something already within your understanding, you'll judge the utterance true. If it conflicts with something already within your understanding, you'll judge it false.

But now suppose this meaning isn't already within your understanding, but doesn't conflict with your understanding either. If you assume the speaker is sincere, then you'll just add the meaning to your understanding of the world. You don't *judge* the sentence true, you simply *accept* what the speaker says as true—you take it to be depicting a situation with the character tag 'real.' (In computer science terms, you update your database.) We saw this sort of situation in Chapter 28, when Gina was telling Phil about the man drinking the martini, and Phil simply accepted her description. That's how we normally use sentences that convey information, like these:

> I've got a pain in my toe.
> My house is the first house in the third block on the right, and it's green.
> The ballgame is on TV at 7 tonight.
> The man drinking a martini is my department chair.
> Millard Fillmore was the thirteenth president of the US.
> You are made of bazillions of tiny molecules.
> When you die, you go to heaven. [a *foundation for religious belief!*]

Of course there are lots of atypical situations in which you don't immediately accept a speaker's statement. For instance, the context may contain one of those formulas that signals a virtual world: "Once upon a time...," "So a priest, a minister, and a rabbi walk into a bar and...," or (from the opening of this chapter) "Imagine: You're looking at a visual scene and..."

Or you may decline to accept the speaker's statement, because you judge that he or she is lying or teasing or just plain unreliable. It isn't always easy to decide whether you can trust the speaker. If you're constantly worried about it, you're probably paranoid. On the other hand, constant worry is probably a useful tactic if you're in, say, a prison camp or 1980s East Germany.

35

Noticing something's wrong

Suppose you're confronted with one of the following situations, in which two different sources of information apparently conflict:

- You see something within reach, but when you reach for it, you can't feel anything (as in a virtual reality situation). Or you walk into a glass door. In either case, there's a strong feeling of confusion. (Conflict between visual and haptic perception)
- You remember having put your keys in your pocket and now when you reach for them, they're not there. Again a momentary confusion. (Conflict between memory and haptic perception)
- You see two of that woman you've seen at the pool. There's a feeling of confusion before you realize she's twins. (Conflict between visual perception and prior understanding)
- You're following my directions to my house ("first house in the third block") and the street ends after one block. Confusion: Are the directions wrong, or did you make a mistake following them? (Conflict between verbal input and visual perception)
- The president says there are nuclear weapons in Lower Slobbovia. Your professor says there aren't. You're confused. Who do you trust? (Conflict between two verbal sources)
- You're a subject in a famous experiment by Solomon Asch: You're shown a line and asked which of three others it matches in length. But before making your judgment, you hear several other subjects (who, unbeknownst to you are in cahoots with the experimenter)

render a uniform but different judgment. Many of Asch's subjects, confronted with this conflict between their senses and what the others said, had a strong tendency to go along with the others, while feeling confused about their own vision and sanity.

- In the same situation, you might instead respond to the confusion by deciding to trust your own judgment—as did some of Asch's subjects. Truth doesn't equal consensus or received wisdom. In some situations, it's a Good Thing to say "The emperor has no clothes!"
- Your brother says "This toy is mine!" and you say "No, it's mine!" Your anxiety might lead to a fight, or you might come to some negotiation, or you might appeal to a higher authority. This scenario also applies to conflicting nations, cultures, religions, and schools of scientific thought. (Conflict between verbal input and your understanding of the situation)

I want to focus on this feeling of confusion or disorientation for a moment. We tend to brush it aside and try to reach a consistent sense of the situation as quickly as possible. No question—it's distressing and we don't *want* to pay attention to it. This is the experiential signal of not being able to make sense of what's going on.

As usual in the cognitive perspective, we can't take this feeling for granted. Again we seem to need some sort of character tag as its cognitive correlate. The situation that leads to this experience is two competing conceptual/spatial structures, each of which on its own would lead to a feeling of conviction. But they're not consistent, and at the moment the mind/brain is unable to commit to one and reject the other. Let's call this character tag *huh?* or *double-take.*

The mind/brain actually is constantly confronting competing analyses of what's going on. Very few of these conflicts reach consciousness as a *huh?* reaction. Suppose you hear the beginning of a sentence:

Put the apple on the . . . .

This could be continued in either of these two ways:

Put the apple on the towel.
Put the apple on the towel in the cup.

The first of these implies that the apple should end up on the towel; the second implies that the apple starts out on the towel.

Put the apple on the towel.   Put the apple on the towel in the cup.

These are clearly in conflict. But if we hear either of these sentences, we experience no sense of confusion at the point when we've only heard *Put the apple on the*. . . . Evidently the brain takes care of this conflict before it generates a character tag that reaches consciousness.

Remember the duck-rabbit? During the time you're seeing it as a duck, your brain is suppressing the rabbit—the conflict has been resolved. When it switches to the rabbit, is there a split-second of *huh?*, as the competition is suddenly opened and then clamped down again? I'm not sure.

A more interesting place where *huh?* doesn't appear is in dreams, where nonsensical things happen all the time. As in Chapter 31, Uncle Sol doesn't look like Uncle Sol at all, he's young and blond instead of old and bald. You may sort of notice it but it doesn't bother you. Or you may not notice it at all until you wake up and are trying to tell someone about it. As in the other dream-situations we've talked about, it's as though the monitor for consistency is turned off, like a broken "check engine" light. So you think everything's fine.

Here's two more places where there's no sense of conflict between verbal input and a perception, because the "check engine" light is broken.

- A schizophrenic hears God speaking. You tell him it's in his imagination. Without hesitation, he tells you you're wrong.
- A patient suffering from left-sided neglect due to brain damage finds this weird hand lying in his bed. The doctor tells him it's his own hand. "No," the patient says, "it's not." "Whose is it, then?" "It must be *yours*, doctor!"

All the other character tags have a converse case: familiar vs. novel, real vs. image, and so on. Does *huh?* have a converse? I suppose it's the feeling of comfort: yes, this makes sense, all's well with the world.

Part Four
Rationality and Intuition

36

What's it like to be thinking rationally?

Descartes was one of the few who think, therefore they are,
Because those who don't think, but are anyhow, outnumber them by far.

(—Ogden Nash)

What do we take rational thinking to be? I think the ideal for rational thinking is to be totally explicit about how to get from assertion A to assertion B, without any assumptions and without any leaps of faith. And being totally explicit means being *verbally* explicit—spelling it all out in sentences, either through overt speech (if you're trying to convince someone else) or at least in verbal imagery (if you're trying to convince yourself). If you can't explain it, you don't really *know* it. Here's the way Descartes puts it, in the *Discourse on Method*:

> The first [rule] was never to accept anything as true that I did not know to be evidently so....
> The second, to divide each of the difficulties... into as many parts as might be possible....
> The third, to conduct my thoughts in an orderly way, beginning with the simplest objects....
> And the last, everywhere to make such complete enumerations and such general reviews that I would be sure to have omitted nothing....

[W]hat satisfied me the most about this method was that, through it, I was assured of using my reason in everything, if not perfectly, at least to the best of my ability.

Modern formal logic grew out of the attempt to build such a theory of totally explicit step-by-step thought, suitable for doing rigorous mathematics and science. And that in turn led to the development of digital computers and all the wonderful things we've gained from them.

But!! There are rock-bottom fundamental reasons why you can't be totally explicit. One reason comes from Lewis Carroll's entertaining little essay of 1895, "What the Tortoise Said to Achilles." Here's a brief version of the argument:

Take the very simplest case of rational thought, a standard syllogism like this one. Let's call it A.[1]

> A: All houses on Goden St are worth over $600,000.
> My house is a house on Goden St.
> Therefore my house is worth over $600,000.

What makes this a logical argument? The time-worn answer (back to Aristotle) is that any argument of the form in B is valid.

> B: All Xs are Y.
> Z is an X.
> Therefore, Z is Y.

Hold your horses! (says the tortoise to Achilles). How does that prove that A is valid? After all, Aristotle's answer relies on a hidden syllogism, which I'll call C:

> C: All arguments of form B are valid.
> Argument A is an argument of form B.
> Therefore, argument A is valid.

---

[1] You might ask how I'm supposed to know the first premise of the syllogism—the value of each house—without first determining the conclusion—the value of *my* house. Well, let's assume somebody told me the first premise. Maybe *they*'ve checked the value of my house, but I haven't, so I still have to do the reasoning.

Okay, but how do we know that argument C is valid? It's actually another argument of form B, and so *its* validity relies on another hidden syllogism:

D: All arguments of form B are valid.
   Argument C is an argument of form B.
   Therefore, argument C is valid.

And how do we know D is valid? Etcetera. There's an infinite regress. So you can't fully prove that argument A is a valid argument. That's more or less the tortoise's story.

It gets worse. One thing Wittgenstein carries on about is: Even if you know what the rules are, how do you know you've applied them correctly? In following the tortoise's reasoning, we've taken it for granted that arguments A and C *are* arguments of the form B. How can we *prove* that argument A is an argument of the form B? To do this, we have to line argument A up with B:

All houses on Goden St   lines up with *All Xs*
worth over $600,000   lines up with *Y*
my house   lines up with *Z*

How do we know we've done it right? Well, we need a further rule that tells us how to line arguments up. And how do we know we've applied *that* rule correctly? Another infinite regress stares us in the face, and so we have another reason we can't prove argument A valid.[2] Kant too notices this problem. He speaks of the "faculty of judgment," the capacity of "distinguishing whether this or that does or does not stand under a given rule."

---

[2] Wittgenstein then takes this argument in a curious direction: he suggests you could never have a "private language"—a rule-governed system that you use to talk to yourself—because there's no independent way to tell that you're following the rules. But if you think about it, the same argument ought to apply just as well to "public" languages. How can you tell that other people are following the rules, or that you're using the same rules they do? By this criterion there are no "public" languages either. In the case of real languages like English, the answer to Wittgenstein is that we almost never ask whether we or anyone else are applying the rules properly, unless we notice that they don't talk the same as we do (see Chapter 2).

(cont.)

Now if this logic wished to give some general direction...how we should distinguish whether this or that did or did not stand under [these rules], this again could not be done otherwise than by means of a rule. But this rule, precisely because it is a rule, requires for itself direction from the faculty of judgment.

Worse still (and Wittgenstein didn't notice this), the rule for lining up argument A with argument B has its pitfalls. Here's another putative argument that lines up with B just as well as A does. But it's not valid. The third line not only doesn't follow from the first two, it's nonsensical.

> E: All houses on Goden St are clumped together in one block.
>   My house is a house on Goden St.
>   *Therefore, my house is clumped together in one block.

You might respond: Well, maybe for some reason argument E is an exception to *All arguments of form B are valid*. Maybe we're not entitled to line up *clumped together in one block* with *Y* in argument B. I'd reply: But how do we know it's an exception? Ah, you say—because if it weren't an exception, then argument E would be valid. Hold on, though: you can only make this argument because you've already judged that argument E is invalid—which of course begs the question.

Or you might say, Aha: Even though *All houses on Goden St are clumped together in one block* looks like an instance of *All X are Y*, it has a different *logical* form, and that's why the first line of argument E doesn't count as an instance of the first line of argument B. This is actually the right reason. In argument B, we thought of property *Y* as something that applies to single individuals, and the first line of argument B asserts that

---

Here's a possible real example of a "private language": Congenitally deaf children who grow up in an environment where a sign language is not in use often develop a "home sign," their own idiosyncratic system of signs that they use to communicate with their family. We know the children have devised it and not their parents, because they're more fluent in it than their parents. Thus in a sense they are the only fluent speakers of their language, the only ones who are really in command of all its rules. Yet research on these languages has shown that they are systematic—probably without any conscious efforts at systematicity on the child's part.

each *X* has this property. *Worth over $600,000* is such a property. But *clumped together* is a property that can only be ascribed to a collection of individuals, not to a single individual, so it can't possibly apply to a single house.

But saying that *clumped together* has a different logical form from *worth $600,000* amounts to admitting that argument C is wrong. We have to replace it with:

> F: All arguments with the *logical* form of B are valid.
> Argument A is an argument with the logical form of B.
> Therefore, argument A is valid.

Now the problem is: how do we determine an argument's logical form? And how do we compare *that* to the logical form of B? We've just seen that the sentence's grammatical form alone isn't a reliable guide. The problem is that logical form is an aspect of *meaning*, not of grammar, and, as we saw way back in Chapter 12, grammar alone isn't enough to determine meaning.

So now we're in big, big trouble. Why? Because, as we've been seeing over the last twenty-some chapters, meaning is hidden. You *can't* inspect it and line it up with other meanings using an explicit rule. So this is yet another obstacle to conducting totally rational, totally explicit reasoning.

In addition to these three arguments, here's an argument from the neuropsychologist Karl Lashley, from a brain and cognitive perspective:

> *No activity of mind is ever conscious.* [Lashley's italics] This sounds like a paradox, but it is nonetheless true. There are order and arrangement, but there is no experience of the creation of that order. I could give numberless examples, for there is no exception to the rule. A couple of illustrations should suffice. Look at a complicated scene. It consists of a number of objects standing out against an indistinct background: desk, chairs, faces. Each consists of a number of lesser sensations combined in the object, but there is no experience of putting them together. The objects are immediately present. When we think in words, the thoughts come in grammatical form with subject, verb, object, and modifying clauses falling into place without our

having the slightest perception of how the sentence structure is produced....Experience clearly gives no clue as to the means by which it is
organized.

I think this observation is right on target. As we saw in Part Two,
research in psychology and neuroscience has revealed how tremen-
dously intricate the processes are that our minds use to construct the
world of our experience. Yet these processes feel totally transparent.
Oh sure, every now and then we experience a sense of effort – it's
hard to see *this*, it's hard to understand *that*, now I'm having trouble
expressing myself, now I'm confused about what's going on. But
that's far from being conscious of the actual processes that give rise
either to our perception or to the sense of effort that comes with it.
Even when we're aware of our *thoughts*, we're not aware of the process of *thinking*.

What does Lashley's observation mean for rational thinking? In order
for us to understand our syllogism A, some process of mental/neural
computation has to make the connection from the premises (the first
two lines) to the conclusion (the third line). The result of this computation is just the third line, *not* the process of getting from the first and
second lines to the third. The part we want to justify, though, is *how* we
get from the first and second lines to the third. And this, according to
Lashley, simply can't be brought into awareness.

What *is* present in awareness is a feeling that we might express as
"Uh-huh, it follows," an intuitive feeling of conviction again. If we try to
justify this intuition, we might appeal to syllogisms B and F. But our use
of them is in the end supported by "Uh-huh" judgments too. In the same
way, our sense that argument E is *invalid* doesn't come from rational
justification, but from an intuitive dissenting feeling, "Nope," the sense
that something's amiss.

By now, you can probably guess what I'm going to say next. All
together now: "As usual, these intuitive feelings don't come by magic!"
Behind the feeling of conviction that syllogism A is valid and syllogism E

is not, your mind/brain is doing hard work—just as it's doing hard work in understanding the sentences in the first place. But because the work is unconscious, it all feels totally transparent.

The conclusion from all of this is that ultimately, you have to trust your gut:

It's logically and psychologically impossible to achieve the ideal of purely explicit rational thought. What we experience as rational thinking is necessarily supported by a foundation of intuitive judgment. We need intuition to tell us whether we're being rational!

Not to be pessimistic, but the situation is actually even less promising. Remember that the meanings of sentences are hidden. What's conscious when you understand a sentence is (a) its pronunciation (or written form), and (b) the feeling that the sentence is meaningful. So it's not just the connections that are unconscious—the meanings of the premises and conclusions are too:

The cognitive correlates of the experience of rational thinking are (a) the pronunciation (or written form) of the premises and the conclusion, (b) the feeling that all of these are meaningful, and (c) the feeling that the conclusion is valid.

You may find this unwelcome, but that's life.

There are the usual two ways to phrase this conclusion. The iconoclastic one is that there's no such thing as rational thinking (just like there's no such thing as sunsets, words, free will, truth, and You). I personally find it more useful to say that rational thinking isn't quite what we thought it was, at least from the cognitive perspective. What is it, then?

Pop science sometimes identifies rationality with the left hemisphere of the brain and intuition with the right. Or sometimes what I'm calling intuition is classified as "emotion" and relegated to the evolutionarily older parts of the brain—like the thoughts of animals. Or rational thinking is characterized as "classical" and intuitive thinking as "romantic."

It's not like that at all. What we call rational thinking simply can't take place without a huge complex background of intuitive thinking that's registering in consciousness only as "Uh-huh, that follows" or "Nope, it doesn't follow." In other words, rational thinking isn't an *alternative* to intuitive thinking. Rather, it *depends* on intuitive thinking, and (as we'll see in Chapter 38) it serves as a *refinement* or *enhancement* of intuitive thinking.

One proposed division of the mind that is supported by considerable experimental research suggests that we have two modes of reasoning, sometimes called "System 1" and System 2." System 1 is supposed to be fast, effortless, automatic, and non-conscious. It corresponds pretty well to what I'm calling intuitive thought. System 2 is supposed to be slow, effortful, controlled, linear, conscious—and unique to humans. It does exactly the kind of reasoning I've been calling rational thought.

What I'm proposing here in effect is that System 2 isn't separate from System 1. Rather, it "rides on top of" System 1. It's thought that's linked to a cognitive correlate of consciousness, namely to the pronunciation of language. Since pronunciation is linear and discrete, rational thought is linear and discrete. Since pronunciation is slow compared to the speed of thought itself, rational thought is slow. Since thought is unconscious, we can gain conscious access to it only if it has a conscious "handle" such as pronunciation. Since only humans have language, only humans have System 2. I tentatively conclude from this that System 2 amounts to nothing more than System 1 plus language (and perhaps other forms of thought that can be linked to conscious "handles").[3]

[3] As mentioned in Chapter 20, this is not to say that if a chimpanzee could master language, it would be as smart as us. Humans' System 1 is doubtless more sophisticated than that of chimps.

And if this is how it is, it behooves us to show intuitive thinking more respect. It's neither sloppy, "irrational," "emotional" thinking nor wondrous mystical magical thinking, it's the workaday cognitive foundation of *all* thinking. It just happens that, like the cognitive processes of seeing the world and understanding language, it's pretty much all unconscious.

37

How much rational thinking do we actually do?

The goal of the Enlightenment, as I understand it, was to rebuild our knowledge of the world on firm rational foundations. You should make your own truth-judgments, you shouldn't take anything on faith, you should question everything, you shouldn't believe mere hunches, and above all, you shouldn't trust the Received Wisdom—especially the Received Wisdom of the Church. This is of course the basic ethos of modern science.

But if you step back, it's obvious that we don't have the luxury of questioning everything in our day-to-day lives. How many people bother to find out where their food comes from, how electricity gets into the plugs in their house, how water gets into their faucets and from their drains into the ocean,[1] how their computers and cellphones work, how the monetary system works, how their clothes and chairs and dishes and tools are manufactured,[2] what happens to their garbage, how the details of the government work, and a bazillion other essential aspects of every-day life? We basically take all these things on trust. The environmentally

---

[1] I'm recalling a very very long *New Yorker* article describing the water supply and sewer systems of New York City. The two parts of the article were joined by the single sentence "The water flows out of the faucet and into the drain"—the only part of the water supply that we're normally conscious of.

[2] How do they make drill bits? How do they make the machines that make drill bits?

and politically conscious among us—and the economic and engineering nerds—may worry about one or another of them from time to time. But if you got serious about all of them, there wouldn't be any time to live. (Believers might say, "Only God has enough time for all that!")

The same is true even in the citadel of science. Who has time to read all the scientific literature, even in their own subspecialty, not to mention in other areas? Much less do all the experiments themselves? We have little choice but to trust other scientists most of the time. Just deciding which Received Wisdom to trust can sometimes be a full-time job. For practical reasons we simply have to accept an "epistemic division of labor," and place our bets on somebody else's truth-judgments.

What about other parts of life? When you pick out a novel to read at bedtime, are you doing it—and could you do it—on rational grounds? When you've just met someone and unexpectedly find yourself in an engaging conversation and maybe even attracted to them, are you doing so—and could you do so—on rational grounds? Did you decide—and could you have decided—to become a scientist (or whatever you are) on totally rational grounds? I'd guess that very little of our lives, and even very little of what's *important* in our lives, is based on rationality.

Intuitive reasoning isn't at all random. Just because we can't be conscious of its workings doesn't mean it's crazy. A lot of experimental research has been devoted to uncovering people's unconscious processes when they're reasoning intuitively. Much of this research is dedicated to showing how often people are *irrational* from a logical or mathematical point of view. Some of it is devoted to finding the quick and dirty strategies that people use to reason, which work perfectly well under most normal circumstances but break down every now and then (like the visual principles that give rise to the illusions in Chapter 21). Some of this research is devoted to finding special principles of reasoning that apply in, say, the social and moral domains.

The overall gist of this research is that our human ability to make intuitive judgments has arisen from an evolutionary process that equipped us to quickly figure out what's going on, predict what's next, and act accordingly. We share many aspects of this ability with our primate cousins. Intuitive reasoning can't be 100% accurate, the way logic is supposed to be, because we rarely have full information about the current situation, because we have limited capacity for processing information, and above all because we have limited time in which to act. Given these constraints, our natural intuitive strategies for reasoning do pretty well a lot of the time.

38

How rational thinking helps

At the end of Chapter 36, I suggested that thinking with the accompaniment of conscious "handles" enhances or refines intuitive thought. Let's see how it does this.

In what we experience as rational thinking (let's just say "in rational thinking" from here on), we're expressing our thoughts as sentences, either out loud or in verbal imagery. According to the Unconscious Meaning Hypothesis (Chapter 15), the part of a sentence that's conscious is its pronunciation, and its meaning remains unconscious. But as we saw in Chapter 20, pronunciation as such can't serve as the vehicle of thought—only meaning can do that. So what difference does the conscious pronunciation make? Does the pronunciation just serve as a "crutch" for thinking? With enough practice, could we toss the pronunciation away and think with "pure meaning"? Well, actually I think the conscious "handle" of pronunciation is a lot more useful than that.

Here's why. The "handle" of pronunciation enables you to give the thought a reference file of its own: it's understood as a self-standing entity in the world (Chapter 29). This enables you to do lots of useful things with the sentence. First of all, even when you're done uttering the sentence, it's like the cat behind the bookcase: it still exists for you, and you can retrieve it when you want it. "Hold that thought!" "As I just said, . . ."

Second, a sentence expresses not just the content of a thought but also the character tags associated with it.

There's a cat on the mat.   [= There's a cat on the mat + *conviction*]
There isn't a cat on the mat.   [= There's a cat on the mat + *dissent*]
Is there a cat on the mat?   [= There's a cat on the mat + *noncommittal*]

So now the character tags aren't just experienced as feelings. You can hear them, remember them, and manipulate them.

An important example of this manipulation arises when a sentence gives rise to a *huh?* experience. You're in Asch's experiment (see Chapter 35), judging the length of one line against three others. You judge that it matches the middle one, but everybody else says "It matches the longest one," and you feel *huh?* With language, you can turn that feeling into a question: "Can that be right? Is the line really that long?" And now you can hold *that* thought and ruminate on it.

Here's another important way you can use language to manipulate thought:

Why is there a cat on the mat?

This sentence expresses a thought to which you assent, and it initiates a search for reasons or causes behind the thought. This manipulation is one of the primary generators of scientific inquiry—and also inquiry into people's motives ("Now why did she say *that*?").

A third thing you can do with thoughts expressed as sentences is make intuitive judgments of the connections among them. This is the activity that's experienced as reasoning.

Today's Tuesday + Tomorrow's Wednesday [character tag: *consistent*]
Today's Tuesday + Tomorrow's Thursday   [character tag: *inconsistent*]

Then you can build these character tags into a sentence in various ways, and you can make truth-judgments on the results:

If today's Tuesday, then tomorrow's Wednesday.   [*conviction*]
"Today's Tuesday" entails "Tomorrow's Thursday."   [*dissent*]

You can manipulate these sentences the same way you do with simple sentences like *There's a cat on the mat.*

If today's Tuesday, is tomorrow Wednesday?
"Today's Tuesday" doesn't entail "Tomorrow's Thursday."

What's interesting is that these last four examples don't make any commitment to the sentences within them. Even if you have no idea whether today is in fact Tuesday, you can assent to *If today's Tuesday, then tomorrow's Wednesday.*

A different manipulation expresses both a connection between the two sentences *and* a commitment to the first one:

Because today's Tuesday, tomorrow must be Wednesday.

These linguistic manipulations are extremely important to our thought. They free us from being bound to the current situation. They enable us to conceptualize virtual worlds, and keep them in mind, and through that we can do hypothetical reasoning.

Another important way two thoughts can be connected is to be understood as alternatives to each other. Language gives us a way to make this sort of connection explicit too.

Either it's snowing or I'm dreaming.

This expresses a conviction about the thought as a whole, while remaining noncommittal about each of the parts.

We can also focus more sharply on exactly where the differences between the alternatives lie:

Either JOHN or BILL ate the leftover pasta.
John ate either the leftover PASTA or the turkey SANDWICH.

With these tools, you can explore the possibilities methodically, using hypotheticals like *If it's snowing, then...*; *If JOHN ate the pasta, then...* When you're trying out one possibility, you don't lose the other, because you still have a "handle" on it and on its connection to the possibility now under consideration. You can start with a thought on which you're noncommittal—a question. You can trace its connections to other thoughts step by step until you reach a thought for which you have a clear conviction or dissent. Then you can trace the connections back to arrive at a yes or no answer to your original question.

These procedures enable us to question our intuitive reasoning and break it down into smaller, explicit steps. The ideal, just as Descartes put it (Chapter 36), is to make the intuitive connections as transparent and trivial as possible—although, as we also saw in Chapter 36, there comes a point of diminishing returns.

These sorts of processes do exactly the things we want rational thought to do. They would be impossible without the phonological "handles" both for the contents of thought and for its character tags. We can't deliberately manipulate unconscious thoughts on their own, we can't hold them in mind, and we can't experiment with their character tags. And as we saw in Chapter 10, visual imagery (except for sign language) can't help in the ways language can. It doesn't provide us with "handles" for all the abstract things that language can express—especially character tags. So language, by providing "handles" for all these aspects of thought, gives us a fantastic tool for enhancing and enriching thinking.

Not to mention its advantages for *communicating* thought. Our understanding is vastly increased through collaborative thinking, which requires continual linguistic give-and-take among participants. Above all, it permits us to communicate the thought of previous generations, so we're not always starting from scratch.[1]

[1] Did language arise in our distant ancestors primarily as an enhancement of communication, or as an enhancement of thought? (More properly, were the reproductive benefits conferred on our ancestors by having language primarily due to their better ability to communicate or due to their better ability to think?) We can't go back there and find out. Nearly everyone assumes that the primary advantage was in communication. But Noam Chomsky, never to be taken lightly, has argued that communication had little to do with it. For him, the primary innovation was structured thought. What he calls "externalization"—the ability to speak one's thoughts out loud—was a later development. But for him, "externalization" includes pronunciation, which provides the very "handles" that make rational thinking possible. So, on the present story, he's got to be wrong. My inclination is to think that the language faculty developed in the service of enhancing communication, but the immediate enhancement of thought was a huge side benefit.

39

Some pitfalls of apparently rational thinking

Using language as a scaffolding for thinking has its limitations too. One has come up a number of times already: the illusion of binarity. Either someone is bald or he's not. Either something is a genocide or it's not. Either you're a scientist or you're not. From the ordinary perspective, the word itself more or less *is* the concept (Chapter 15). And words have a tendency to sharpen boundaries—the "handle" is more discrete than the concept it's a handle *for* (Chapter 11). So relying on the word makes it easy to avoid the fragile middle ground and the slippery slope. The world comes to be divided up into black and white, and you don't have to (or aren't allowed to) recognize its full color.

As we saw in Chapters 11, 13, and 14, *not* having a word for some concept can render it invisible. Going back to one of our examples there: If you think that thinking equals *rational* thinking, then by definition monkeys can't think, because they don't talk. But what *do* they do? If the only other term you have is "(mere) instinct," it's hard for you to appreciate how sophisticated their behavior actually is. They might as well be no different from turtles. So how can we talk about whatever it is that monkeys do? Well, okay, if you don't want to call it thinking, then let's call it something else, say "shminking." Now we're in business. We can ask: do turtles shmink too? If so, how is monkey shmought different from turtle shmought? Does human thinking amount to shminking plus language, or is it something else altogether? And so on. Without this new word, discourse is stymied. By adding it to our repertoire, we're off and running.

It's not just words that lead to pitfalls. You can put words together in a way that conforms to grammatical structure but fails to convey a unified meaning. Here are two examples from Chapter 21, which obviously make no sense.

Colorless green ideas sleep furiously.
I've forgotten the score of the sonata I hope to compose someday.

More dangerous is when a speaker or writer combines words to create an "aura" of meaningfulness, for instance in this sentence from an interview with the philosopher Alva Noë:

I don't think of consciousness as something that happens in us or to us but as something that we achieve or something that we do through our action and interaction with the world around us.

At first this might sound convincing enough. But if we take it apart and reconstruct its relative clauses, we find some pretty questionable pieces:

Consciousness doesn't happen in us.
*Consciousness doesn't happen to us.   [What could this mean?]
We achieve consciousness.
*We do consciousness through our action and interaction with the world around us.

Even the first and third sentences, even though they sound sort of okay, are a bit fishy. What could it mean to say "Consciousness happens"? Is it like "Shit happens"? I'm not sure. And usually when we say "We achieve consciousness," it's in the passive sense of 'waking up.' But the author seems to have in mind something more active and intentional, more like "We achieve a victory." Again, I don't think being conscious is something we "intend" to do. The writer is apparently groping for something, but maybe it's kind of like the gap between "thought" and "instinct": there's no appropriate word for what he has in mind.

224

The linguistic therapy I've been applying here to words like *smoke*, *meaning*, *consciousness*, and *true* is intended to help guard against this kind of foggy use of language as a crutch for foggy thinking. Sure, it's sometimes useful and necessary to stretch the use of language (Chapters 11 and 12). But this requires care and close attention.

In addition, remember that rational thinking relies not just on understanding sentences but also on forming intuitive connections *among* sentences. So it's only as reliable as our intuitive judgments of connection. This is why we're always encouraged to check our reasoning—to question every connection and make sure it makes sense. Unfortunately, it's all too easy to be complacent, especially when our reasoning leads us to a conclusion we like. It's only when somebody *else*'s reasoning leads to a conclusion we *don't* like that we're likely to look hard for the flaws in the argument. (Psychologists call this "confirmation bias.")

One place where people are prone to being complacent about connections is in explaining reasons for their actions. One of my favorite examples comes from an experiment by Richard Nisbett and Timothy Wilson. They asked customers in a department store to judge which of a number of pairs of stockings they liked best, and then to say *why* they liked them best—that is, to explain their intuitive judgment. What the customers didn't know was that all the stockings were identical. Yet they gave all sorts of reasons for their preferences, with full conviction.

This is an experimental situation, a trick. It's more pernicious when it turns up in real life. One day as I was writing this, thousands of dead birds fell out of the sky in Arkansas, and certain people asserted with full conviction that this was because God disapproved of Congress's vote to allow gays to serve openly in the military. This is an especially blatant example. But the same sort of reasoning occurs far more subtly all the time. I'm sure you've known someone who gives you a different reason every time for the same unfortunate outcome—turning in assignments late, getting into car accidents, failing in relationships, failing in jobs, reducing taxes, starting wars, and so on. It's not that they're lying and think they can put one over on you. They sincerely believe their stories with utmost conviction. Only *you* suspect that these are self-justifying excuses, and that there has to be some deeper reason for their doing the same thing over and over again. In fact, if you suggest there might be such an underlying cause, they may well get angry at you. They really are convinced of the connection, and they see no flaw, logical or otherwise, in their reasoning. Their therapist will say they're in denial.

And what are you and I in denial about? Are we being rational, or are we just rationalizing? From the inside, we have no way to tell. The best we can do is to watch for cues from our physical and social environments that conflict with our convictions. Being alert to the possibility that one may be wrong at least keeps one modest, I guess.

40
Chamber music

I'd like to talk a bit more about how rational thinking is integrated with intuition. My example will be, of all things, playing chamber music.

Some people think that playing music is a question of "inspiration." Other people think that, at least for classical music, it's just a matter of playing the notes the composer wrote. Actually, figuring out how to "play the notes" isn't always so easy. A well-known way to damn someone's performance by faint praise is to say "Um, he played all the notes . . . ." In the same vein, a composer friend of mine recently told me about a performance of one of his pieces, in which the performers had played brilliantly, but they "really didn't get it." I once had this experience from the other side, when I was asked to perform a piece of traditional Japanese music on the clarinet. I had no problem playing all the notes in time and in tune, but I didn't have a clue what was going on. My playing was wooden and incomprehending, I had no idea how to improve it, and I'm sure my Japanese hosts knew. It was as if I had tried to read them a Japanese poem from a phonetic transcription.

When musicians try to figure out how to go beyond (or read between) the notes, here's the kind of thing that happens. I'm rehearsing with four colleagues for a performance of the Brahms Clarinet Quintet, one of the great pieces of all time. It seems to me that the violins, Colin and Lena, aren't playing the opening with enough character—it sounds too wimpy. I consult the score and discover that the violins are marked f (for *forte*, 'loud').

I ask Colin and Lena if they can play with more force. This turns out not to be so easy, because of the passage's sustained character and the part of the violin's range it falls in.

Ken, the violist, notices that the only dynamic markings Brahms uses in the whole first movement are *forte*, *piano* ('soft'), and *pianissimo* ('very soft'). So he suggests that *forte* here doesn't have to mean 'loud.' It just has to contrast with 'soft'—anywhere from 'healthy sound' to 'ferocious', depending on the musical context. We settle on 'healthy' for this passage.

I still don't like what I'm hearing. It seems too mechanical, it's not expressive enough. My attention is drawn to the *decrescendi* ('getting softer') in the first two measures, notated by the long wedges. What do *they* mean? Taken at face value, they would tell us that the second meas-ure should be played softer than the first, and the third measure still softer. But this doesn't make sense, because the viola and cello enter in the third measure with an accompaniment marked *forte*, and they shouldn't be louder than the violins.

Colin and Lena try starting upbow, which, because of the way the bow naturally exerts pressure on the string, creates a *crescendo* ('getting louder') in the first half of the measure. The downbow in the second half then creates a natural *decrescendo*. We're not convinced. For one thing, it means the violins have to start softer than *forte*. And besides, if Brahms had meant *crescendo* in the first half of the measure, he could have written it. So what does he mean by the *decrescendo*?

I suggest that the sense of the *decrescendi* might not be so much a matter of volume as of emphasis: bringing out the first note of each group of six by slightly lengthening it, and then gradually speeding up, almost "throwing away" the last three notes in the group. (A technical term for this is *rubato*. A non-technical term is "schmaltzy.") I demonstrate by singing: "Do it like this . . . ." My description sounds artificial, but (to me at least) my demonstration sounds expressive, and its flexibility suits Brahms's Romantic genre. Of course, Brahms never comes out and tells you to do things like this. They're just part of the tradition.

(Recalling Chapter 12, you may notice that this is a bit like some things that happen in language: Why are you asking me *Can you pass the salt*, when you know perfectly well that I can? Aha, you must be asking me to pass the salt! Similarly, why does Brahms write *decrescendo* without corresponding *crescendo*, when he can't mean it? Aha, he must mean something else, maybe *rubato*.)

Colin and Lena hate this interpretation of the *decrescendi*. They find it mannered and self-indulgent. At this point, the discussion has consumed ten or fifteen minutes of rehearsal time for six seconds of music, so we drop the subject and move on. We never do reach agreement about what Brahms means, Colin and Lena more or less ignore the *decrescendi*, and I remain dissatisfied. So it goes.

(Some months later, I hear a recording of the Quartetto Italiano playing this passage just the way I had imagined it. I think it sounds great, and I feel vindicated. Meanwhile, looking back, I can think of other ways to play the *decrescendi* that might have made Colin and Lena happier.)

I want to draw two things out of this little episode. The first has to do with what *mean* means. The questions "What does *forte* mean?" and "What does Brahms mean by *decrescendo*?" aren't supposed to be answered by sentences. Sentences can only give hints toward the real answers, which are how the music is to be played. Verbal descriptions can talk about instrumental technique ("start upbow"), timing ("make this note longer and this one shorter"), or about emotional state ("play more urgently here"), or even metaphor ("healthy," "throw these notes away", "at this point the bottom drops out"). But the meaning can also be expressed directly by playing the music—*"Decrescendo* here means playing like this" [demonstrating]. Any of these might work in describing how to play a passage. Or they might not. It depends on the players' sensibilities—whether they catch on to your (or "the") meaning.

Among the uses of *mean* that we discussed back in Chapter 7, the closest analogues to these uses are the explanation of symbols ("A red light means you should stop"), and demonstration (*"Osculating* means doing *this"* [demonstrating]). They're quite different from the sense that the music theorist Leonard Meyer had in mind when he entitled his book *Emotion and Meaning in Music*. Meyer is interested in the "emotional impact" sense: What makes music *meaningful*? (I suspect that what we call "meaningfulness" in music is connected to a character tag: we respond to some emotional impact the music has on us, and we attribute the depth of feeling to the music itself. But I digress.)

The more important thing I want to get from this episode is that my colleagues and I are having a rational discussion of how to interpret the symbols in Brahms's music—we're consciously reasoning about how to play the piece. But this rational discussion begins and ends with intuitive judgments. At the beginning, it's triggered by an intuitive *huh?* reaction: "This somehow doesn't sound right." And the conclusions we reach aren't truth-judgments of sentences, they're intuitive judgments about the music: "Yes, now it sounds better!" or "Nope, it still doesn't sound right!"

In between the *huh?* and the *uh-huh*, though, our conversation has all the hallmarks of the language-aided manipulations of thought that we saw two chapters back. "If the *decrescendo* marking means to get softer, the accompaniment will be louder than the melody. The accompaniment shouldn't be louder than the melody. Therefore the marking must mean something else. What else could it mean? It could be *this*, or *this*, or *this*. If it's *this*, ...," and so on. What's different from our earlier cases is that our reasoning is in the service of satisfying intuition. We're using rational thinking to help us decide not what is *true*, but what to *do*.

Overall, the goal is a collective sense that the five of us are all understanding the music the same way—just as when (in Chapter 28) Gina and Phil had to converge on the guy with the martini. And even though our goal isn't a linguistic utterance, we need the language of rational thought to work towards it. In this case, thanks to time constraints—plus differences in taste—we unfortunately end up without complete convergence, and we have to settle for something less. Still, we know we're all in this together, and we're trying to create a coherent performance that satisfies us and the audience—and that would, we hope, satisfy the composer.

You may have noticed that all our discussion is about a place in the Brahms where I'm not even playing. Why should I be jumping in and making suggestions here? Well, it has to do with the need for a collective sense of rightness. In chamber music, you can't just play your own part. You have to be constantly listening to everyone. The lead shifts from moment to moment. Sometimes I have the lead, and sometimes I have to follow the viola or the second violin. Even when I'm not playing, the way everyone else plays affects what I do when I come in next.

Not to be too heavy-handed, but I think science is a lot like chamber music. You can't just do your own stuff. You have to be constantly listening to everyone. Sometimes the crucial facts come from your own field, sometimes from the most unexpected place in someone else's. We're all in this together, and the goal is to create a coherent story about thought and meaning and the mind and the brain that will satisfy us—and, we hope, posterity.

41
Rational thinking as a craft

It's all well and good to be able to use language as a "handle" to manipu-late thoughts. But where do the thoughts we manipulate come from? Of the gazillions of thoughts we *could* turn into questions, how do we choose which ones we're actually going to spend our time on? And where do the candidate answers ("Try upbow," "Try a little *rubato*") come from? We generally call it imagination. And imagination's not rational. What is it? It feels a little like magic.

At this point you should be expecting me to jump into the cognitive perspective. But this time I have no idea how to do it. (And I don't think anyone else does either.) So please indulge me as I go at this question indirectly, looking at music a little more from the ordinary perspective.

Whatever musical understanding is, it lies somewhere behind the notes, in the relations among them and the shapes of the patterns they make. No matter how many markings composers may put in the written music to make their intentions more explicit, it's never enough. Perfor-mers still have to make that intuitive leap to the sense of the music.

Doesn't this sound a lot like what I've been saying about language? The main difference is that in music there's no demand for truth-conditions—only for faithfulness to the composer's intention, as much as you can divine it, and for the satisfaction of the players and the listeners.

When you're learning to make music, an important element in improving is endless practice of all the low-level technical things you need even just to play all the notes. That too can be a subject of rational analysis. But I'm interested here in what it takes to go beyond the notes, as we were trying to do in the Brahms.

You learn from a good teacher how to take the situation apart when your musical intuitions reach their limit. The advice is mostly about the particular piece you happen to be working on. Here's how to get the right tempo for this place. Don't get too loud too soon here. A little accent right there makes the point of the phrase. You have a tendency to go flat here, so be careful. You have to listen to the second violin here, and then the cello here. This is how Casals used to play this place. Here the sun comes out. Here's how this phrase fits into the whole piece, and here's how that changes the way you should play it. Your teacher illustrates these suggestions with sung or played demonstrations, and above all, conveys them with great passion.

With enough attention, openness, desire, and luck, you successfully imitate the demonstrations—and you "get" them. You resonate with your teacher's passion, you play your heart out, as though your life depends on every note, and you find things that you didn't know you had in you. If all goes well, these messages sink in and you can apply them to other pieces too. Your intuitions become sharper. You begin to hear what better players than you are doing, and why that makes them better. And you hear yourself better, more "objectively," you avoid bad habits that you didn't even know you had, and you find ways to play with ever greater vitality and depth of expression.

I think that through this process you end up with two important things. One is a heightened sensitivity to *huh?* You notice more of the little sloppy infelicities—slightly out-of-tune notes, slight unintended distortions of rhythm, slight miscoordinations between players, slight letdowns in intensity. And you also notice more opportunities—places where a little adjustment suddenly brings out an expressive detail.

The other thing you end up with is a grab bag of tools—things to try when you encounter a *huh?* These might be tricks of fingering, tricks of rhythm, how to find the rhythmic and harmonic point of a phrase, how to build gradually to a climax, when to think of metaphors, when it's important to think ahead, how to communicate with the other players, how to look elsewhere in the piece or even in other pieces for hints on how to play this passage, and so on and so on. A lot of our "imagination" consists of noticing a *huh?* and having a hunch about what trick might fix it. That's what my colleagues and I are doing when we're working on the Brahms.

None of the details you improve on are necessarily so important by themselves. But collectively they add up to the difference between a vivid performance and a routine one. A lot of listeners will be able to tell the difference, but they may not be able to say why.

And every so often there comes one of those times you live for. Everything "clicks," no discussion is needed, it all happens by intuition. You and the other players play off of each other, inspire each other, you don't know where it's coming from. And when it's over, there's nothing to do except look at each other in astonishment and say "Oh my!"

I'm only talking about music because it's something I know well. But I think the same thing goes on with theater directors, sports coaches, art and writing teachers. Through the teacher's spirited suggestions and demonstrations, the student learns how to attend to more and more details, how to be sensitive to possible pitfalls and possible opportunities, and how to relate every step to a vision of the finished product. This is what's involved in learning the craft.

I'm beginning to think this is an attractive model for rational thinking (or, as it's sometimes called, "critical thinking"). We need rational thinking when intuition isn't enough to do the job—when we don't "get it" or it's "not working." I've tried to show you that the ideal of totally explicit rational thinking, with no appeals to intuition, is logically and psychologically impossible. What I'm suggesting is that people's actual use of rational thought is a lot more flexible than that. When we're thinking well, we appreciate more subtleties and we have better tools for analyzing them. We can avoid pitfalls and find opportunities. Our intuitions become better at telling us what we shouldn't take for granted, what we should question—the *uh-huh* and *nope* are finer-grained. We're able to anticipate what questions could be raised by someone with interests other than ours—we can see our argument more "objectively." We're able to come up with apt metaphors, and we notice appropriate parallels in tradition. In the ideal case, the overall vision of where we're trying to go informs our appreciation of every detail.

Again, a huge part of this is possible only through the ability to articulate all the parts verbally, to hold them in memory, to retrieve them, manipulate them, and compare them. At the same time, the end result is judged by how well it satisfies intuition. The craft is in the proper mixture of intuition and rationality.

If I'm right about this, then learning to think rationally can't be taught explicitly. Here's why. Nobody can tell you how to serve a tennis ball or play Brahms without giving you a demonstration. Your teacher's words are only hints about what to pay attention to. They can't capture that intuitive step of "getting it." Some teachers rely more on words, some rely more on demonstrations—and some students respond better to more words and some to more demonstrations.

Just because rational thinking is carried out in words doesn't mean the situation is any different than in tennis or Brahms. Take science, the epitome of rational thought. You don't start to learn science by having someone tell you all about the scientific method or the philosophy of science. (In fact, philosophy of science ties itself in knots over everyday notions that working scientists know "by the seat of their pants," such as what counts as *evidence* or as an *explanation*.) To learn science, you need lots of demonstrations, lots of supervised practice in the lab, lots of practice on your own. You have to build up your repertoire of data, literature, techniques, and questions, so that you have material for unconscious understanding to build on, and so that when you need to make rational connections, you have a rich store of imagination at your disposal. The craft of doing science, like making music, lies in the proper mixture of rationality and intuition.

And every once in a long while, something takes hold and intuition sweeps you along. It all "flows," you don't know where the ideas came from. Sometimes they even turn out to be good ones! This too is something we live for.

Here's a version of the same thing, from an artist:

> When you start working, everybody is in your studio—the past, your friends, enemies, the art world, and above all, your own ideas—all are there. But as you continue painting, they start leaving, one by one, and you are left completely alone. Then, if you're lucky, even you leave.

I want to ratchet this up just one more level. How should you teach—teach anything, say reading or mathematics? There seem to be these two opposing poles in philosophy of education. If I may caricature them, one pole insists on breaking things down into the smallest parts, doing things by rote, by the book, with lots of drill, for the test—allegedly the "rational" way. This is ridiculously stultifying, students hate it, and they never get the big picture. The other pole advocates "intuitive" holistic understanding, the big picture, and believes the details will take care of themselves. The students may like it better, but they don't really learn to read or do math. The trouble with both approaches is that they don't recognize how important it is to get the right mixture of rationality and intuition. And because that mixture is intuitive, you can't articulate a formula for it. You can only give useful hints and point out noteworthy cases. Wise teachers know how to use this mixture—if their school's educational policy lets them.

And how do you teach teachers to have these intuitions? Teaching is a craft too. I don't have to go around the circle again. You get the idea.

42

Some speculation on science and the arts

Half a century ago, C. P. Snow complained about the mutual incomprehension and lack of respect between the "two cultures" of the humanities and science. The situation is pretty much the same now. The main difference is that, in Snow's time, the humanities controlled the British intellectual establishment and science was relatively low-status, whereas now (at least in the US) science is flourishing, and it's the humanities that are starved for resources and prestige. Books and articles appear with titles like *What's Happened to the Humanities?*, *Does Literary Studies Have a Future?*, "A world without literature?," and "Will the humanities save us?"

I want to put the questions posed by these titles in a larger context. By "humanities," Snow and everyone else in this conversation mean essentially literature and literary theory as taught in departments of English, foreign languages, and classics. These studies are actually less closely related to other traditional humanities such as philosophy and history than they are to the arts – fine arts, music, theater, film, and architecture. So I want to rephrase these questions as: What's the point of the arts?

It's not hard to justify science. It leads to concrete results that translate into our prosperity—better food, better health, better transportation, better access to information, and so on. Well, yes, but don't forget that it's also brought us nuclear weapons and other unpleasant side effects like global warming. And not all science has concrete benefits. What practical good is there in knowing about dwarf planets, or the first thousandth of a second after the Big Bang, or the color of some dinosaur's feathers? Still, on balance it's clear that Science is a Good Thing.

By these standards it's hard to justify the arts. A degree in English Literature doesn't prepare you for a job the way a degree in chemistry does. Economic statements like "Every dollar of arts funding brings $10 into the community" don't really speak to what the arts are about.

Less materialistic justifications ring a bit hollow: "Students learn to enter into conversations with great authors" about "the meaning of life" and "the human condition." Reading a classic "helps you to define yourself in relation or even in opposition to it." One learns "ways of reading," "making the ordinary strange," and "bringing what is hidden into the open." The classics "provide models of response to misfortune that . . . will outlast us." "The defining quality of the arts is the expression of the human condition by mood and feeling." "Arts project the human presence on everything in the universe." These all carry a nice aura of **profundity**, but what do they actually say?

The literary theorist Stanley Fish rejects arguments of this sort, and proclaims

> To the question "of what use are the humanities?," the only honest answer is none whatsoever. And it is an answer that brings honor to its subject . . . . The humanities are their own good.

Conclusions like this don't win a lot of hearts on the university's board of trustees or at the Department of Education.

I suspect that "Of what use?" is the wrong way of putting the question, and that part of the trouble comes from the concentration on literature. A work of literature necessarily is *about* something— anything from a small scene to a historical epic. If the purpose of literature is to convey something about the human condition or the meaning of life, why isn't a journalist's or a historian's way of conveying it just as useful?

The answer is that in the arts, there's something important about the *form* in which the material is conveyed. It matters that the content is embodied in a novel or a poem or a play, and it matters that the form in itself yields satisfaction. So let's ask the same question about an artistic medium that's *all* form. What's the point of *music*? Why play and study Brahms? People sometimes say that music too expresses the "human condition." But the Clarinet Quintet doesn't tell us about life experiences, moral imperatives, or models of response to misfortune, at least not in any direct way.[1] Nor do the facts of Brahms's life and the conditions under which he wrote the Quintet give much insight into the music. Rather, we understand the music better, both as listeners and as performers, through coming to appreciate the originality and depth with which Brahms has put all its details together from basic musical materials. This deeper insight into the form gives us a deeper experience of the music. And one can say the same for literature and the visual arts.

Let's cast the net wider. Why do people *like* novels, plays, music, dance, art, and film—and not just the classics? Why do *kids* like poetry— maybe not Wallace Stevens, but poetry nevertheless? Even more broadly: Why do people in every culture like to decorate their houses, their pots, and themselves? (Why do I care that there's a frog on my coffee mug?) Why do we like gourmet food? Why do we like all kinds of beautiful stuff—so much that we spend huge amounts of time and effort on creating it, acquiring it, experiencing it?

In light of what we've been doing here, I'd like to offer a conjecture: Science resonates with the rational parts of thinking, and the arts resonate with something in the intuitive parts. (Whatever "resonate" means!) Science can be justified on rational and often utilitarian grounds. The point of science is to answer explicit questions, to explain observations, to draw connections among phenomena, to make statements that are

---

[1] Indirectly, yes. My friend Henry reported (hyperbolically, of course) that during our performance of the Brahms Quintet, at least three members of the audience were so moved that they committed suicide.

subject to truth-judgments. With luck it also leads to material improvements in our lives—even if not all scientists care about that.

This isn't the point of the arts at all. Art isn't about being true. Its "rightness" doesn't lie in its "correctness." As we saw in the rehearsal of the Brahms, reasoning about a work of art leads not to a truth-judgment, but to a judgment of artistic quality or artistic integrity. Where science seeks ever greater generalizations, artistic appreciation seeks ever more intricate and subtle details and patterns. The works of art that we call great are the ones that you can keep going back to and finding more.

Science seeks abstraction from the surface of appearances. Art revels in the character of the surface—it's not just *what*'s said, it's very much *how* it's said. And more fundamental than reasoning about art is the pure experience of it. This is especially the case in music, dance, abstract art, and architecture, where there's no "propositional" content, only form. But it's certainly true of literature as well.

The improvements the arts make in our lives definitely aren't material. In studying literature, music, and art, we get better acquainted with great works, we grow to appreciate what's great about them, we learn to unfold more and more from them—in short, we deepen our sense of their beauty and increase our satisfaction in knowing them.

I suspect the traditional importance of studying the artistic canon—all the dead white men like Shakespeare, Rembrandt, and Beethoven—doesn't have to do with helping you define *yourself* so much as giving you a sense of who *we* are—our cultural community and heritage. Arguments about what might replace the traditional canon are implicitly about how broad a community we want our students to learn to identify with.

None of this makes a lot of sense rationally. Louis Armstrong said about jazz, "If you have to ask what it is, you'll never know." The arts speak to us on some level other than conscious rationality. It's probably the fact that we can't explain it rationally that leads to all the profound stuff about the human condition and so on—pretty much all of which is rationalization.

If there's to be any explanation of art's value to us, I suspect it's going to come from the cognitive and neural perspectives. What's going on in your mind/brain when you're experiencing art? How does the experience draw on ordinary seeing and hearing, and how does it go *beyond* them? And why does that make a difference to us? I'd guess that the answers to these questions won't be found just in Great Art, but also in less exalted things like pueblo pottery, folk music and garage bands, and even comic strips. E. O. Wilson, in *Consilience*, is right in seeing the forms of art as shaped by the character of the human mind/brain, at a very general level, and possibly in very particular ways as well.

On the other hand, Wilson seems to think that the whole goal is to explain our aesthetic response to art in terms of human biology and human evolution. That's the cognitive/neural perspective. But, as with sunsets and free will, this doesn't erase the ordinary perspective—studying and experiencing art *as* art. And here the goal is to appreciate the glorious particularities of individual works of art on their own terms.

There's now a flourishing tradition in the cognitive neuroscience of music. I don't know about the other arts. But even in music, the neuroscience of the aesthetic response is still a mystery. And by the way, finding its location in the brain still won't tell us how it *works*, nor why Brahms is so great.

A rational enterprise like science is good at justifying its existence: you just keep talking. Fundamentally intuitive enterprises like music and literature aren't so good at justifying their existence. Because intuition is thought *without* linguistic expression, it's easy for all the language of rationality to crowd it out, both inside and outside your head. And the language of rationality by its very nature misses the point.

If there's any message in what we've been doing here, it's that rational thinking isn't what people think it is, and that it requires the underpinning of intuition to work at all. To understand a rational argument, you have to "get it." The arts go right to the "getting it" without the intervention of all the talking. And when you "get it," the experience is richer in ways that can never be conveyed by language.

Again, this isn't to say there's anything wrong with rational thought—only to suggest that it isn't the single highest goal of our mental life, and that intuition calls for at least equal billing. And also to suggest that the arts aren't just foolish decoration in our lives. They may not bring in as much money, but they're as essential to us human beings as science is.

43
Learning to live with multiple perspectives

Let me try to tie this all together. One thing I've been trying to develop here, over these many tortuous chapters, is a better understanding of the distinction between rational thinking and intuitive thinking. Rational thinking is allegedly completely conscious, and every step is spelled out explicitly. Intuitive thinking is unconscious, and only the result comes to consciousness, as if by magic.

I've tried to show that this distinction ought to be understood rather differently. What we experience as rational thinking consists of thoughts linked to language. The thoughts themselves aren't conscious. Rather, what's conscious is the "handles" of pronunciation that are linked to the thoughts, plus some character tags that lend the pronunciation a sense of meaningfulness and conviction. And the conscious sense that one sentence logically follows from another—that your reasoning is rational—is itself an intuitive judgment. So rational thought isn't an *alternative* to intuitive thought—rather, it rides on a foundation of intuitive thought. To state it a bit iconoclastically, rationality is intuition enhanced by language.

This isn't to say that there's something wrong with rational thinking. I've talked a lot about its amazing benefits. Maybe the most important is the ability it gives to ask questions. Intuitive thinking gives us little beyond *huh?*—a sense that something's the matter. Rational thinking, using the "handles" provided by language, allows us to make the *huh?* more explicit and precise, to focus on different alternatives, to follow up

243

hypothetical consequences, and to pay attention to many more fine details. We need rational thinking to do science. We need rational thinking to understand intuition!

On the other hand, thinking enhanced by language has its pitfalls, partly because it conceals all the parts of meaning that language doesn't express. We can use rational thought more effectively if we learn to appreciate the intricate and not entirely systematic relation of spoken and written language to meaning.

I've been stressing, though, that whatever advantages rational thought offers, it still relies on a grounding in intuitive thinking. This has led us to pay some attention to the deep role intuitive thinking plays in all sorts of other activities at the core of our lives. In doing so, we don't have to glorify intuitive thinking at the expense of rationality. We should just recognize the importance of finding the appropriate balance between the two—which may differ from problem to problem and from moment to moment. And finding this balance may itself take a combination of reasoning and hunches.

Rationality vs. intuition is only one dimension of what we've been looking at here. Another dimension has been in the background from the beginning. In Chapter 4, I called it the "perspectival perspective"— the idea that our understanding makes use of a set of partially connected perspectives. Each perspective has its strengths and its weaknesses, each contributes its own part to our understanding, and none can be completely reduced to any of the others.[1]

---

[1] The "perspectival perspective" bears some resemblance to what Richard Rorty approvingly calls the "ironic" position. He too rejects the notion of absolute truth and absolute reality. However, he comes to the issue from a Wittgensteinian and Davidsonian point of view: rather than different perspectives (i.e. ways of understanding), there are just different vocabularies, different metaphors, different language games, different traditions. Although the cognitive perspective that I've focused on here does introduce some new vocabulary, I don't think that's what distinctive about it. Its vocabulary follows from the structure of its concepts, not the other way around. And I don't think the cognitive perspective is a metaphor for anything. On the other hand, it does have this in common with Rorty's "traditions": it takes a lot of work to get comfortable with it.

The ordinary perspective is the one from which we conduct our daily lives. I'm inclined to think it's the one nature has equipped us with. With no effort, we experience a world full of objects and people, words and sentences, events happening, things causing other things, people acting of their own free will. Sentences are true or false on the basis of how they correspond to the world. We also experience an inner life of images and thoughts. If we examine our thoughts, they turn out to be sentences in our head, and from this we may conclude that our thought is inner language.

Intuitively, all this is perfectly satisfactory. We can live our lives without questioning it. But our language capacity allows us to frame questions that don't have immediate answers. What makes the sun rise and set? What are words, *really*? Where does our free will come from? What happens to us when we die? And so on. Some sorts of answers involve just adding things to the ordinary perspective, new entities that maybe we can't see. There's a god with a chariot hauling the sun around. Words live in an eternal space of essences. Free will is given to us by God. When we die, we go to heaven or hell.

Other kinds of answers are more radical: you have to construct a new perspective. Perspectives other than the ordinary are always to some degree jarring to intuition. They rely far more on rational thinking than does the ordinary perspective. So, for instance, to understand sunsets, you have to imagine stepping off the earth into space. Then you'll see that the sun isn't going up and down. Rather the earth is rotating, so that from the earth it *looks* like the sun is going up and down.

In this book, we've kept stepping into the cognitive perspective, asking what's going on inside a person's mind that accounts for his or her experience of the world—including the conviction that there's really a world out there. None of the entities in the ordinary perspective can be taken for granted, not even physical objects. From this perspective, the issues are things like: what gives you the conviction that there's an object out there, that *this* caused *that*, that this sentence implies this other sentence, that you're acting out of free will? And from this perspective, we've been able to make some better sense of the way we experience our thought.

(Another question for the cognitive perspective is: How do we create and manage new perspectives, including the cognitive perspective itself? I suspect that this ability is a fundamental aspect of human intelligence.)

We can step into perspectives even more distant from the ordinary. We can ask how the neurons in our brains create the phenomena of the cognitive perspective such as pronunciation, spatial structure, reference files, and character tags. And we can go even further and ask how neurons do these things by virtue of their chemistry and physics.

But look what happens. As we move from an earth-centered to a sun-centered perspective, and then on to larger and larger cosmological perspectives, persons fade from view—we're just insignificant specks on a piece of dust. In the same way, as we move from the ordinary perspective to the cognitive and neural perspectives, and eventually to a physical/chemical perspective, we also lose sight of the person entirely—persons are kind of too big. Neither direction offers room for notions like human dignity any more.

Even basic things like physical objects dissolve. From a subatomic perspective, physical objects are mostly empty space. From a cognitive perspective, we *perceive* a physical object when a certain kind of spatial structure is linked to a reference file and a certain character tag. And look how the answers from these two perspectives have absolutely nothing to do with one another.

From the perspectival perspective, it's important to keep track of what perspective you're in. If you start mixing perspectives, you end up with weird assertions: There are no sunsets. There is no such thing as a language. There is no such thing as free will. There is no such thing as truth. The whole world is just a product of my mind. There is no such thing as Me. And so on.

It's important to keep asking which perspective is right for your current purpose. If you're trying to understand what makes sentences true, the ordinary perspective leads to confusion and paradox. The cognitive perspective says that's the wrong question—you can make much more progress if you ask how *people judge* sentences true. If you're trying to understand why the sky is blue, it turns out that you need a subatomic quantum perspective, in order to explain the wavelengths of light that strike your eyes. But you also need a cognitive/neural perspective to explain why we experience that mixture of wavelengths as the color blue.

And there are still lots of activities for which the ordinary perspective is right where you want to be: playing the Brahms Clarinet Quintet, planning a party, advocating for social justice. The cognitive perspective may be able to explain why we have morals, but it can't answer moral questions—what's the right thing to do, which set of morals we should adopt. These too are questions for the ordinary perspective.

Finally, from the perspectival perspective, it's important to recognize that there's no overarching, perspective-free Truth About The World. Our questions about our world don't converge on a single mutually consistent set of answers. There are only different ways of understanding our world, some of which work better for some kinds of questions, and some of which work better for others. This is not the ideal solution to the Problem of Knowledge, but it's the best we can do, so we'd better learn to live with it.

This is not to say there's no point in trying to understand, that everything is relative, so why bother. Rather, I'm hoping to sharpen our tools so we can try harder.

References and further reading

Chapter 1

Two expositions of the cognitive perspective on language that focus on grammar are Noam Chomsky, *Reflections on Language* (Pantheon, 1975); Steven Pinker, *The Language Instinct* (Morrow, 1994).

Chapter 2

Early expositions of the notion of mental grammar: Noam Chomsky, *Syntactic Structures* (Mouton, 1957); *Aspects of the Theory of Syntax* (MIT Press, 1965).

The notion of "speech community": Judith T. Irvine, "Speech and language community," *Encyclopedia of Language and Linguistics*, 2nd edition (Elsevier, 2006), pp. 689–96.

The language situation in the former Yugoslavia: Robert D. Greenberg, *Language and Identity in the Balkans: Serbo-Croatian and its Disintegration* (Oxford University Press, 2004).

The notion of "social construction" comes from Peter L. Berger and Thomas Luckmann, *The Social Construction of Reality* (Anchor Books, 1966).

On Nicaraguan Sign Language, see Judy Kegl, Ann Senghas, and Marie Coppola, "Creations through contact: Sign language emergence and sign language change in Nicaragua," in Michel DeGraff (ed.), *Language Creation and Language Change* (MIT Press, 1999), pp. 179–237.

The quote from David Lewis is from p. 5 of his "Languages and language," in Keith Gunderson (ed.), *Language, Mind, and Knowledge* (University of Minnesota Press, 1975), pp. 3–35.

Chapter 3

Chomsky's terms "E-language" and "I-language" come from his *Reflections on Language* (Pantheon, 1975).

For the distinction between systems strictly for language and more general mental systems, see Marc Hauser, Noam Chomsky, and Tecumseh Fitch, "The faculty of language: What is it, who has it, and how did it evolve?," *Science* 298 (2002), pp. 1569–79; Steven Pinker and Ray Jackendoff, "The faculty of language: What's special about it?," *Cognition* 95 (1975), pp. 201–36. For a different take, see Michael Tomasello, *Constructing a Language* (Harvard University Press, 2003).

David Lewis on conventions: see references to Chapter 2.

Language as a Platonic object: Jerrold Katz, *Language and Other Abstract Objects* (Rowman & Littlefield, 1981); D. Terence Langendoen and Paul Postal, *The Vastness of Natural Languages* (Basil Blackwell, 1984).

Consilience: E. O. Wilson, *Consilience: The Unity of Knowledge* (Alfred A. Knopf, 1998).

Chapter 4

Navigation by the stars: Thomas Kuhn, *The Copernican Revolution* (Random House, 1957).

Manifest image: Wilfrid Sellars, *Science, Perception, and Reality* (Routledge & Kegan Paul, 1963).

"Institutional" vs. "brute physical" facts: John Searle, *The Construction of Social Reality* (Free Press, 1995).

The meaning of *gold*: Hilary Putnam, "The meaning of 'meaning,'" in Keith Gunderson (ed.), *Language, Mind, and Knowledge* (University of Minnesota Press, 1975), pp. 131–93.

Chapter 5

For a treatment of some of the questions in this chapter and the next from a philosophical viewpoint, see Brian Epstein, "The internal and external in linguistic explanation," *Croatian Journal of Philosophy* 8.22 (2008), pp. 77–111.

Time as metaphor: George Lakoff and Mark Johnson, *Philosophy in the Flesh* (Basic Books, 1999). For discussion of the limitations of the cognitive linguistics view of metaphor, see Ray Jackendoff and David Aaron, review of Lakoff and Turner, *More Than Cool Reason, Language* 67 (1991), pp. 320–38; Ray Jackendoff, *Language, Consciousness, Culture* (MIT Press, 2007), pp. 342–4.

Acoustics of speech: Alvin Liberman, "Some assumptions about speech and how they changed," Haskins Laboratories Status Report on Speech Research SR-113 (1993); online at: http://www.haskins.yale.edu/sr/sr113/SR113_01.pdf

Chapter 6

Psycholinguistic research on different forms of the same word: Steven Pinker, *Words and Rules* (Basic Books, 1999).

The many senses of *over* and similar phenomena: George Lakoff, *Women, Fire, and Dangerous Things* (University of Chicago Press, 1987). (Disclaimer: I don't necessarily endorse all of his analyses.)

Chapter 7

Ludwig Wittgenstein, *Philosophical Investigations* (Basil Blackwell, 1953). "One cannot guess how a word functions" (p. 109); "We must do away with all explanation" (p. 47).

Situation Semantics: Jon Barwise and John Perry, *Situations and Attitudes* (MIT Press, 1983).

Chapter 8

I discuss evaluative terms like *adore* and *interesting* in much more detail in chapter 7 of *Language, Consciousness, Culture*, and I extend the analysis to notions of value in chapter 9 of that volume.

Chapter 9

Wittgenstein on the meaning of *this*: *Philosophical Investigations*, p. 18.

See my *Foundations of Language* (Oxford University Press, 2002), chapters 9 and 10, for discussion of many of the alternative notions of meaning (sets etc.). Section 4.2 discusses the notion of Deep Structure, its relation to meaning, and how it echoes Wittgenstein's term *Tiefengrammatik* ('deep grammar').

For discussion of how idioms, compounds, prefixes, and suffixes can behave like words, see *Foundations of Language*, chapter 6.

Douglas Hofstadter's *Gödel, Escher, Bach* (Basic Books, 1979) is an entertaining introduction to the theory of computation and its application to theories of the mind. Noam Chomsky's *Syntactic Structures* and *Aspects of the Theory of Syntax* revolutionized linguistics; see *Foundations of Language*, especially chapters 1–6, for a more contemporary assessment.

Chapter 10

Wittgenstein on the boxer: *Philosophical Investigations*, p. 11.

Chapter 11

For many more examples and discussion of the experimental literature on color naming and other categorization, see Gregory Murphy, *The Big Book of Concepts* (MIT Press, 2002); and chapter 1 of Eric Margolis and Stephen Laurence's *Concepts: Core Readings* (MIT Press, 1999).

The proposal that words like *climb* are actually ambiguous was once proposed by the philosopher of language Jerrold Katz, in his *The Philosophy of Language* (Harper & Row, 1966), p. 73. This analysis of *climb* first appears in Charles Fillmore, "Towards a descriptive framework for deixis," in R. Jarvella and W. Klein (eds), *Speech, Place, and Action* (Wiley, 1982), pp. 31–52; Ray Jackendoff, "Multiple subcategorization and the theta-criterion: The case of *climb*," *Natural Language and Linguistic Theory* 3.3 (1985), pp. 271–95.

Wittgenstein on *game*: *Philosophical Investigations*, pp. 31–2.

George Lakoff's example of *mother* is one of many discussed in his *Women, Fire, and Dangerous Things*. For more cases, see my *Foundations of Language*, pp. 352–6.

The quotation about Pluto is from Mike Brown, *How I Killed Pluto and Why It Had It Coming* (Spiegel & Grau, 2010), as quoted in a review in the *Boston Globe* (Jan. 1, 2011).

Chapter 12

Paul Grice discusses cases like "Will you be going near a mailbox?" in his *Studies in the Way of Words* (Harvard University Press, 1989). See also chapter 8 of Steven Pinker's *The Stuff of Thought: Language as a Window into Human Nature* (Penguin Books, 2007).

The Rodgers and Hart song is given a haunting performance by Peggy Lee in a memorable 1941 recording with Benny Goodman.

On ellipsis: Peter Culicover and Ray Jackendoff, *Simpler Syntax* (Oxford University Press, 2005), chapter 10.

Chapter 13

Wittgenstein on what a clarinet sounds like: *Philosophical Investigations*, p. 36.

For discussion of the cognition of non-human primates, see Wolfgang Köhler, *The Mentality of Apes* (Kegan Paul, 1927); Jane Goodall, *In the Shadow of Man* (Dell, 1971); Richard Byrne and Andrew Whiten, *Machiavellian Intelligence: Social Expertise and the Evolution of Intellect in*

Monkeys, Apes, and Humans (Clarendon Press, 1988); Dorothy Cheney and Robert Seyfarth, *How Monkeys See the World* (University of Chicago Press, 1990); Cheney and Seyfarth, *Baboon Metaphysics* (University of Chicago Press, 2007); Frans de Waal, *Good Natured: The Origins of Right and Wrong in Humans and Other Animals* (Harvard University Press, 1996); Daniel Povinelli, *Folk Physics for Apes* (Oxford University Press, 2000); Michael Tomasello (ed.), *Primate Cognition* (special issue of the journal *Cognitive Science* 24.3) (2000).

On "nonconceptual content," see José Bermúdez and Arnon Cahen, "Nonconceptual mental content," in Edward N. Zalta (ed.), *The Stanford Encyclopedia of Philosophy* (Spring 2010 edn): http://plato.stanford.edu/archives/spr2010/entries/content-nonconceptual/

On the concepts of paramecia: Jerry Fodor, "Why *paramecia* don't have mental representations," *Midwest Studies in Philosophy* 10 (1987), 3–23.

On the language of thought: Jerry Fodor, *The Language of Thought* (Harvard University Press, 1975).

Chapter 14

The Sapir–Whorf hypothesis: John B. Carroll (ed.), *Language, Thought, and Reality: Selected Writings of Benjamin Lee Whorf* (MIT Press, 1956); Geoffrey Nunberg, *The Great Eskimo Vocabulary Hoax and Other Irreverent Essays on the Study of Language* (University of Chicago Press, 1991).

Tzeltal sense of space and related topics: Stephen Levinson, *Space in Language and Cognition* (Cambridge University Press, 2003); Peggy Li and Lila Gleitman, "Turning the tables: Language and spatial reasoning," *Cognition* 83 (2002), pp. 265–94; Peggy Li, Linda Abarbanell, Lila Gleitman, and Anna Papafragou, "Spatial reasoning in Tenejapan Mayans," *Cognition* 120 (2011), pp. 33–53.

The domains of spatial expressions, colors, and grammatical gender are the main areas stressed by Guy Deutscher in his *Through the Language Glass: Why the World Looks Different in Other Languages* (Metropolitan Books, 2010), which attempts to show (unsuccessfully in my view) that language profoundly affects thought.

On the language Pirahã: Daniel Everett, *Don't Sleep, There Are Snakes* (Pantheon, 2008); Peter Gordon, "Numerical Cognition without Words: Evidence from Amazonia," *Science* 306 (Oct. 15, 2004), pp. 496–9.

On children learning numbers: Rochel Gelman and C. R. Gallistel, *The Child's Understanding of Number* (Harvard University Press, 1978); Stanislas Dehaene, *The Number Sense* (Oxford University Press, 1997);

Heike Wiese, *Numbers, Language, and the Human Mind* (Cambridge University Press, 2003).

Chapter 15

Much of the material in Part Two is drawn from my *Consciousness and the Computational Mind* (MIT Press, 1987) and chapter 3 of *Language, Consciousness, Culture*. What I'm calling here the Unconscious Meaning Hypothesis is called there the "Intermediate Level Theory."

John B. Watson quote: "Psychology as the behaviorist views it," *Psychological Review* 20 (1913), pp. 158–77.

Peter Carruthers quote: *Language, Thought, and Consciousness* (Cambridge University Press, 1996), p. 51.

Chomsky quote: *On Nature and Language* (Cambridge University Press, 2002), pp. 75–7. Similar remarks appear in Robert Berwick and Noam Chomsky, "The Biolinguistic Program: The current state of its development," in Anna Maria Di Sciullo and Cedric Boeckx (eds), *The Biolinguistic Enterprise: New Perspectives on the Evolution and Nature of the Human Language Faculty* (Oxford University Press, 2011), pp. 19–41.

Wittgenstein quotes: *Philosophical Investigations*, pp. 107–8.

Cherokee: quoted in Boston *Globe* (Dec. 24, 2010).

Chapter 16

"How can I know what I think until I see what I say?" Google tells me this quote has been attributed variously to Henry David Thoreau, W. H. Auden, the political theorist Graham Wallas, the novelist E. M. Forster, a little girl quoted by Graham Wallas, and an old lady quoted by E. M. Forster. Well, for our purposes I guess it doesn't really matter *who* said it.

Tip-of-the tongue: William James, *Principles of Psychology* (1890; Dover reprint 1950).

Feeling of knowing: Asher Koriat, "How do we know that we know? The accessibility model of the feeling of knowing," *Psychological Review* 100 (1993), pp. 609–39; Valerie A. Thompson, "Dual-process theories: A metacognitive perspective," in Jonathan Evans and Keith Frankish (eds), *In Two Minds: Dual Processes and Beyond* (Oxford University Press, 2009), pp. 171–95.

Tip-of-the-fingers sensation: Robin Thompson, Karen Emmorey, and Tamar H. Gollan, "'Tip of the finger' experiences by deaf signers," *Psychological Science* 16 (2005), pp. 856–60.

Nicaraguan Sign Language: See references to Chapter 2.

Chapter 17

Daniel Dennett on the "Cartesian theater": *Consciousness Explained* (Little, Brown, 1991).

Chapter 18

Descartes' view of the "vessel of consciousness," for instance in the *Discourse on Method*, Discourse 5.

Max Eastman quote: *Einstein, Trotsky, Hemingway, Freud, and Other Great Companions* (Collier Books, 1962), p. 132.

John von Neumann, *The Computer and the Brain* (Yale University Press, 1958).

The "Hard Problem" of consciousness: David Chalmers, "Facing up to the problem of consciousness," in Jonathan Shear (ed.), *Explaining Consciousness: The Hard Problem* (MIT Press, 1997), pp. 9–30; John Searle, "Minds, brains, and programs," *Behavioral and Brain Sciences* 3 (1980), pp. 417–24; William Robinson, "The hardness of the Hard Problem," in Shear (op. cit.), pp. 149–61; Daniel Dennett, "Are we explaining consciousness yet?", in Stanislas Dehaene (ed.), *The Cognitive Neuroscience of Consciousness* (special issue of *Cognition* 79) (2001), pp. 221–37; Paul Churchland and Patricia Churchland, "Recent work on consciousness: Philosophical, theoretical, and empirical," in Naoyuki Osaka (ed.), *Neural Basis of Consciousness* (John Benjamins, 2003), pp. 123–38.

Neural correlates of consciousness: Francis Crick, *The Astonishing Hypothesis* (Charles Scribner's Sons, 1994); Francis Crick and Cristof Koch, "Toward a neurobiological theory of consciousness," *Seminars in the Neurosciences* 2 (1990), pp. 263–75; Cristof Koch, *The Quest for Consciousness* (Roberts, 2004).

Chapter 19

For the three linked data structures in language—phonology, grammatical structure, and meaning—see my *Foundations of Language*, chapters 1 and 5.

Chapter 20

Antonio Damasio quote: "A neurobiology for consciousness," in Thomas Metzinger (ed.), *Neural Correlates of Consciousness* (MIT Press, 2000), pp. 111–20. Bernard Baars quote: "Working memory requires conscious processes, not vice versa: A Global Workspace account," in Osaka (ed.), *Neural Basis of Consciousness*, p. 11.

Primate cognition: See references to Chapter 13.

Consciousness as quantum activity: Stuart Hameroff and Roger Penrose, "Conscious events as orchestrated space-time selections," in Shear (ed.), *Explaining Consciousness*, pp. 177–95.

Consciousness as the activity of certain receptors on neurons: Hans Flohr, "NMDA receptor-mediated computational processes and phenomenal consciousness," in Metzinger (op. cit.), pp. 245–58.

"Proto-awareness" connected to the receptive fields of neurons: Bruce MacLennan, "The elements of consciousness and their neurodynamical correlates," in Shear (op. cit.), pp. 249–66.

"Executive" theory of consciousness: James, *Principles of Psychology*; Jerome Bruner, *In Search of Mind* (Harper & Row, 1983); Marvin Minsky, "Matter, mind, and models," in Minsky (ed.), *Semantic Information Processing* (MIT Press, 1968), pp. 425–32; Karl Popper and John Eccles, *The Self and its Brain* (Springer International, 1977).

Koch, *The Quest for Consciousness*. First quote, p. 234; second quote, p. 233; third quote, p. 318.

I talk about the role of attention in *Consciousness and the Computational Mind*, section 13.4, and in *Language, Consciousness, Culture*, section 3.4. Victor Lamme makes a similar distinction between awareness and attention, in his "Why visual attention and awareness are different," *Trends in Cognitive Sciences* 7 (2003), pp. 12–18.

Phenomenal vs. access consciousness: Ned Block, "On a confusion about the function of consciousness," *Behavioral and Brain Sciences* 18 (1995), pp. 227–87.

Consciousness as produced by higher-order or reflexive representations: Hofstadter, *Gödel, Escher, Bach*; David Rosenthal, "Two concepts of consciousness," *Philosophical Studes* 94 (1986), pp. 329–59; Peter Carruthers, *Language, Thought and Consciousness* (Cambridge University Press, 1996); Wolf Singer, "Phenomenal awareness and consciousness from a neurobiological perspective," in Metzinger (ed.), *Neural Correlates of Consciousness*, pp. 121–37; Gerald Edelman and Giulio Tononi, "Reentry and the dynamic core: Neural correlates of conscious experience," in Metzinger (op. cit.), pp. 139–51; Josef Parvizi and Antonio Damasio, "Consciousness and the brainstem," in Dehaene (ed.), *The Cognitive Neuroscience of Consciousness*, pp. 135–60.

"Global workspace" theory of consciousness: Bernard Baars, *A Cognitive Theory of Consciousness* (Cambridge University Press, 1988); Baars, "Understanding subjectivity: Global Workspace Theory and the resurrection of the self," in Shear (op. cit.), pp. 241–8. The quote from Baars is from the latter of these, p. 241. The quote from David Chalmers is in "Facing up to the problem of consciousness," in Shear (op. cit), p. 22. The quote from Stanislas Dehaene and Lionel Naccache is in "Towards a cognitive neuroscience of consciousness: Basic evidence and a workspace framework," in Dehaene (op. cit.), p. 15.

Chapter 21

Wittgenstein on the duck-rabbit and related phenomena: *Philosophical Investigations*, p. 193–214.

Examples of visual illusions: Donald Hoffman, *Visual Intelligence* (W. W. Norton, 1993); Richard Gregory, *The Intelligent Eye* (McGraw-Hill, 1970); Richard Gregory, *Eye and Brain* (Princeton University Press, 1990); Béla Julesz, *Foundations of Cyclopean Perception* (University of Chicago Press), 1971; Irwin Rock, *The Logic of Perception* (MIT Press, 1983). Some impressive videos can be found at V. S. Ramachandran's website: http://cbc.ucsd.edu/ramaillusions.html

Visual understanding: references above plus David Marr, *Vision* (Freeman, 1982); Koch, *The Quest for Consciousness*; Naomi Eilan, Rosaleen McCarthy, and Bill Brewer (eds.), *Spatial Representation* (Basil Blackwell, 1993).

Immanuel Kant, *Critique of Pure Reason*.

Gestalt psychologists: Wolfgang Köhler, *Gestalt Psychology* (Liveright/Mentor Books, 1947); Kurt Koffka, *Principles of Gestalt Psychology* (Harcourt, Brace & World, 1935).

George Miller quote from "Trends and debates in cognitive psychology," *Cognition* 10 (1980), pp. 215–25; this quote from p. 222.

Chapter 22

On intentionality: Searle, "Minds, brains, and programs"; Jerry Fodor, *Psychosemantics: The Problem of Meaning in the Philosophy of Mind* (MIT Press, 1987).

Primate social world: Cheney and Seyfarth, *Baboon Metaphysics*.

For more discussion of social concepts, see my *Language, Consciousness, Culture* and Erving Goffman, *Frame Analysis* (Harper & Row, 1974).

Chapter 23

Long-lived resonance in conscious brain activity: Stanislas Dehaene, Jean-Pierre Changeux, Lionel Naccache, Jérôme Sackur, and Clair Sergent, "Conscious, preconscious, and subliminal processing: A testable taxonomy," *Trends in Cognitive Sciences* 10 (2006), pp. 204–11.

Being able to judge categories without being able to say how: Michael Polanyi, *Personal Knowledge* (University of Chicago Press, 1962). Polanyi discusses many cases of knowledge of this sort, which he calls "connoisseurship."

"Exemplar" theories of category learning: Gregory Murphy, *The Big Book of Concepts* (MIT Press, 2002); Edward Smith and Douglas Medin, "The exemplar view," in Eric Margolis and Stephen Laurence (eds), *Concepts: Core Readings* (MIT Press, 1999), pp. 207–21.

Chapter 24

The issue of how sight and touch are correlated goes back to John Locke's *Essay Concerning Human Understanding* (1690). Locke cites a letter from William Molyneux, asking whether a blind man whose sight was restored could distinguish shapes by sight that he previously knew only by touch. Recent discussions include Irwin Rock, *The Logic of Perception* (MIT Press, 1983); J. Farley Norman, Hideko F. Norman, Anna Marie Clayton, Joann Lianekhammy, and Gina Zielke, "The visual and haptic perception of natural object shape," *Perception and Psychophysics* 66 (2004), pp. 342–51; Marc Ernst and Martin Banks, "Humans integrate visual and haptic information in a statistically optimal fashion," *Nature* 415 (Jan. 24, 2004), pp. 429–33; and several articles in Eilan, McCarthy, and Brewer, *Spatial Representation: Problems in Philosophy and Psychology*.

Blind children navigating a room: Barbara Landau and Lila Gleitman, *Language and Experience: Evidence from the Blind Child* (Harvard University Press, 1985).

The woman lacking proprioception: Oliver Sacks, *The Man Who Mistook His Wife for a Hat* (Summit Books, 1985), chapter 3.

Beethoven's thought processes: Paul Mies, *Beethoven's Sketches* (Dover Books, 1974); Lewis Lockwood and the Juilliard String Quartet, *Inside Beethoven's Quartets* (Harvard University Press, 2008).

Chapter 26

The "feeling of familiarity" is discussed in Valerie A. Thompson, "Dual-process theories: A metacognitive perspective," in Evans and Frankish, *In Two Minds: Dual Processes and Beyond*, pp. 171–95.

Visual agnosia: Sacks, *The Man Who Mistook His Wife for a Hat*.

Unreliability of eyewitnesses: Elizabeth Loftus, *Eyewitness Testimony* (Harvard University Press, 1979).

Somatic markers: Antonio Damasio, *Descartes' Error: Emotion, Reason, and the Human Brain* (G. P. Putnam's Sons, 1994).

Free will: Daniel Wegner, *The Illusion of Conscious Will* (MIT Press, 2002); Daniel Dennett, *Freedom Evolves* (Viking, 2003).

McGurk effect: Harry McGurk and John MacDonald, "Hearing lips and seeing voices," *Nature* 264 (1976), 746–8; Dominic Massaro, *Perceiving Talking Faces* (MIT Press, 1997).

Chapter 27

Theories of compositionality and inference: Ray Jackendoff, *Semantics and Cognition* (MIT Press, 1983); *Semantic Structures* (MIT Press, 1990); *Foundations of Language*; *Language, Culture, Consciousness*; *Meaning and the Lexicon* (Oxford University Press, 2010). In formal semantics (assuming Fregean compositionality): Irene Heim and Angelika Kratzer, *Semantics in Generative Grammar* (Blackwell, 1998). In Cognitive Grammar: Ronald Langacker, *Cognitive Grammar: A Basic Introduction* (Oxford University Press, 2008).

On Spatial Structure: David Marr, *Vision* (Freeman, 1982); Paul Bloom, Mary Peterson, Lynn Nadel, and Merrill Garrett (eds), *Language and Space* (MIT Press, 1996).

Experiments on infants' token features: Karen Wynn, "Addition and subtraction by human infants," *Nature* 358 (1992), pp. 749–50; Fei Xu and Susan Carey, "Infants' metaphysics: The case of numerical identity," *Cognitive Psychology* 30 (1996), pp. 111–53.

Chapter 28

Misfiring reference in conversation: Keith Donnellan, "Reference and definite descriptions," *Philosophical Review* 75 (1966), pp. 281–304.

Chapter 29

The material in this chapter is discussed in greater detail in my *Semantics and Cognition*, chapter 3, and *Foundations of Language*, section 10.8.

"Descriptive metaphysics": P. F. Strawson, *Individuals: An Essay in Descriptive Metaphysics* (Methuen, 1959).

Mirror neurons: Vittorio Gallese, Luciano Fadiga, Leonardo Fogassi, and Giacomo Rizzolati, "Action recognition in the premotor cortex," *Brain* 119 (1996), pp. 593–609; Christian Keysers, "Mirror neurons," *Current Biology* 19 (Nov. 17, 2009), pp. R971–R973.

Chapter 30

Frame analysis: Goffman, *Frame Analysis*.

"I thought your yacht was longer than it is": Bertrand Russell, "On denoting," *Mind* 14 (1905), pp. 479–93.

Theory of Mind: David Premack and G. Woodruff, "Does the chimpanzee have a theory of mind?" *Behavioral and Brain Sciences* 1 (1978), pp. 515–26; Simon Baron-Cohen, *Mindblindness: An Essay on Autism and Theory of Mind* (MIT Press, 1997).

My earlier account of pictures and beliefs: *Semantics and Cognition*, chapter 11. Gilles Fauconnier has expanded this analysis to a large number of complex situations in *Mappings in Thought and Language* (Cambridge University Press, 1997).

Chapter 31

On the body/soul split: Paul Bloom, *Descartes' Baby* (Basic Books, 2004); see also my *Language, Consciousness, Culture*, chapter 5.

Capgras syndrome: Ryan McKay, Robyn Langdon, and Max Coltheart, "'Sleights of mind': Delusions, defences, and self-deception," *Cognitive Neuropsychiatry* 10 (2005), pp. 305–26.

Cross-cultural studies of religion from a cognitive perspective: Pascal Boyer, *Religion Explained* (Basic Books, 2001); Scott Atran, *In Gods We Trust* (Oxford University Press, 2002).

There's no such thing as a soul: Damasio, *Descartes' Error: Emotion, Reason, and the Human Brain*; Crick, *The Astonishing Hypothesis*.

Evolutionary origins of the human mind: Daniel Dennett, *Darwin's Dangerous Idea* (Simon & Schuster, 1995); Steven Pinker, *How the Mind Works* (W. W. Norton, 1997); Richard Dawkins, *The Selfish Gene* (Oxford University Press, 1989).

Evolutionary sources of morality: Robert Boyd and Peter Richerson, *The Origin and Evolution of Cultures* (Oxford University Press, 2005); Richard Alexander, *The Biology of Moral Systems* (Aldine de Gruyter, 1987).

The form of human moral concepts: my *Language, Consciousness, Culture*; Marc Hauser, *Moral Minds* (HarperCollins, 2006); John Mikhail, *Elements of Moral Cognition* (Cambridge University Press, 2011).

Attacks on religion: Richard Dawkins, *The God Delusion* (Houghton Mifflin, 2006); Daniel Dennett, *Breaking the Spell* (Viking Penguin, 2006); Sam Harris, *The End of Faith* (W. W. Norton, 2005).

Reasons why we conceptualize people in terms of souls: One interesting suggestion is Daniel Dennett's "self as center of narrative gravity" in *Darwin's Dangerous Idea*.

Chapter 33

" 'Snow is white' is true if and only if snow is white": Alfred Tarski, "The concept of truth in formalized languages," in his *Logic, Semantics, and Metamathematics* (Oxford University Press, 1956), pp. 152–97. This approach forms the foundation of modern formal semantics, such as in Irene Heim and Angelika Kratzer, *Semantics in Generative Grammar* (Basil Blackwell, 1998).

"The distance from Boston to New York is 200 miles": Jerrold Katz, "Chomsky on meaning," *Language* 56 (1980), pp. 1–41; Ray Jackendoff, "On Katz's autonomous semantics," *Language* 57 (1981), pp. 425–35; James Higginbotham, "Jackendoff's conceptualism," *Behavioral and Brain Sciences* 26 (2003), pp. 680–81.

"The present king of France is bald": Bertrand Russell, "On denoting," *Mind* 14 (1905), pp. 479–93.

William James on fictional characters: *Principles of Psychology*, vol. 2, p. 292.

Chapter 35

Asch experiment: Solomon E. Asch, "Opinions and social pressure," *Scientific American* 193 (1955), pp. 31–5. Online at: http://www.panarchy.org/asch/social.pressure.1955.html

Denying ownership of one's own body parts: V. S. Ramachandran and Sandra Blakeslee, *Phantoms in the Brain* (HarperCollins, 1998). See also Sacks, *The Man Who Mistook His Wife for a Hat*, chapter 4.

Chapter 36

Descartes, *Discourse on Method*, Discourse 2.

Lewis Carroll, "What the tortoise said to Achilles," *Mind* 4 (1895), pp. 278–80. Reprinted in Hofstadter, *Gödel, Escher, Bach*, pp. 43–5.

Wittgenstein on how you know you've applied the rules correctly: *Philosophical Investigations*, pp. 38–9, 85–6.

"Home sign": Susan Goldin-Meadow, *The Resilience of Language* (Psychology Press, 2003).

Kant quote: *Critique of Pure Reason*, Introduction to Book II, *Analytic of Principles*.

Karl Lashley quote: "Cerebral organization and behavior," in H. Solomon, S. Cobb, and W. Penfield (eds.), *The Brain and Human Behavior* (Williams &Wilkins, 1956), pp. 1–18. This quote is from p. 4.

System 1 and System 2: Evans and Frankish, *In Two Minds: Dual Processes and Beyond*.

Chapter 37

Some of the more accessible recent expositions of the research on intuitive thinking are Gerd Gigerenzer, *Gut Feelings: The Intelligence of the Unconscious* (Viking, 2007); Malcolm Gladwell, *Blink: The Power of Thinking Without Thinking* (Little, Brown, 2005); Jonah Lehrer, *How We Decide* (Houghton Mifflin Harcourt, 2009). Two earlier expositions are Michael Polanyi, *Personal Knowledge* (University of Chicago Press, 1962); Daniel Kahneman, Paul Slovic, and Amos Tversky (eds), *Judgment Under Uncertainty: Heuristics and Biases* (Cambridge University Press, 1982).

Chapter 38

Chomsky on the evolutionary source of language: *Reflections on Language* (Pantheon, 1975); *New Horizons in the Study of Language and Mind* (Cambridge University Press, 2000).

Chapter 39

"I don't think consciousness is something that happens to us...": Alva Noë in *The Nation* (Mar. 16, 2009), quoted with sincere apologies.

The experiment on judgments of stockings: Richard E. Nisbett and Timothy DeCamp Wilson, "Telling more than we can know: Verbal reports on mental processes," *Psychological Review* 84 (1977), pp. 231–59.

Chapter 40

Similar conversations about musical interpretation are reported by Arnold Steinhardt of the august Guarneri Quartet, in his *Indivisible by Four* (Farrar, Straus, and Giroux, 1998), pp. 93, 99, 163, and 284.

A different sense of musical meaning: Leonard Meyer, *Emotion and Meaning in Music* (University of Chicago Press, 1956).

Chapter 41

"When you start working...": Philip Gaston, quoted by Barry Schwabsky in *The Nation* (Jan. 10–17, 2011).

Chapter 42

Humanities vs. science: C. P. Snow, *The Two Cultures* (1959; repr. Cambridge University Press, 1998); Alvin B. Kernan (ed.), *What's Happened to the Humanities?* (Princeton University Press, 1997); Eugene Goodheart, *Does Literary Studies Have a Future?* (University of Wisconsin Press, 1999); Michael Wood, "A world without literature?" *Daedalus* (Winter 2009), pp. 58–67; Stanley Fish, "Will the humanities save us?": http://opinionator.blogs.nytimes.com/2008/01/06/will-the-humanities-save-us/

"Students learn...": Anthony Kronman, quoted in Fish (op. cit.); "helps you define yourself...": Italo Calvino, quoted in Wood (op. cit.); "ways of reading," "making the ordinary strange": Wood (op. cit.); "bringing what is hidden into the open": Kronman, quoted in Fish (op. cit); "provide models of response": J. M. Coetzee, quoted in Wood (op. cit.); "The defining quality of the arts...": E. O. Wilson, *Consilience: The Unity of Knowledge* (Alfred A. Knopf, 1998), p. 213; "Arts project...": Wilson (op. cit.), p. 200; "To the question 'of what use are the humanities?'..." Fish (op. cit.).

Cognitive neuroscience of music: Aniruddh Patel, *Music, Language, and the Brain* (Oxford University Press, 2008); Fred Lerdahl and Ray Jackendoff, *A Generative Theory of Tonal Music* (MIT Press, 1983).

Chapter 43

The "ironic" position: Richard Rorty, *Contingency, Irony, and Solidarity* (Cambridge University Press, 1989).

Index